American Indian Culture

American Indian Culture

Volume 3

Symbolism in Art—Zapotec Civilization
Appendices
Indexes

Edited by

Carole A. Barrett
University of Mary

Harvey J. Markowitz
Washington and Lee University

SALEM PRESS, INC.
Pasadena, California   Hackensack, New Jersey

∞ The paper used in these volumes conforms to the American National Standard for Permanence of Paper for Printed Library Materials, Z39.48-1992 (R1997)

Most of the essays appearing within are drawn from *Ready Reference: American Indians* (1995), *Great Events from History: Revised North American Series* (1997), and *Racial and Ethnic Relations in America* (1999); essays have been updated and new essays have been added.

Library of Congress Cataloging-in-Publication Data

American Indian culture / edited by Carole A. Barrett, Harvey J. Markowitz.
    p. cm. — (Magill's choice)
    Includes bibliographical references and index.
    ISBN 1-58765-192-0 (set : alk. paper) — ISBN 1-58765-193-9 (vol. 1 : alk. paper) — ISBN 1-58765-194-7 (vol. 2 : alk. paper) — ISBN 1-58765-247-1 (vol. 3 : alk. paper)
    1. Indians of North America—Social life and customs. I. Barrett, Carole A. II. Markowitz, Harvey. III. Series.
    E98.S7A44 2004
    970.004'97—dc22

2004001362

First Printing

Contents

Contents

Alphabetical List of Contents

Volume 1

Alphabetical List of Contents

Volume 2

Alphabetical List of Contents

Volume 3

American Indian Culture

Symbolism in Art

Tribes affected: Pantribal
Significance: *The seemingly abstract designs that appear on American Indian structures, baskets, and pottery represent various aspects of Indian cosmology.*

Art historians distinguish between abstract and representational Native American art, but in the sense that all design elements are significant, all can be said to be representational. A ubiquitous element is the circle. Oglala mystic Black Elk explained the importance of circularity as imitating an important principle of the universe; hence tipi design, the whole tipi village, and designs on clothing and houses signify the circular wholeness of the earth and the circle of the seasons. Circularity also represents the sun, the central divinity and astronomical anchor of the nomadic Plains people, and a circle or concentric circles with branches or rays appears in beadwork, painted on hides, and worked into other artifacts.

Circularity is significant in house design in many tribes, whether grass houses in California or the Southwest, Navajo hogans, Eskimo winter dwellings or Apache wickiups; the house is a symbolic microcosm of the earth, and some groups place the opening to the east to receive the day's first light, symbolizing the creative mating of earth and sky. On a smaller scale, circularity is inherent in such artifacts as coiled baskets and pottery, where applied or inlaid design often reflects natural forms such as spider webs or coiled snakes. Tiny pottery seed pots from the southwestern pueblos symbolize the earth, with a minute hole representing the maternal opening through which the first people emerged in the process of creation.

The complementary abstract figure is the cross or X-shaped figure. This design element most often signifies the four directions; when placed within a circle, it represents a centering of the individual within the community and of the community within the universe. Black Elk alludes to such a figure in describing his great vision, and the figure of the quartered circle appears in such creations as Navajo sand paintings. The quartered circle is also part of the general patterning of four that recurs in many Plains and Southwest cultures: Sets of pairs and multiples of four recur in all aspects of art, including numbers of repetitions of songs during ceremonies, figures in sand paintings and on woven blankets, jewelry, household implements, and other artifacts. A major significance of such quarternary patterning is the idea of balance: matched pairs of opposites represent the balance between male and female, light and dark, hard and soft, life and death, and good and evil that must be maintained in the universe. Not all groups have four as their significant number; five and seven are also significant, as are other numbers.

Color symbolism is highly elaborated in many traditions, though different meanings may be associated with colors. Hence, black may signify the north in one context, while white is the color for the north in another; in body painting, black may signify mourning for one people, whereas it is part of a warrior's outfit for another. The idea of balance is also expressed through color symbolism, as in the alternating black and white stripes of Hopi clowns.

The distinction between art and non-art is not central to native traditions, and symbolic significance permeates the creation of almost every object, whether for practical use or aesthetic contemplation.

Helen Jaskoski

Source for Further Study
Berlo, Janet Catherine. *Native North American Art*. New York: Oxford University Press, 1998.

See also: Art and Artists: Contemporary; Bragskins; Paints and Painting; Petroglyphs; Pictographs; Sand Painting; Sculpture.

Tanning

Tribes affected: Pantribal
Significance: *Tanning enabled animal hides to be preserved and used.*

The tanning of deer, elk, bison, and small animal hides was accomplished by women, using the brains of the animals or human urine. Most hides were tanned on both sides, but sometimes the hide was tanned only on the underside (if the hair was left in place). In the Arctic, the Inuit tanned only with urine, which was often stored during the winter in ice troughs. Plains and Plateau peoples would mash animal brains with moss into small cakes for later use in tanning. A woman's status was determined by her ability to do hide work, which included preparing the hide, tanning, and sewing.

To remove the hair, a woman could bury the hide in ashes for several days, or she could use a sharpened hand stone or one hafted to a leg bone as a scraper. The hide was next beamed with an animal rib to break the grain, then pegged to the ground or placed on a vertical rack to facilitate rubbing the brains or urine into the hide. After tanning, the hide could be smoked with "punk" wood in a small tipi structure in order to prevent it from cracking when it was dried after being wet.

John Alan Ross

See also: Buffalo; Hides and Hidework.

Tattoos and Tattooing

Tribes affected: Widespread but not pantribal
Significance: *Tattooing was one of the most widespread native practices in pre-contact North America and later.*

Tattooing was one of the most widespread native practices in the Americas. Techniques ranged from cutting with blades to pricking with needles or other sharp instruments. Among the Aleut and Northwest Coast peoples, a common technique was to "sew" the design into the flesh with a needle. The most common pigment was charcoal, and all parts of the face and body were tattooed.

Tattooing was used to enhance physical beauty, indicate social status, and commemorate rites of passage. High-ranking Bella Coola men were tattooed with their parents' totemic animals. Among the Mandan, chiefs were usually the only men with tattoos, often on one arm and breast. Natchez nobility wore tattoos on their faces, arms, legs, chests and backs. Osage shamans tattooed their chests with symbols associated with their heritage of knowledge. The Tlingit often made tattoos during the final potlatch of the mortuary cycle, and they used hand tattoos as a sign of nobility.

Tattooing was often undertaken as medicine. Ojibwa healers used tattooing to treat arthritis, toothaches, broken bones, sprains, dislocated joints, and backaches. Instruments included three or four fish spines, bone splinters, or needles inserted and fastened into a split stick handle. Charred birchbark, gunpowder, or other medicines were applied either to the affected area or to the pricking instruments. Tattoos were made in the form of circular spots above the source of pain. When the affected area was large, marks were made in rows or lines.

Tattoos appear to have been most frequently worn by women. Women in the Great Plains tattooed their faces between the mouth and the chin. Tattoos were considered among the most attractive features of Netsilik Eskimo women, for whom there were separate afterlives for women with tattoos (who joined skillful hunters) and without them (who sat through eternity with bowed heads).

John Hoopes

Sources for Further Study
Dubin, Lois Sherr. *North American Indian Jewelry and Adornment: From Prehistory to the Present*. New York: Henry N. Abrams, 1999.

Caplan, Jane, ed. *Written on the Body: The Tattoo in European and American History*. Princeton, N.J.: Princeton University Press, 2000.

See also: Dress and Adornment; Grooming; Medicine and Modes of Curing: Pre-contact; Paints and Painting; Rites of Passage.

Technology

Tribes affected: Pantribal
Significance: *Technology has had a powerful impact on Native Americans, resulting in both improvement and deterioration of their quality of life.*

There is an old story about a group of Quechan Indians who were being brought to Mexico City by train to be wined and dined by politicians who wanted to buy some of their land. As the locomotive left the station, one of the Quechan, Yellow Feather, pointed at a nearby bluff and said something calmly in his native tongue that the Mexicans who were with them did not understand. Soon passing an enormous cactus, again Yellow Feather pointed and spoke, though he spoke more quickly this time because the train was moving faster now. As the train picked up steam, now racing through his ancestral lands, Yellow Feather pointed here and there, every moment speaking more quickly and frantically. Then it was quiet. Startled by the sudden silence, one of the Mexican escorts looked over and noticed that Yellow Feather was now only looking out the window and weeping. "What's wrong with him?" the escort asked. "It is our custom," replied one of the other Quechan, "to recall who we are and where we come from as we travel through our lands. Landmarks, such as the Coyote's Blood Cliffs or the Cactus Giant, have stories attached to them, which we tell as we travel by them. This not only helps us to remember who we are, but it is also an honor to the spirits who inhabit each place.

Yellow Feather cries because the locomotive travels so fast that it is impossible for him to remember himself."

Technology and Change. Technology has always been an agent of change. Typically, "technology" refers to the application of an idea to a particular problem. In other words, technology solves problems. When a weight needs to be lifted but is too heavy for a human to lift alone, perhaps a lever and fulcrum may be applied to the weight to shift it. The lever, as simple as it is, constitutes "technology" because it solves the problem of how to move a heavy weight. For the same reason, using a sharp rock to scrape the hair from a hide or tying a piece of leather to one's forearm to prevent chafing from a bowstring are also technologies. It is important to understand, however, that when a particular technology solves a particular problem, new problems frequently arise from the solution. In the story above, Yellow Feather solves the problem of taking weeks to travel to Mexico City for an important meeting by agreeing to go by train; but because the train moves so quickly, Yellow Feather must forgo the ancient tribal custom of geographic storytelling.

The application of technology accomplishes several things simultaneously. First, it makes living easier in some way—since it solves a problem—though it can make other aspects of life more difficult. Second, technology helps humans control their environment. By building huts with mud-covered stone, many Native Americans were able to keep cool in the heat and warm in the cold. By cutting channels from rivers to farm fields with specially made stone tools, agriculturally based Indians were able to irrigate land that would otherwise have been unusable. Third, technology changes people's relationship with the environment. An undesirable environment—dry soil, predators, clay that makes fragile pottery—can be changed with irrigation ditches, bows and arrows, and fiber-tempered clay. Finally, technology changes people's relationship with others. Perhaps a member of a tribe discovers that a harpoon point that rotates freely on the end of its shaft is a more effective weapon for hunting seals than a harpoon with a fixed point. That inventor may become greatly admired among the tribe, and on a more extended level, that tribe may come to be more respected, or despised, by other neighboring tribes. Thus, technology initiates change in both obvious and desirable ways, and in ways unexpected and sometimes disastrous. For both pre- and post-contact Native Americans, the most significant technological developments were made in five general areas: tools, hunting and gathering, agriculture, battle gear, and transportation.

Pre-contact Influences—Tools. Technology, by its nature, requires tools. For pre-contact Native Americans, tools were often as simple as specially shaped stones, bones, and wood. With these materials, hand axes, scrapers, hammers, chisels, files, grinders, and knives were made. As the tools were improved, so were the crafts that they helped make. A good tool can help a craftsperson make an even better tool, which, in turn, can help make the craftspeople develop better technology. For example, early North American spears were tipped with stones that were somewhat sharp, though their characteristics were not uniform because stone-shaping was difficult. To offset the weight of the stone points, hunters used long, heavy shafts; these ensured a more controlled flight. The drawback with these early spears was that because they were so cumbersome, they were difficult to carry and throw, especially in a forest or with heavy garments on. Eventually, hunters found that a dull-pointed piece of bone could flake off small pieces of a stone much more easily than a piece of rock, which had been their previous tool. Using the bone tool, they found that they could better control the shaping of a stone, which subsequently allowed them to make smaller, lighter, and sharper blades than before. This meant that spears and arrows could be lighter, and so could travel farther, and were more deadly.

Hunting and Gathering. North American natives originally drew their sustenance from hunting and gathering food that grew in the wild. Crudely made stone axes and knives were in use more than seventy thousand years ago for activities such as scraping and cutting hides, stripping the bark from branches, and chipping other stones into new tools. By the 1500's, Native Americans were using their tools to design and build complex equipment that helped to make their lives easier. They were perfecting stone arrow and spear points and shafts for maximum penetration; they were experimenting with improved nets and weirs, and were developing highly efficient traps and snares; they were inventing new ways to prepare foods, including stone ovens and nonmetallic containers that could contain and store hot liquids; they were developing airtight and waterproof baskets; and they were becoming increasingly aware of how best to protect themselves from the elements using a combination of natural fibers and leather. These improvements were changing the Native Americans.

Provided that the natural resources were available, hunting and gathering became more effective and efficient: With a bow and arrow, a hunter's stealth becomes less important than his or her accuracy with the weapon. Airtight containers meant food could be preserved longer, making wandering tribes less dependent on locating wild crops. Better garments meant fewer injuries, which meant more healthy workers to help support the tribe. All of these technological improvements created new problems, such as having too many healthy, hungry people for a given area to support and migration delays that resulted in the people arriving late to areas and finding that the region's food had rotted and that the game had already migrated or hibernated.

Agriculture. Many anthropologists attribute the waxing of Native American agriculture and the waning of hunter-gatherer societies to technological development. According to this theory, as tools, weapons, and pottery became more effective, it became less necessary for the people to wander from location to location looking for food. With their improved tools, it was now easier to stay in one place, harvesting the local crops and hunting the local animals, and storing the surplus for difficult times. By developing ways of planting and irrigating soil, that is, by controlling their environment, the agriculturally inclined Native Americans were better able to control their food supplies, and thus their lives. As their technology improved, they became less subject to the whims of nature.

Battle Gear. As in any other culture, desperation, envy, jealousy, and greed often compelled Native American neighbors to fight with each other, sometimes quite ruthlessly. The tools of war were developed along with hunting tools and weapons. Wooden and leather shields were constructed to protect against arrows and spears. Arrow tips were designed to pierce the new shields, as were more powerful bows. Stories abound as to the power of these weapons, one of the most telling being found in a nineteenth century diary that describes a man's skull suspended from a tree trunk and held in place by a single deeply embedded arrow piercing both sides of the bony cranium. Simple forms of body armor and helmets were developed by some tribes to protect them in battle from throwing knives, throwing sticks, and clubs. Like other technologies, the development of weapons was self-perpetuating. Curved arrow shafts gave way to artificially straightened arrow shafts that dramatically improved the arrow's flight and the archer's accuracy. Spears went from being heavy and short-ranged to being lighter and having more range. Even in these early times there was an arms race.

Transport. Because other developing technologies were encouraging the transformation of the hunter-gatherer into a farmer, the technologies involving transportation remained fairly undeveloped in pre-contact times. The primary means of getting around were by foot, raft, and canoe. Improved footwear in the form of sandals, moccasins, and boots made foot travel more comfortable. This comfort made the traversal of longer distances and difficult terrain more possible. Pre-contact rafts, usually fashioned from logs and branches lashed together with vine and water weeds, were more often grasped than ridden. More often than transporting people, rafts carried supplies. Canoes at this time were mainly hollowed-out tree trunks, sometimes with an outrigger for stability. In general, a tribe's transport by land or water increased its contact with other people, environments, and customs. This created situations that were sometimes complementary and sometimes hostile.

Post-contact Influences. After 1500 C.E., Native American technology changed more than it had in the previous fifty thousand years. Along with the technological changes, there were also tremendous social and cultural changes. The primary catalysts for these changes were the Europeans, who, having discovered the "new world," were now enduring danger and hardship to explore it and claim it as their own. As they encountered Native Americans, they sought to "civilize" them by encouraging them in more or less coercive ways to abandon their natural developmental process and to adopt a way of living, technologically speaking, that was hundreds of years in the Native American's future. After contact, Native American technological changes were not so much developmental as they were adoptive.

As trade began between the Europeans and the natives, stone knives and axes gave way to the metal knives and axes that were more easily handled and that could hold a sharper edge better. Iron and steel tools, such as chisels and plows, became highly desirable among the tribes, especially among those that were quickly adopting European ways of life.

While early European guns were inferior to bows and arrows both for hunting and warfare, their foreignness, complexity, and loudness impressed Native Americans. Oral and written accounts of how natives used guns suggest that, prior to the development of a reliable repeating rifle, natives used guns as symbols of their wealth, rather than as weapons; it required many supplies to trade for a single firearm, and more still to get the lead and black powder to fire it. Frontier journals indicate that a skilled archer could powerfully and accurately shoot at least ten arrows in the time it took an early rifler to shoot once, reload, and fire again.

The development of railroads and commercial waterways also changed the ways of Native Americans, especially since both of these transportational technologies helped bring in more invaders. Eventually, Native Americans learned to distrust the European Americans, who with increasing frequency broke treaties and invaded their lands with large machines.

In the nineteenth and twentieth centuries, the technologies that govern natural resources became particularly important for Native Americans. For more than a century, Native Americans have fought for the right to exploit the natural resources that exist on their lands but that are being stolen by European American technologies such as dams, artificially made canals, oil drilling, strip mining, and timbering. Using legal and political power, contemporary Native Americans are slowly regaining some of the rights over the oil under their land, the ores in their mountains, and the waters that flow through their land.

Technology allows people to solve problems and to dominate particular forces. When the Europeans came to North America with their more advanced technologies, Native Americans were often awed, impressed, and afraid. In the diaries and journals written on the early American frontier by Europeans making their way through "Indian country," one gets the sense that, for these invaders, the Native Americans were the problem to be solved. The old saying, "The pen is mightier than the sword" is particularly relevant to the issue of Native American technology, because with both of these technologies—the pen that wrote treaties never meant to be kept, that wrote bills of sale for millions of acres of land for a few supplies, that signed away the children of illiterate Native American parents to European mission schools; and the sword, which was brought to bear on natives who would not cooperate with the pen—the European invaders dominated all of North America, ultimately changing the oldest inhabitants on the continent into one of the most exploited peoples in the Western Hemisphere.

Kenneth S. McAllister

Sources for Further Study

Ambler, Marjane. *Breaking the Iron Bonds: Indian Control of Energy Development*. Lawrence: University Press of Kansas, 1990. A well-researched and developed book that introduces the history of federal Native American policies, particularly those that relate to reservation energy development. Includes numerous illustrations, maps, and tables, as well as an excellent bibliography and index.

Browman, David L., ed. *Early Native Americans: Prehistoric Demography, Economy, and Technology*. New York: Mouton, 1980. An anthology of articles with varying perspectives addressing the issues surrounding the entry and early technological development of human beings in North America. Many excellent photographs, charts, and time lines, along with an index of names and an index of subjects.

Johnson, Jay K., and Carol A. Morrow, eds. *The Organization of Core Technology*. Boulder, Colo.: Westview Press, 1987. A collection of essays that reexamine the way that tool manufacturing developed in North and Central America up to the contact period. Several dozen tables detail locations, materials, and types of early tools.

Laubin, Reginald, and Gladys Laubin. Photographs by Gladys Laubin. Drawings by Reginald Laubin. *American Indian Archery*. Norman: University of Oklahoma Press, 1980. An engagingly written book about bows, arrows, spears, and darts that combines scholarship and anecdote. Includes both black-and-white and color photographs along with numerous drawings, a bibliography, and an index.

Sassaman, Kenneth E. *Early Pottery in the Southeast: Tradition and Innovation in Cooking Technology*. Tuscaloosa: University of Alabama Press, 1993. A book that discusses the socio-economic and political importance of early pottery and cooking technology, refuting long-held interpretations about the significance of these technologies on the Native Americans' change from hunters and gatherers to farmers. A lengthy bibliography and an index.

Van Buren, G. E. *Arrowheads and Projectile Points: With a Classification Guide for Lithic Artifacts.* Garden Grove, Calif.: Arrowhead, 1974. Basically intended for field researchers, this book details a system by which stone tools can be correctly identified and archived. There are many excellent photographs and drawings of tools such as scrapers, arrow points, and spear heads, as well as historical and formative information about them. Contains a bibliography and index.

See also: Agriculture; Irrigation; Metalwork; Pottery; Tools; Transportation Modes; Weapons.

Tipi

Tribes affected: Arapaho, Cheyenne, Crow, Dakota, Kiowa, Pawnee, others

Significance: *Undoubtedly the most widely known of all American Indian structures, the tipi is a practical and comfortable form of shelter that was ideally suited to life on the Plains.*

The tipi (or tepee) is a cone-shaped dwelling made of wooden poles covered with skin or bark that was used primarily by the Plains peoples. The word is Dakota in origin and combines the words *ti,* meaning to dwell, and *pi,* which refers to the third-person plural, or "they." Thus the word in translation means "they dwell."

The tipi was made of three primary poles, usually of willow because of its smoothness and strength, 20 to 30 feet long tied together at the top. Fifteen to sixteen more poles, slightly shorter, were added, along with the lifting pole used to raise them. Two smoke flap holes were used to aid in the control of air flow. The conical structure was tilted slightly to keep rain out and assist air circulation. It was covered with animal hides, usually buffalo or deer, or with bark of various sorts, depending on locale. A flap was used for the door, which was secured with wooden pegs.

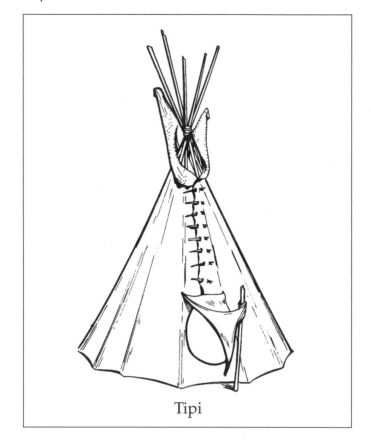

Tipi

Before the introduction of the horse, these portable lodgings would be about 12 to 15 feet across at the base and could be readily and rapidly assembled and disassembled. They were dragged along behind large domesticated dogs, the main poles slung across their backs, with the secondary poles and skin covering carried between them. After the horse became an integral part of Plains life, the tipi increased in size and could be from 20 to 30 feet across at the base.

For winter use a secondary lining was made for the interior to increase the insulating properties of the outer covering. A fire pit was dug in the middle of the floor, and the ground was often cleared and packed hard, then covered with grasses, leaves, and hides. These dwellings were very warm and comfortable in the winter, and they could be made open and airy in the warmer seasons by removing the lining, opening the flap, and raising the outer covering a few inches above the ground to increase air flow.

Modern tipis are made using a variety of materials for the poles. They are often covered with canvas and can measure up to 40 feet across at the base.

Michael W. Simpson

See also: Architecture: Plains; Hides and Hidework; Horses.

Tobacco

Tribes affected: Pantribal but especially Southeast and Southwest tribes

Significance: *Tobacco was an important recreational and ceremonial substance for many Indian tribes.*

As early as 1500 B.C.E., the Tamaulipas farmers of Mesoamerica (Central America) cultivated tobacco. In the Southwest, tobacco was grown as early as 630 C.E., though the tobacco grown by eastern Indians was not introduced until after the Spanish conquest. The Southwest Pima tribe approached tobacco farming scientifically, cultivating seed crops and rotating planting sites. Their neighbors, the Tohono O'odham, simply planted all the seed from a previous year. Only old men and some women smoked, as both the Pima and Tohono O'odham believed that tobacco inflicted a cough and made one lethargic and less resistant to cold. Southwest Indians did not chew tobacco. They still grow a small amount of tobacco today.

Exploring Florida in 1539, John Hawkins reported that the Indians were smoking a dried herb. This tobacco was apparently introduced to the Florida Indians by Spanish explorers. In the piedmont and the Cumberland Plateau, Algonquin farmers raised tobacco plants three feet high, dried the leaves over a fire, and ground them to smoke in pipes. They eventually adopted a milder tobacco from the West Indies, introduced into Virginia by John Rolfe. In the north, the explorer Jacques Cartier reported that the Indians around present-day Montreal were growing and using tobacco. By the eighteenth century, tobacco cultivation had become a major enterprise among the Cherokee, Choctaw, Chickasaw, Creek, and Huron Indians. Much of the agricultural process of growing tobacco was ultimately learned from the Indians by white agricultural interests.

David N. Mielke

Sources for Further Study

Champagne, Duane, ed. *Contemporary Native American Cultural Issues*. Walnut Creek, Calif.: AltaMira Press, 1999.

Winter, Joseph C., ed. *Tobacco Use by Native North Americans: Sacred Smoke and Silent Killer*. Norman: University of Oklahoma Press, 2000.

See also: Calumets and Pipe Bags; Pipestone Quarries; Tobacco Society and Dance.

Tobacco Society and Dance

Tribes affected: Widespread but highly developed among the Crow

Significance: *Tobacco societies controlled the complex rituals surrounding planting, caring for, and harvesting tobacco.*

Of all North American tribes, the Plains Crow developed the most elaborate Tobacco Society. The tobacco species *Nicotiana multivalvis* was considered holy, a supernatural gift having its own ceremony and mystically associated taboos. After the earth was formed, the Creator saw a human, transformed a star into a tobacco plant, and decreed that the Crow should honor tobacco with ceremony. Consequently, tobacco was their mainstay of living.

From this founder or ceremonial "father" came adopted novices, newcomers who had independent visions that revealed unique revelations for adopting further novices. Approximately thirty groups, under the leadership of a Mixer, possessed their own distinctive songs and emblems. These groups formed independent military societies, each with its own bird and animal symbols.

The main function of the Tobacco Society was to perpetuate the welfare of society and integrate society with the supernatural, and natural worlds by controlling the complex ritual required to plant, care for, and harvest this sacred plant. Tobacco was believed to be capable of conferring special benefits to its votaries. A main element of the tobacco complex was dreaming and visions, ones prophetic of future deeds. Tobacco visions helped decide who should become a member. A man or woman was adopted by a "father," and usually a husband and wife were initiated together. The candidate was instructed in songs and rituals during the winter, and in the spring was formally initiated, after the tobacco planting. Installed members encouraged nonmembers with gift-giving.

The four-day spring Tobacco Dance was staged in a specially built conical lodge of ten large pine trunks, with an altar strewn with juniper to represent the Tobacco Garden. Drummers participated, but the distinctive instrument was the rattle to imitate thunder. The specially painted participants laid their bundles of sacred tobacco seed in a row. Participants sang individual songs, danced, and then sweated in a willow sweatlodge and were washed with wild carrot root infusion or scrubbed with sagebrush to purify them and help them resist disease for one year.

John Alan Ross

See also: Dances and Dancing; Tobacco; Visions and Vision Quests.

Tomahawks

Tribes affected: Pantribal
Significance: *Tomahawks were both weapons and tools that aided North American Indians in fundamental survival.*

"Tomahawk" comes from the Algonquian word *otomahuk*, meaning "to knock down." Tomahawks are small axes that were used by North American Indians as tools, weapons, and hunting devices.

This poster illustrates the European fear of Native Americans and their weapons. *(Library of Congress)*

Originally, tomahawks consisted of a head made of stone or bone mounted on a wooden handle. These tomahawks generally measured eighteen inches in length or less and were light in weight. Following the arrival of the Europeans, hatchets with metal heads were made by white artisans. These tomahawks became a valuable trading item between whites and Indians.

Indians used tomahawks as throwing hatchets against their enemies in battle. They were also used to chop wood, to drive stakes into the ground, and to hunt food. Some tomahawks were used simply for ceremonial purposes. One example of this type of tomahawk is a "pipe tomahawk," which had a pipe bowl attached to its head and a hollow handle. These tomahawks were smoked during ceremonies. It is widely believed that the expression "bury the hatchet" came from the Indian custom of burying a tomahawk as part of a peace ceremony at the end of hostilities among Indians.

Jennifer Raye James

Source for Further Study

Taylor, Colin F. *Native American Weapons*. Norman: University of Oklahoma Press, 2001.

See also: Scalps and Scalping; Tools; Warfare and Conflict; Weapons.

Tools

Tribes affected: Pantribal

Significance: *The many tools that were manufactured by American Indians enabled them to hunt, fish, farm, make clothing, build their homes, and protect themselves from both wild animals and hostile strangers.*

Before European traders and settlers emigrated to North America, American Indians were limited in the materials available to them for the preparation of their tools. Inland Indian tribes utilized stone, wood, and animal bone almost exclusively. Indians living near the oceans also used seashells. In most tribes each man or woman made his or her own tools, and considerable time was spent in searching for the right piece of a useful mineral or for a type of wooden branch to make into the desired tool. Effort was spent in the conceptualization of how to prepare a desired tool most appropriately from the few materials available and how to make it most attractive. Tool preparation was arduous in most cases, and the tools that Indians used—axes, arrowheads, arrows, bows, clubs, hammers, harpoons, knives, farm and home implements, nets, scrapers, spear heads, tomahawks, traps, and so on— combined ingenuity and aesthetic sensibility.

Hammers, Axes, and Adzes. Preparation of these tools first required the choice of an appropriate stone. Hammers, very common Indian tools, were prepared in several stages. First the chosen stone was chipped roughly with another stone and a bone chisel to produce the general shape of the desired hammer. Then more careful chipping yielded a more exact hammer shape. Finally, grinding with wet sand or sandstone completed the process. The stone most often chosen for hammers was granite, because the repeated pounding that is involved in hammering does not easily split or shatter this exceptionally tough stone.

Good stone axes were rare because minerals that could yield a sharp enough point to shape logs were scarce. Even the best axes Indians could make (prior to their contact with Europeans, who provided metal tools) were poor shaping tools. Only in the American Northwest did Indians do extensive woodworking. There, available minerals such as serpentine could be used to make adzes (cutting tools with thin, arched blades).

Clubs and Tomahawks. Two other very common Indian tools were clubs and tomahawks, although these Indian artifacts were most commonly used as weapons in warfare. Clubs were often made by shaping a heavy piece of wood with a knot at one end. The eastern Indian tribes, especially the Algonquian groups, are credited with the invention of the tomahawk. The first tomahawks were clubs with a pointed stone inset into the knot in the club. Tomahawks were heavier, sharper, and deadlier than were clubs and spread slowly through the Indian tribes. They reached the height of deadliness and wide use only after European traders introduced the axlike metal tomahawks that many tribes came to favor.

Arrowheads, Harpoons, Knives, Scrapers, and Spearheads. These ubiquitous Indian implements were very often made of flint, chert, or black obsidian (volcanic glass), all stones that can be chipped to produce very sharp cutting edges. In order to make them (an arrowhead, or projectile point, for example), the Indian artisan positioned a bone chisel against a chosen place at the edge of the stone to be used. Then the chisel was struck repeatedly with a hammer, until a stone chip was knocked off by the percussion. After chipping away at the entire edge of the chosen stone, a sharp, serrated edge was produced. Then, carrying out the same overall procedure on the other edge of the stone produced a typical arrow-

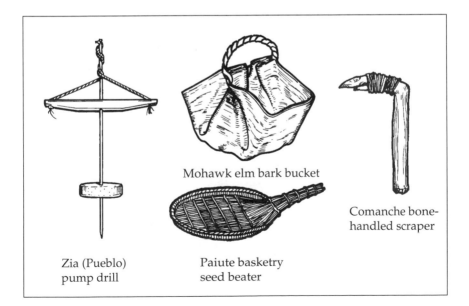

Mohawk elm bark bucket

Comanche bone-
handled scraper

Zia (Pueblo)
pump drill

Paiute basketry
seed beater

head. Longer stones of various sizes, edged on one side only, became knives or scrapers. The blades of harpoons and spears were made in a similar fashion, but they were much larger.

In a great many instances, these implements were attached to short handles (such as knife hafts) or long handles (spear or arrow shafts). Stone implements were thus necessarily engineered so that the haft or the shaft could be attached by the use of rawhide or sinew straps. Harpoons were designed so that a long rope was firmly attached to the harpoon head. This was necessary for efficient recovery of the fish or other aquatic creatures hunted with these tools.

Bow and Arrow Design. The bow-and-arrow combination derived from efforts of Indians to cast spears for longer distances than was possible when they were simply thrown by hand. The wooden or reed shafts of arrows were chosen for straightness, strength, and lightness. The arrow's back end was notched to fit a bow string and fletched with two or three bird feather pieces. Fletching facilitated straight flight upon release from a bow. Arrows were considered to be quite valuable and were very time-consuming to make, so most Indians marked them so that they could be easily identified and reclaimed for reuse.

Bows were made of strong, springy wood (such as hickory, oak, or ash) that was reinforced for even greater strength by use of added bone and sinew. These tools of the hunt and of war varied according to whether the Indian using them traveled on foot or on horseback. Those who rode on horses used short, curved bows. Such bows were often double-curved compound bows of the shape sometimes called a Cupid's bow. Made mostly of wood or animal horn, they were strengthened in the middle by pieces of bone or sinew. Indians who traveled on foot often used very simple wooden bows usually as long as the bow wielder was tall; they were much less curved than the bows of horsemen. The bow strings utilized by various Indians varied from twisted plant fiber cords to animal sinew, depending on the tensile strength that was required by the user.

Farm and Home Implements. The axes, hammers, knives, and scrapers previously described were everyday tools that were used both in the home and in the fields. In addition to stone tools, many bone implements were utilized because of their hardness, the plentiful occurrence of bone in game animals eaten, the varied shapes and sizes of animal bones, and the fact that bones could be broken into very sharp fragments when struck with hammers or even with unworked stones. Sharp bone slivers could be used as awls that drilled holes in skins to make into footwear and other clothing or as chisels utilized in toolmaking. The shoulder blades of large animals were also made into hoes by some tribes that farmed. Deer antlers were used as picks for the digging of the ores and gemstones (copper and turquoise, for example) used to make jewelry. Bone, stone, or wood hooks used to catch fish were also made by many tribes.

Sinew, Tools, Nets, and Traps. Animal sinews were highly valued items widely used in Indian toolmaking. Their use was based on their strength and on the fact that a wet sinew shrinks when it dries. It has already been mentioned that sinew was used for bowstrings wherever possible. In addition, sinew lashings were the preferred way to affix bladed tools to their handles. Where sinew was used, it was first wet thoroughly. Then it was used to tie the stone part of the tool to its handle tightly and allowed to dry. The shrunken, dried lashings held the parts of the tool together firmly and became quite hard.

Nets and other types of animal traps were also widely utilized by American Indians in their hunting and fishing activities. Nets were made of the fibrous inner bark of trees, of grasses woven into cordage, or of combinations of these materials and strips of animal hide or sinews. They were used to catch fish or smaller land animals. Sometimes they were also incorporated into traps into which aquatic animals or land animals were driven by large groups of Indians. Other traps for catching solitary, large game included wooden pens, spring traps, and deadfall traps. These last two types of traps caught animals by dropping heavy weights on them or by catching them by a foot after they were attracted by bait. It is now believed that many Indian tribes obtained more food animals with nets and traps than with archery, spear casting, and hook fishing.

Simple Wooden Tools. Many tools used by Indians were made of wood only. For example, many arrows used to hunt birds and other small game were merely sharpened sticks. Such arrows were more expendable, and stone points were not necessary to kill such animals. Planting sticks used by Indians who farmed were usually long branches, forked near the bottom. One fork end was sharpened to be used in the actual planting; the other end was a foot rest. In addition, many hoes and clubs were made of wood only.

Sanford S. Singer

Sources for Further Study

Adair, James. *Adair's History of the American Indians*. Edited by Samuel Cole Williams. 1930. Reprint. New York: Promontory Press, 1974. This book, first published in 1775 and edited by Williams, describes the lifestyle of many American Indians, therein illustrating the preparation and the use of many Indian tools.

Cobb, Charles R., ed. *Stone Tool Traditions in the Contact Era*. Tuscaloosa: University of Alabama Press, 2003. A review of the various types of stone tools used by Native Americans.

Hothem, Lar. *Arrowheads and Projectile Points*. Paducah, Ky.: Collector Books, 1983. This well-illustrated book describes arrowheads and other projectile points, their preparation by various Indian tribes, the materials and techniques used, and ways to identify fakes of various types. It is interesting and contains very good illustrations.

_____. *Indian Flints of Ohio*. Lancaster, Ohio: Hothem House Books, 1986. Illustrates Indian tools and their provenance from 8000 B.C.E. to 1650 C.E. Engenders an understanding of the evolution of Indian toolmaking and of how the tools were mated with components that completed them.

Montgomery, David R. *Indian Crafts and Skills: An Illustrated Guide for Making Authentic Indian Clothing, Shelters, and Ornaments*.

Bountiful, Utah: Horizon, 1985. Most interesting here are the illustrated descriptions of the preparation of common Indian tools and of several types of traps. Tools and traps are related to other aspects of Indian life.

Russell, Virgil Y. *Indian Artifacts*. Boulder, Colo.: Johnson, 1981. Describes and illustrates most types of Indian tools and other artifacts. Explains how many of the Indian artifacts were fabricated.

See also: Bows, Arrows, and Quivers; Knives; Lances and Spears; Technology; Tomahawks; Weapons.

Torture

Tribes affected: Pantribal
Significance: *Torture was widespread among indigenous tribal peoples for military, social, and religious reasons.*

Many, if not most, indigenous tribal peoples practiced one or more forms of physical torture of enemies, prisoners, captives, and miscreants within the tribe. Some tribal groups, such as the Puebloan cultures of New Mexico, may have committed very little or no torture. European Americans, themselves no strangers to torturous acts, commented regularly on what seemed to them purposeless or completely sadistic actions by "devilish savages." Numerous accounts of scalpings and bodily mutilations, such as the famous ones including Colonel Charles Crawford in northern Ohio in 1782 or the Hungate family near Denver in 1864, became standard conversation fare of the frontier and parlor alike. Certainly European Americans misunderstood the reasons behind such actions; falling into stereotyping and feeding readers what they wanted to read, European American writers also undoubtedly overstated the case. Yet actual torture occurred frequently, especially in the Eastern Woodlands and on the Plains.

Torture took place in several varieties. Often the captors tied enemies to a stake or other framework and burned them with bonfires, firebrands, or coals. Stabbing, beating, and cutting the victims often occurred along with the burnings, as did mutilation and dismemberment. Torturers often shot arrows or, after obtaining guns, bullets into the suffering captives. Some of the unlucky experienced the horrors of feeling themselves disemboweled, flayed, or scalped while they were still alive. On many occasions, however, the goal of torture was not death. With such customs as the gauntlet, in which victims had to run or stagger through rows of kicking, punching, and beating tribal members lined up in parallel or spiral formations, a tribe was often testing captives as potential adoptees or slaves. If a captive showed pluck or fortitude, he or she might even be rewarded with freedom.

To individual tribal groups, torture probably had many and different meanings. On one level it was surely an expression of simple revenge. Yet for most groups, torture also served military, social, and religious needs. Tribes could earn a terrifying and fearsome reputation through renowned torture. Members who had not participated in the actual battle or capture could join communally in a torture ceremony. Many indigenous peoples also believed that enemies would haunt them in an afterworld, and mutilation would distinctly disable those enemies. Sometimes torture was propitiation of certain spirits, manitous, or windigos. Whatever the case, torture was not, as many European Americans feared and believed, random, unthinking violence, but rather a custom integrated into the tribal worldview.

Thomas L. Altherr

See also: Adoption; Captivity and Captivity Narratives; Ethnophilosophy and Worldview; Scalps and Scalping.

Totem Poles

Tribes affected: Northwest Coast tribes

Significance: *The cultural hallmark of the native peoples of the Northwest Coast is the totem pole, a meticulously carved column representing family history, social rank, and ethnic identity.*

Totem poles are among the largest wooden sculptures ever created. Typically carved from the single trunk of a western red cedar, they reached up to 80 feet in height in the nineteenth century, with one twentieth century piece from Alert Bay in British Columbia being an astounding 173 feet high.

There are different types of carved poles that are usually collectively referred to as "totem poles." These include freestanding poles erected in front of houses or along village beaches, interior house posts that make up part of the framing, and frontal poles set alongside the main entrance. A dramatic variant of this latter type has an entrance right through the pole itself. A Haida pole at Ninstants, for example, depicts a grizzly bear devouring a human being, and the entrance passes right through the bear's stomach. Funeral customs are also reflected by the erection of memorial poles, grave markers, and mortuary poles which contain the ashes or support a box with the remains of the deceased chief. Not all tribes had all types of pole.

The images on the poles are not really "totems." They are best seen as valuable family crests which depict a mythic or historic event in their past. This might include the encounter of a clan ancestor in the origin times with a supernatural creature, who bestowed upon him the right to use his crest as well as entitlements to hunting and fishing territories, wealth, or other distinctions. Sometimes historic events were recounted, such as how one clan outsmarted another or how a rival chief had been humiliated. These stories helped to legitimize social standing for the chief, his clan, and his children and to lay claims to new rights. By socially manipulating crest images on totem poles and other works of art, chiefs energetically competed for rank, prerogative, and privilege.

Although abstracted and complex, crests could usually be identified by the inclusion of conventionalized features. Beaver always had a cross-hatched tail and two large incisors. A toothy "V"-shaped smile with spines over the eyes revealed Sculpin. Similar iconic devices disclosed Sea Grizzly, One-Horned Goat, Giant Rock Oyster, Fog Woman, Lightning Snake, Thunderbird, and a host of others.

The carving of totem poles flourished in the mid-1800's because of an influx of metal tools and commercial paints. Along with these aids, however, came acculturative forces that led to the virtual extinction of the art form by the early 1900's. The potlatch, a ceremonial feast central to the erection of totem poles and the telling of their stories, was outlawed by the Canadian government in 1884. Disease as well as missionary and other pressures undermined the social and ceremonial fabric that supported carving.

Totem poles on Queen Charlotte Island, British Columbia, during the early twentieth century. *(Thomas Lunt, American Museum of Natural History)*

A resurgence of ethnic pride has reversed this trend. A revised Canadian Indian Act of 1951 dropped the ban on potlatching. Church-related groups such as the Alaska Native Brotherhood gave up resistance to traditional ceremonialism. Training schools for artists were established, and totem poles once again began to be raised. Carving began to be accepted as art rather than merely as an ethnic curiosity, and poles can now be found from museums to malls and internationally from Germany to Japan.

Gary A. Olson

Source for Further Study

Hawker, Ronald W. *Tales of Ghosts: First Nations Art in British Columbia, 1922-61.* Vancouver: University of British Columbia Press, 2003.

See also: Architecture: Northwest Coast; Arts and Crafts: Northwest Coast; Potlatch; Sculpture; Totems.

Totems

Tribes affected: Pantribal
Significance: *Totems were animal spirit guardians who helped individuals and families survive.*

American Indians share the concept of the totem, or guardian spirit, with many aboriginal peoples, including those of Australia. Help with survival in a demanding environment was sought by individuals and families, and among some tribes, an individual might have a personal guardian spirit as well as a clan totem associated with his or her extended family.

Creation myths and other oral tales of American Indians refer to a time when animals talked and behaved much as people do, and the idea of a totem spirit that communicates with those seeking its assistance may be linked to those stories.

Many of the Pacific Northwest and Alaskan tribes carved elaborate wooden totem poles that served as illustrations of the lineage of the clan. The totem pole also served to trace the history and interrelationship of the clans, with important events recorded symbolically on the poles.

The acquisition of a personal guardian spirit was made through a visitation of the spirit, usually in animal form, in a dream or during a vision quest. The spirit might take the form of a bear, eagle, beaver, or other familiar animal. Less often, the spirit was associated with natural forces such as lightning, and an individual associated with such a totem would be regarded as powerfully protected. The spirit might teach the chosen individual certain songs to call forth its power, and different types and levels of power were associated with various totem spirits.

During its appearance, the spirit would also convey certain taboos or activities necessary to observe in order to keep the totem's favor. Entire families of the Bear Clan, for example, would refrain from killing or eating bears, for the spirit was believed to take the animal's form to appear, and they could not risk angering it.

While not all tribes believed that people were descended from animals, some tribes might consider the animal spirits to be their ancestors, and worthy of the highest respect.

One may be born into a family already possessing a certain totem, but the protection of any particular spirit was never actively sought. It was believed that the spirit chose whom it believed to be worthy. Not every seeker received a guardian, and the totem could withdraw its favor and protection if something was done to displease it.

Patricia Masserman

Source for Further Study
Berlo, Janet Catherine. *Native North American Art*. New York: Oxford University Press, 1998.

See also: Guardian Spirits; Religion; Totem Poles; Visions and Vision Quests.

Tourism

Tribes affected: Pantribal
Significance: *Tourism has become a valuable economic resource for many tribes, but it may also involve catering to popular stereotypes and sometimes the jobs it provides offer low wages.*

Until the late nineteenth century, the European Americans who made contact with Native American tribes were mainly explorers, trappers, and pioneers. By the end of that century, though, two historical developments turned the native groups into tourist attractions. First, conflict had ended with the victory of European American society. This meant that the earlier inhabitants had to find ways of adjusting to the dominant civilization. Second, railroads and other means of transportation made possible travel to reservations and other native settlements.

Native American tourism was encouraged in the 1960's and 1970's by cultural trends and political events. Fascination with Native American cultures and ways grew in the larger population, particularly among those involved with the youth "counterculture" of the time. During the same decade, the control of many tribes over their own lands and resources increased. In 1975, the U.S. Congress passed the Indian Self-Determination and Education Assistance Act of 1975, designed to provide federal assistance to enable tribes and reservations to achieve greater economic and social independence. During the late 1960's and 1970's, also, the legal sophistication of a number of native groups, such as the Native American Rights Fund, enabled tribes to enlarge their territories and to expand their rights to use their own lands.

Tourism was one way that Native Americans could profit from these lands. Throughout the late twentieth and early twenty-first centuries, Native Americans sought to use tourism to retain their ethnic identities while surviving economically. With the help of government assistance and business partnerships, tribes developed recreational facilities and organized powwows and other cultural attractions. In Arizona, for example, the White Mountain

This father and son are displaying examples of ethnic art to be sold to tourists. *(Jay Foreman, Unicorn Stock Photos)*

Apache Tribe developed the Apache Cultural Center, a ski resort, and facilities for camping and fishing. Farther north, the Wisconsin Native American Cultural Tour brought visitors to the Oneida Nation, Menominee Nation, Stockbridge-Munsee Band of Mohicans, and the Forest County Potawatomi. In Colorado, the Western American Indian Chamber was formed in Denver in 1989. With funding from the American Express Company, the Chamber promoted tourism to reservations. It also sponsored a yearly Native Tourism Alliance Conference in Denver in the spring of each year.

Gambling on reservations was one type of tourism that became especially common and controversial. The 1988 Gambling Regulatory Act legalized casinos on reservations in many states, promoting this kind of tourist attraction. Researchers have found that gambling does bring profits, but that it may also result in problems such as increases in crime and bankruptcy.

Many Native Americans see tourism in general as a mixed blessing. It is a substantial source of income for many tribes. It enables members of some groups to remain in their homelands, instead of seeking work elsewhere. However, many of the jobs generated by most forms of tourism provide relatively low wages. Appealing to a mass tourist market may also involve catering to Euro-American stereotypes about Native American ways. For example, tipis may be erected in tourist areas to represent dwellings of native groups that historically did not live in tipis; likewise, natives in various parts of the country may be called on to dress in costumes of the Plains Indians, made familiar in films, even though such dress is foreign to their particular band or tribe.

Carl L. Bankston III

Sources for Further Study

Berkhofer, Robert F. *The White Man's Indian: Images of the American Indian from Columbus to the Present*. New York: Vintage Books, 1978.

Bordewich, Fergus M. *Killing the White Man's Indian: Reinventing Native Americans at the End of the Twentieth Century*. New York: Anchor Press, 1996.

Cantor, George. *North American Indian Landmarks: A Traveler's Guide*. Detroit, Mich.: Visible Ink Press, 1989.

Lew, Alan A., and George A. Van Otten. *Tourism and Gaming on American Indian Lands*. New York: Cognizant Communication, 1998.

See also: Employment and Unemployment; Gambling; Metalwork; Stereotypes.

Toys

Tribes affected: Pantribal
Significance: *The toys with which American Indian children played were meant both to amuse and to prepare children for their roles as adults.*

In traditional American Indian societies, children played with toys, as children in every society do. Many traditional Indian toys were similar to the types of toys widely found in other cultures, such as dolls, spinning tops, noisemaking toys, items (such as balls and sticks) used in games, and miniature versions of tools used by adults. Toys were generally made of materials that could easily be found locally—wood, stone, bone, or clay.

Toys designed for infants were intended to be amusing and to hold attention. These types of toys included rattles and attractive objects hung on the bow of the cradleboard, such as strings of carved bones that would rattle when the baby moved them by hand.

Children often made crude clay figurines of sheep, goats, horses, dogs, cats, cradleboards, canoes, and humans. They utilized bits of stone, wood, and rags in their play, much as children do today when pretending. Dolls were common, and it was not unusual for dolls to have clothing, cradleboards and houses. Some dolls were actually hollow pottery with pebbles inside. Small play utensils and implements helped children learn the work that would be required of them as adults. Children of most tribes made cat's-cradles with string, jumped rope, spun tops, bowled hoops, and played with balls. The tops were made of wood, stone, or bone and spun with a long thong of buckskin. The handles for the tops were made of sticks, sometimes whittled into a spoonlike shape. As the children matured they played with checkers, dice cut from sticks, knucklebones, or shells, and pitched quoits.

"Buzzer" or "hummer" toys operated by strings were common. Boys in some tribes had bull-roarers, which were made of a flat piece of wood, tapered at one end, with a stout cord that passed through a hole at the other end. When this toy was swung rapidly at arm's length, its blade rotated and produced a roaring noise that could be heard for some distance. Some tribes regarded this to be an important sound producer and used it in ceremonies, but most thought it a child's toy. Boys were given miniature bows and arrows and were taught to stalk game and hunt very early. During play, boys would imitate medicine men and had medicine bags made of squirrel or bird skins with small white shells or pebbles for charms. Boys of the Sioux tribe, and probably others, imitated white traders, using fur for a beard and birchbark for hats and shirts. They would smear their faces with light-colored dirt to imitate pale skin.

Hopi children received kachina dolls and toy weapons from adults during the kachina dances. Children also had drums and peashooters. Inuit children possessed sleds, boats, hunting outfits, bows and arrows, carved figures of ducks or seals, and dolls (often with fur clothing), which were carved from ivory, wood, or stone. The children of Plains Indians had dolls, sleds, clay blocks, balls, and tops. Ojibwa children had dolls and small animals made of cattails.

Lynn M. Mason

See also: Children; Games and Contests; Hand Games.

Trade

Tribes affected: Pantribal
Significance: *Before Europeans arrived in the Americas, American Indians had well-established systems and routes of trade; the European concept of trade soon altered the traditional ways.*

Pre-contact Indian tribes had philosophies about property that differed dramatically from those of most Europeans; their philosophies limited the notion of what was to be traded and by whom. Most Indian property was personal, such as clothing, weapons, and subsistence items. This personal property did not usually include land. Indian tribes and kin groups, rather than individuals, had rights to land. There was no concept of real estate as being privately owned. Among agricultural groups of Indians, garden areas were tended by groups; produce from these areas was shared. When Indians gathered or fished, they had the right to do so at will anywhere within their group's or tribe's territory. The same was the case for hunting. In addition, Indians interpreted land rights as rights to use the land productively. Land was not to be destroyed or even left unused, and if land were left unused for some time, it was ordinarily allotted to other groups within the tribe. Since land could not be traded or sold in the ethic of most tribes, there was an inevitable conflict with Europeans who wanted to purchase tribal properties.

Traditional Trade Patterns. With a great range of climate, topography, and flora and fauna, Indian peoples conformed to their environments in diverse ways. East of the Mississippi, in heavily forested areas, tribes traded extensively with one another by traveling on established trails or on rivers. In the Southeast, among the Creeks, for example, corn was a product communally produced and offered to other tribes. Plains tribes subsisted largely on buffalo, and they traded buffalo meat and skins with other tribes that came west such as the Sioux, Cheyennes, and Arapahos. In the Southwest, the Navajos planted crops on the floors of canyons and arroyos, while the Indians of the Great Basin and California wandered in small family groups, gathering seeds and nuts and snaring small animals. Each of the above cultures considered itself a self-sufficient people with communal functions and responsibilities. None considered itself an owner of properties in a European sense. Trade entailed gift-giving and a mutual exchange of items of use. It was not commerce with the European idea of accumulating material toward wealth. It was also not commerce in the sense of acquiring material that would be considered personally owned indefinitely.

Trade with Europeans. Many Indian tribes, however, were increasingly fascinated by European goods. French and English, and later Dutch and Swedish, explorers viewed trade with Indians as a way of acquiring domination over them. After 1600, with colonies established on the eastern coast of North America, trade was not only a simple exchange of goods from which each side benefited; the process of post-contact interaction became a cultural conflict and a struggle over land rights and uses. Initially, some Indians converted European articles to functions other than those originally intended, such as tools and body ornaments. This changed, however, with European objects such as guns and farming tools. Indian cultures were being changed by trade with whites, while European settlers and adventurers were acquiring large tracts of Indian territories through trade. Commercial hunting began to overtake traditional Indian subsistence hunting, and it demanded

A depiction of Indians trading at a frontier town that appeared in an 1875 edition of Harper's Weekly. *(Library of Congress)*

far more time and effort. Indians were soon becoming more dependent on European markets for their raw materials and were affected by fluctuating European prices. Hunted species dwindled, hunters traveled to other tribes' territories, and intertribal conflicts ensued. A debtor dependency developed, with Indians often being forced to give up land in this new commercial process.

The forced transition to reservation life was the final blow to the hope that Indian groups could effectively participate in large-scale trade with the dominant culture as the United States became increasingly populated and industrialized. It was not until the second half of the twentieth century that tribes began to enter the mainstream economy in significant numbers, and success has varied widely among tribes. Types of participation in the modern economy included ranching, the production of resources (such as gas and oil), the tourist trade, the sale of Indian art and crafts (such as jewelry), and, most recently, running gambling casinos on Indian land. In the case of bingo halls and other gambling centers, the federal Indian Gaming Regulatory Act (1988) recognized the right of tribes to engage in this type of economic activity on their own land without having to follow the same restrictions that apply to non-Indians. A number of controversies and questions have arisen, however, over the possible participation of organized crime groups in some operations, over non-Indian management of some centers, and over whether this type of "trade" should be considered appropriate use of a group's environment. Nevertheless, gambling centers represent one Indian adaptation to the European American concept of trade that has resulted from the extremely limited possibilities that exist on the land to which most Indian groups were restricted.

Max Orezzoli and William T. Osborne

Source for Further Study
Kennedy, Margaret A. *The Whiskey Trade of the Northwestern Plains: A Multidisciplinary Study.* New York: P. Lang, 1997.

See also: Gambling; Gifts and Gift Giving; Money; Resources.

Transportation Modes

Tribes affected: Pantribal
Significance: *Long before their contact with European civilization, American Indians had developed a number of unique modes of long-distance transportation, many of which, in their original or modified forms, are in use today.*

American Indians have traditionally used a wide variety of modes of travel, especially watercraft. Some of these modes are still in use today and have been adopted by the descendants of European settlers. In other cases, traditional ways of transport have been replaced by those made possible by European technology.

Transportation on Land. The North American Indians never developed the wheel, which was basic to European land travel. In South America, the wheel was developed but was used only in children's toys; apparently it was never considered a serious means of transportation. The probable reason for this is that wheeled vehicles require a flat, well-maintained road, and Indian cultures never built these to any great extent.

Traveling on foot was therefore the only means of land transportation practiced in the temperate climates of North America until Europeans brought horses to the Americas. A variety of containers, frequently of animal skin or of woven fibers, were developed for carrying necessary travel provisions or trade goods. The Plains tribes used a device called the travois, which consisted of two shafts that could be pulled by a dog (or a person); the shafts supported the load, hung or suspended between them. In snowy conditions, snowshoes were commonly worn for winter travel. They were often made of local wood, wetted and heated to make it pliable; the snowshoes were shaped, then webbed with hide. In other cases they were made entirely of woven hide.

Apart from walking, the major mode of land transportation in temperate climates was horseback riding. Although fossil evidence suggests that a small type of horse was once native to the

Americas, they were extinct before European explorers arrived. The Europeans introduced modern horses at the end of the fifteenth century, and many American Indian tribes, especially in the Great Plains, quickly adopted this mode of transportation.

Sleds were a common mode of transportation, especially in the Arctic and Subarctic regions. Among some Inuit groups, dogs were originally considered sacred, and sleds were pulled by humans. At some point, dogs were used, possibly because of the influence of the Athapaskans, the other major group of Arctic and Subarctic natives, who had long been using dogs to pull sleds. Dogsleds were very often quite large, up to 14 feet in length, and could carry heavy loads.

Boats. As was the case in pretechnological European society, water travel was considered far more important than land travel for several reasons. Lakes and rivers already existed—no trails needed to be blazed. Many Indian tribes lived by the shores of lakes, rivers, or oceans, as waterways provided an excellent source of food. Travel was faster and easier because waterways are generally unobstructed. Finally, once a route along a waterway was known, it would always be there, and previous travelers could easily explain the routes to others.

The type of boat most commonly used by Indians was the canoe, and there were a number of varieties. Dugout canoes were widely popular. These were formed by splitting large trees and hollowing out the middle of half the tree by fire or simply by scooping or chipping out the inside with stone or wooden implements. Also common were canoes made of bark or skin, sometimes caulked with the resin from trees or with animal fat.

Canoes varied widely in size. At one extreme, the Iroquois of New York and southeastern Canada made canoes up to 40 feet long. Many other tribes made canoes for one or two persons. The Tlingit of Alaska made dugout canoes of cedar, sometimes as long as 45 feet, which could hold up to sixty people; they also made much smaller canoes for one or two persons.

Canoes were paddled in a variety of ways. Usually there were a

Nootka Indians in a canoe carved from a tree. *(Library of Congress)*

number of paddles used by people on both sides, with steering accomplished by means of one side paddling while the other side sat idle. Sometimes, however, especially in the longer canoes containing a larger number of people, there was a short paddle used in the back of the boat. The Inuits used kayaks, a variation on the canoe that was paddled with a single oar, swung from side to side.

Marc Goldstein

Sources for Further Study

Bancroft-Hunt, Norman. *People of the Totem.* New York: G. P. Putnam's Sons, 1979.

Hamilton, Charles, ed. *Cry of the Thunderbird: The American Indian's Own Story.* Norman: University of Oklahoma Press, 1972.

Oswalt, Wendell H. *This Land Was Theirs: A Study of North American Indians.* 7th ed. Mountain View, Calif.: Mayfield, 2001.

Spencer, Robert F., Jesse D. Jennings, et al. *The Native Americans.* 2d ed. New York: Harper & Row, 1977.

Viola, Herman J. *After Columbus: The Smithsonian Chronicles of the American Indians.* Washington, D.C.: Smithsonian Institution Press, 1990.

See also: Birchbark; Boats and Watercraft; Dogs; Horses; Technology.

Tribal Colleges

Tribes affected: Pantribal

Significance: *Tribal colleges were founded and chartered by American Indian tribes to ensure that their members receive culturally relevant and sensitive education.*

Though appearing under many guises, a consistent aim of nearly all of the first two centuries of United States Indian policy was the assimilation of America's native peoples into the national mainstream. From the late eighteenth century through the first third of the twentieth century, the federal government sought to achieve this goal through educational curricula and institutions that were designed to strip Indian children of their tribal traditions and replace them with the values and practices of Euro-American society. A major instrument of this policy was the federally operated or contract boarding school, in which students were isolated from their home communities for extended periods of time in the hope that they would become white in all but their physical makeup. Informing this aspiration was a philosophy of cultural development that deemed Euro-American culture as the highest stage of human progress, superior to the reputedly savage and barbarous lifeways of American Indian tribes and other non-Western societies. Given this understanding, it is not surprising that General Richard Henry Pratt, the founder and director of the Carlisle Indian Industrial School in Pennsylvania, should have espoused the aim of Native American education to "kill the Indian to save the man."

By the 1960's, condemnations of the methods and goals of federal educational policies were being voiced by Indians and governmental officials alike. Many of these critics maintained that although government policies had failed to achieve their assimilationist goals, their ethnocidal legacy could nevertheless be witnessed in the high incidence of alcoholism and other social pathologies plaguing American Indian communities. In order to eradicate these evils, tribes sought increased control over the nature and content of the curricula to which their children were exposed. They insisted that classes be both culturally and socially sensitive and relevant, contributing to the survival of tribal languages, customs, and values. These demands were both consistent with and supported by a number of federal initiatives that encouraged bilingual and bicultural education, including Title VII of the 1968 Bilingual Education Act, the Indian Education Act of 1972, and the 1975 Indian Self-Determination and Education Assistance Act.

One of the landmark developments to emerge during this period was the Rough Rock Demonstration School, which was founded in 1966 at Chinle, New Mexico, on the Navajo Reservation. Supported by grants from the Office of Economic Opportunity (OEO) and the Bureau of Indian Affairs, Rough Rock was the first Indian school to be controlled and operated by an American Indian tribe. The success of the school's bilingual curriculum and community-based programs soon made it an inspiration and model for other Indian communities seeking to initiate indigenous educational programs for their children.

Rough Rock's achievements spawned an additional innovation among the Navajos that was destined to transform the face of American Indian Higher Education. Up through the early 1970's, it was rare for Navajos or other Native Americans to pursue post-secondary degrees. In the first place, going to college required Indians from reservations to leave their communities and live in populations overwhelmingly composed of non-native peoples. Second, those few individuals who did matriculate often found the values and goals of non-Indian academic culture so alienating and the class offerings so foreign to tribal interests and needs that they dropped out before graduating. Aware of these dismal conditions, many of Rough Rock's founders believed the time was ripe to attempt to found a community-based institution of higher education that would offer Indian-centered majors and programs. Pooling funds from the Office of Economic Opportunity (OEO), the Bureau of Indian Affairs (BIA), the Navajo tribe, and private foundations, they opened Navajo Community College (NCC) in 1968.

Located in the BIA high school at Many Farms, NCC (now Diné College) was the first institution of higher education that was directed by Native Americans. At the center of the school's curriculum was a Navajo Studies Program, which included courses in Navajo history, language, and culture. However, the college also offered a wide variety of vocational classes intended to help tribal members find on-reservation employment. The school operated out of Many Farms High School until 1971, when the U.S. Congress passed the Navajo Community College Act, which earmarked $5.5 million to construct its center at Tsaile, Arizona.

The success of Diné College motivated action by citizens of other tribes who wished to establish community-based institutions of higher education among their own peoples. In 1970, members of the Rosebud Sioux Reservation launched Sinte Gleska College (now University), followed by the opening of Oglala Lakota College on the Pine Ridge Sioux Reservation and D-Q University in Davis, California, in 1971. Between 1971 and 1978, eight new tribally controlled colleges opened their doors. These included

Turtle Mountain Community College in Belcourt, North Dakota (1972); Nebraska Indian Community College in Macy, Nebraska (1972); Cankdeska Cikana Community College in Spirit Lake, North Dakota (1974); Chief Dull Knife Memorial College in Lame Deer, Montana (1975); Keweenaw Bay Ojibwa Community College in Baraga, Michigan (1975) Salish-Kootenai College in Pablo, Montana (1977); Si Tanka (formerly Cheyenne River Community College) at Eagle Butte, South Dakota (1978); Fort Peck Community College in Poplar, Montana (1978).

In the quarter century between 1978 to 2003, nineteen more tribally controlled colleges commenced operation. The reason for this steady growth was partly economic. In 1978, the U.S. Congress passed the Tribally Controlled Community College Assistance Act, making funds available to tribal communities that would otherwise have been unable to found institutions of higher education. This legislation allocated grants of $4,000 per full-time stu-

Representatives from American Indian tribes, education, and business sectors watch as President George W. Bush signs an executive order expected to help Indian tribal colleges and universities. *(AP/Wide World Photos)*

dent (later increased to $6,000) for those tribally chartered institutions whose student bodies and governing boards were formed predominantly of American Indians and whose missions and plans met the criteria the act set forth. These colleges included: Blackfeet Community College, in Browning, Montana (1979); Little Big Horn College at Crow Agency, Montana (1980); Lac Courte Oreilles Ojibwa Community College in Wisconsin (1982); Northwest Indian College, in Bellingham, Washington (1983); Bay Mills Community College in Brimley, Michigan (1984); Fort Belknap College in Harlem, Montana (1984); Sisseton-Wahpeton College in Sisseton, South Dakota (1984); Stone Child College in Box Elder, Montana (1984); Sitting Bull College in Fort Yates, North Dakota (1986); Fond du Lac Tribal and Community College in Cloquet, Michigan (1987); United Tribes Technical College in Bismarck, North Dakota (1987); Fort Berthold Community College in New Town, North Dakota (1988); Leech Lake Tribal College in Cass Lake, Minnesota (1992); College of the Menominee Nation in Kesheena, Wisconsin (1993); Crownpoint Institute of Technology in Crownpoint, New Mexico (1993); Little Priest Community College in Winnebago, Nebraska (1996); White Earth Tribal and Community College in Mahnomen, Minnesota (1997); Saginaw Chippewa Tribal College in Mount Pleasant, Michigan (1998); and Tohono O'odham Community College in Sells, Arizona (1998).

In 1972, representatives of the then-existing tribal colleges established the American Indian Higher Education Consortium (AIHEC) to act as their major lobbying agency. AIHEC began to publish a periodical entitled *Tribal College Journal* in 1981. In 1989, this consortium created the American Indian College Fund (AICF) as a fundraising arm for its member colleges and their students.

Historian Cary Michael Carney reported that as of 1997 approximately one-fifth or 25,000 of the 127,372 American Indian students attending institutions of higher education were enrolled in tribal colleges. These students represent more than 250 Indian nations.

Harvey Markowitz

Sources for Further Study

Carney, Cary Michael. *Native American Higher Education in the United States.* New Brunswick, N.J.: Transaction, 2000.

Deloria, Vine, Jr., and Daniel R. Wildcat. *Power and Place: Indian Education in America.* Golden, Colo.: Fulcrum, 2001.

Szasz, Margaret Connell. *Eduation and the American Indian: The Road to Self-Determination Since 1928.* Albuquerque: University of New Mexico Press, 1998.

See also: American Indian Studies; Boarding Schools; Education: Post-contact.

Tribal Councils

Tribes affected: Pantribal

Significance: *Tribal councils, established by the U.S. government as reservation-based decision-making bodies representing tribal members, were opposed by many native people.*

At one time each native tribe ruled with a form of government unique to its culture but usually based on a consensus process. As the tribes were conquered, they were deprived of their sovereignty and subjected to the rule of the U.S. government through the agents of the Bureau of Indian Affairs (BIA). In 1871, Congress ended treaty-making with the tribes, and the relationship of the government to the tribes became one of guardian to ward.

In 1934, Congress passed the Indian Reorganization Act (IRA), which has been the subject of heated debate ever since. Under the provisions of this act, any tribe, or the people of any reservation, could organize themselves as a corporation, adopt a constitution and bylaws, and exercise certain forms of self-government.

Because the IRA did not recognize existing traditional forms of government, such as those provided by spiritual leaders and elders, many people boycotted the process of voting in these IRA-sanctioned governments. As a result, only a minority of tribal members voted to establish the tribal councils, which are structured after European American and hierarchical models.

The matters with which these councils could deal were strictly limited, and decisions and actions were subject to the approval of the BIA. In fact, the reservation superintendent, an agent of the secretary of interior, had full control over the property and financial affairs of the tribe and could veto anything the council did. Because of this, tribal councils were often labeled puppet governments of the BIA.

Various attempts have been made by tribal members to address this situation. In 1944, tribal leaders formed a pan-Indian organization called the National Congress of American Indians (NCAI). In 1961, several hundred native activists issued a "Declaration of Indian Purpose," which called for, among other things, the government's recognition of the rights of tribes. As tribes continue to assert their sovereignty, power has moved from the BIA to the individual tribal councils, which represent the needs of the people.

Lucy Ganje

Source for Further Study
Canby, William C., Jr. *American Indian Law in a Nutshell*. St. Paul, Minn.: West Group, 1998.

See also: Political Organization and Leadership; Tribal Courts.

Tribal Courts

Tribes affected: Pantribal
Significance: *All tribes had aboriginal mechanisms for resolving disputes; with the establishment of reservations, however, new courts were created by the U.S. Department of the Interior, and most of these courts have been replaced by tribal courts.*

Prior to European contact all American Indian tribes and bands had institutional mechanisms for settling disputes. The mechanisms varied from Eskimo song duels and Yurok mediation to Cheyenne and Pueblo councils. Under United States law, tribal governments have the right to retain or modify adjudication procedures unless Congress limits that right.

For example, in the nineteenth century the Cherokee legal system went through a series of changes from a clan- and council-based system to a system based on an Anglo-American model. In the late nineteenth century Congress expanded federal court jurisdiction in Cherokee territory and finally passed the Curtis Act (1898), which abolished Cherokee tribal courts.

Pueblo adjudicatory systems have been influenced by Spanish and U.S. institutions and policies but were never abolished by federal edict and continue to develop. For example, many Keresan pueblos have a council which decides cases. Many disputes are settled before a partial council or single official acting as a mediator. Important cases are decided by the full council; the presiding officer may act as both prosecutor and a judge. Litigants may be advised by kinsmen or ceremonial group members. In a modification of this system, Laguna Pueblo has a full-time judge while retaining the council as an appellate court.

In the mid-nineteenth century a number of tribes were confined to reservations, creating new problems of social order. In 1883 the Department of the Interior established Courts of Indian Offenses. The judges, tribal members appointed by reservation superintendents, enforced administrative rules established by the Department of the Interior. The superintendent had appellate power over the judges' decisions. In 1888 Congress implicitly recognized the legitimacy of these courts by appropriating funds for judges' salaries.

By 1900 Courts of Indian Offenses had been established on about two-thirds of the reservations. These courts were even established in some pueblos, where they competed with indigenous legal systems. Courts of Indian Offenses have an enduring legacy as a model for the procedures and codes of many contemporary tribal judicial systems.

In 1935 substantive law administered by the Courts of Indian Offenses was revised. Moreover, the Indian Reorganization Act (1934) made it easier for tribes to establish court systems less dominated by the Interior Department. Insufficient tribal economic growth slowed replacement of the Courts of Indian Offenses. By 1992, however, only twenty-two remained. By contrast, there were more than 150 tribal courts.

Tribal courts vary in size, procedure, and other matters. The Navajo Nation, for example, now has an independent judicial branch which processed more than eighty-five thousand cases in 1992. There are seven judicial districts and fourteen district court judges. The practice of law before these courts is regulated. Appeals may be taken to the high court. Appellate decisions of note are published. In addition, there are local "peacemaker" courts with 227 peacemakers who act generally as mediators.

Eric Henderson

Sources for Further Study

Carrillo, Jo, ed. *Readings in American Indian Law: Recalling the Rhythm of Survival*. Philadelphia: Temple University Press, 1998.

Pommersheim, Frank. *Braid of Feathers: American Indian Law and Contemporary Tribal Life*. Reprint. Berkeley: University of California Press, 1995.

See also: Indian Police and Judges; Tribal Councils.

Tricksters

Tribes affected: Widespread but not pantribal
Significance: *Tricksters are ambiguous supernatural figures common to North American Indian mythology who are said to have helped in creating human culture.*

Tricksters were common features of North American Indian mythology. Supernatural in origin, tricksters played an important mythological role in giving significant technologies or cultural traits, such as fire or food plants, to a particular cultural group, though often unintentionally. Tricksters were not thought to be basically concerned with human welfare; rather, their gifts to humanity were usually the result of a joke or an accident. Tricksters were often seen as good-natured buffoons, and trickster tales were a source of entertainment as well as morality tales for children.

Ambiguous Natures. The fundamental characteristic of a trickster figure was its ambiguity. Tricksters were seen as being supernatural in their origins, but they were definitely not godlike: They laughed, played jokes, and reveled in bawdy or scandalous behavior. They most often took the form of an animal, especially a coyote, raven, or hare, but an animal that could talk and act like a human; alternatively a trickster could be portrayed as an old or ageless man. Whatever their form, tricksters could usually transform themselves, as from male to female or from animal into human form. Never the biggest, strongest, or best-looking of supernatural characters, tricksters lived by their wits. Nevertheless, they were usually too clever for their own good, with their schemes or jokes rebounding on them to get them into trouble. In fact, the sly trickster was also a numbskull, fooled by his own guile into fighting with his own reflection or eating his own body parts. Even successful tricks seldom paid off for the trickster; after securing a meal through a trick, for example, the meal would be lost through the trickster's foolishness. Many of a trickster's actions might seem heroic, such as fighting with a monster or giving humanity some key skill such as flint-knapping, but the heroic behavior was usually unintentional. Moreover, the hero trickster often turned around and next did something disrespectful or disreputable. Tricksters wandered the earth, with their enormous appetites for food and for sex getting them into one tight fix after another. Tricksters were ageless. They could die, and often did as a result of their exploits; however, the trickster was able to survive death and would rebound in another form or be caught in another predicament.

Creators of Humankind. Tricksters were often seen as the creators of a particular culture. For example, among the Nez Perce, the trickster was Coyote. In the Nez Perce origin myth, a monster exists that eats all the animals except Coyote, who ties himself to a high mountain to escape. Finding he cannot reach Coyote, the monster befriends him instead. Using his friendship, Coyote asks if he can go into the monster's stomach and visit his animal friends who were eaten, and to this the monster agrees. Once inside the monster's stomach, Coyote builds a fire and then cuts out the monster's heart with a knife; all the animals are able to escape. Coyote dismembers the monster with his knife and throws the parts around the earth. Everywhere a piece lands, a tribe of Indians is created. When Coyote is finished, his friend Fox points out that there is no tribe on the spot where the monster died. So Coyote washes the monster's blood from his hands and lets the drops fall to the ground; the Nez Perce are created in this way. Coyote says, "Here on this ground I will make the Nez Perce. They will be few in number, but they will be strong and pure." The tale is typical of trickster myths in which the trickster acts as the creator of humankind.

In other tales humans already exist, but they lack the necessary skills or social behavior really to be human beings. Among the usual gifts the trickster bestows on humanity are fire, flint, tobacco, food animals, or cultivated plants, and the regulation of weather or the seasons. In the Northwest, Raven as trickster creates dry earth as well for humans to stand on. In addition, the trickster often brings mortality, portrayed as natural or necessary, to humanity. In the Winnebago trickster tale, Hare originally makes humans immortal but soon realizes that immortality will cause humanity to cover the earth, which would create great suffering from insufficient food supplies. He thus undoes his gift to create a natural balance between humanity and the ability of the earth to support life.

Telling the Tale. Trickster tales were usually narrated by highly respected specialists in the community. These specialists memorized the tales, which were maintained by an oral tradition, and presented them in creative and dramatic tellings. Most of the members of the community knew the outline of the tales, but the specialist's acting ability brought them alive. These specialists were permitted to expand or embellish on the tales as they saw fit; the fundamental plot and the primary actors were retained, but considerable liberty could be taken with the details. Trickster tales were among the most entertaining these specialists presented; the combination of buffoonery, scandalous behavior, and drama in the tales made them good listening. In addition, trickster tales were presented as morality tales for children. As the trickster found himself in trouble because of excessive pride, lust, or greed, children could be reminded of proper behavior. Some authorities believe that the trickster tales served as safety valves for adults as well by making fun of serious rituals or difficult social situations. When the trickster joked with his mother-in-law—ordinarily a very formal relationship among North American Indians—or flaunted the fasts which accompanied many rituals, he was doing something many would have liked to have done but could not because of social requirements. All in all, the trickster was—and is—a popular figure in North American mythology. Even if he was too vain, clever, or greedy for his own good, he was always amusing, and he accomplished much for humankind, even if by accident.

David J. Minderhout

Sources for Further Study

Boas, Franz. *Race, Language, and Culture.* New York: Macmillan, 1940.

de Waal Malefijt, Annemarie. *Religion and Culture: An Introduction to Anthropology of Religion.* 1968. Reprint. Prospect Heights, Ill.: Waveland Press, 1989.

Kidwell, Clara Sue, Homer Noley, and George E. "Tink" Tinker. *A Native American Theology.* Maryknoll, N.Y.: Orbis Books, 2001. An examination of the role of the trickster in Native American religious beliefs.

Leeming, David, and Jake Page. *The Mythology of Native North America.* Norman: University of Oklahoma Press, 1998. Includes a chapter on tricksters.

Pandian, Jacob. *Culture, Religion, and the Sacred Self.* Englewood Cliffs, N.J.: Prentice Hall, 1991.

Radin, Paul. *The Trickster: A Study in American Indian Mythology.* London: Routledge & Kegan Paul, 1956.

Wilson, Samuel M. "Trickster Treats." *Natural History,* October, 1991, 4-8.

See also: Clowns; False Face Ceremony; Humor; Manibozho; Religion; Sacred Narratives.

Turquoise

Tribes affected: Great Basin, Mesoamerican, Southwest tribes
Significance: *Turquoise was made into jewelry used in burial ceremonies and was an important trade item in Mexico and the Southwest.*

Turquoise is a carbonaceous mineral that was prized by many Native American groups primarily for its bright blue-green color. Major turquoise sources were located throughout the American Great Basin, the Southwest, and western Mexico, and turquoise was traded extensively throughout the western United States and Mexico.

As early as 300 B.C.E., the Anasazi Basket Maker culture as far north as Utah worked turquoise for jewelry, which was commonly interred in burials, and traded it as far south as central Mexico. Native American craftsmen from the American Southwest traded turquoise for shell from the Gulf of California and the Pacific coast. Turquoise was frequently worked into thin tesserae used in mosaic inlays over shell ornaments. Similar mosaics covered burial masks from the central Mexican site of Teotihuacán during the fifth and sixth centuries, as well as later Aztec and Mixtec sculpture. By 1000 C.E., large-scale Anasazi sites such as Chaco Canyon in northwestern New Mexico contained specialized turquoise workshops and served as distribution centers for interregional turquoise trade networks. Modern Navajo and Pueblo artisans, particularly Hopi and Zuñi, have maintained a strong tradition of turquoise jewelry and carved fetish figures during the nineteenth and twentieth centuries. In addition, ground turquoise frequently provided pigment for blue paint.

Turquoise held high symbolic import because of its distinctive bright color and relative scarcity. Turquoise stones or nuggets were believed to possess spiritual power and were common components of shaman's medicine bags as curing charms. The color blue commonly symbolized concepts of rain or water, freshness, fertility, and the western horizon, the direction of the setting sun. Mesoamerican cultures revered jade for similar reasons. In Pueblo mythology, turquoise was so revered that a specific divinity, called *Huruing Wuhti* in Hopi (loosely translated as "Hard Substances Old Woman"), was considered the patron deity of turquoise, shell, and coral.

James D. Farmer

Source for Further Study
Dubin, Lois Sherr. *North American Indian Jewelry and Adornment: From Prehistory to the Present*. New York: Henry N. Abrams, 1999.

See also: Arts and Crafts: Southwest; Dress and Adornment; Metalwork; Mosaic and Inlay; Shells and Shellwork; Silverworking; Trade.

Twins

Tribes affected: Widespread but especially the Navajo, Pueblo tribes, Seneca, Sioux

Significance: *The concept of twins formed an important part of religious mythology, explaining the process and structure of creation and providing models for human behavior.*

Twins are common in Native American mythology, but their roles have tribal variants. For the Seneca, the twins Sprout and Flint represent the bipolar structure of existence, the tension between good and evil. Sprout makes deer, and Flint makes mountain lions to eat them. Sprout creates fruits and berries; Flint, thorns and poison ivy.

More common is the myth of the War Twins, who are sons of the Father Sun. In the Zuñi tradition, they help with creation, leading the Zuñi to the surface world and transforming them into humans. Like the Navajo twins, Monsterslayer and Born of Water, they receive weapons from Father Sun and rid the world of monsters, becoming protectors of the tribe. They also often have astronomical significance, creating constellations from the monsters they have slain. In Zuñi myth, the twins are identified with the evening and morning stars.

In Navajo culture, the twins serve as models for boys as they develop into adulthood. Like the twins, male children receive toy weapons from their father. The twins are important figures in rites of passage. In Lakota Sioux culture, twins have a special sacredness, and many healers claim that their power comes from a previous existence as a twin.

Charles Louis Kammer III

See also: Ethnophilosophy and Worldview; Religion.

Urban Indians

Tribes affected: Pantribal

Significance: *As of July, 2002, the U.S. Census Bureau reported that nearly two-thirds of American Indians resided in urban areas. Although this is the lowest percentage among U.S. "racial" (ethnic) groups, the percentage has risen over the years.*

The term "urban Indians" is problematic for most non-Native Americans. Whether thinking of Native Americans brings forth positive, negative, or neutral images, most non-natives do not imagine natives as members of an urban, technological society, and this lack of urban image has led to a blindness regarding the presence and needs of Native Americans in the cities. Identification of the urban Native American has therefore been one of the central problems surrounding government policy making regarding American Indians since the early 1960's.

Relocation and Migration. All members of a federally recognized tribe in the United States, according to the U.S. Constitution, are due certain benefits and services, by right of their heritage. This unique legal relationship with the U.S. government was never meant to end once an individual moved to a metropolitan area, but in effect that is what has happened. In the mid-1950's, the Bureau of Indian Affairs (BIA), in accord with Congress, began the Voluntary Relocation Program. BIA officers on each reservation were instructed to "sell" the idea of city living to likely candidates. Individuals, and sometimes families, were given a one-way ticket to the chosen city, where housing and employment awaited, all arranged by the BIA. Subsistence money was guaranteed for six weeks, after which these newest immigrants were on their own. It was informally known as a "sink-or-swim policy." As anthropologist Sol Tax noted twenty years after relocation, however, "Indians don't sink or swim, they float."

Most Indians who arrived in the city under the relocation program left as soon as they got a good look at their new way of life.

Many of the jobs were unskilled, and Native Americans found they were able to afford only the worst housing available in the city. Under these conditions, transition to city dwelling was, for many, impossible. Yet the BIA did not recognize the shortcomings of its multimillion-dollar program and continued to relocate as many Native Americans as possible. Noticing that many of their clients were returning to their reservations, the BIA began relocating people as far away from their reservations as could be managed, to make it as difficult as possible to return. Part of the plan was to terminate the reservations eventually.

Watt Spade and Willard Walker illustrated one Indian view of this phase of the relocation program, relating a discussion between two American Indian men about the government's wanting to land a man on the moon. It could be done, one man said, but nobody knew how to get the man home again after he landed on the moon. All the government had to do, he said, was put an Indian in the rocket ship and tell him he was being relocated: "Then, after he got to the moon, that Indian would find his own way home again and the government wouldn't have to figure that part out at all." The Voluntary Relocation Program was a failure according to its own goals. This program was based on the prejudiced notion that Native American culture and lifeways would, and should, disappear. The BIA and the U.S. Congress of the 1950's counted on America's cities to speed that process.

Most Native Americans who now live in urban areas did not arrive through the relocation program but migrated independently, usually looking for employment, and settled near relatives or friends from their reservation or hometown. Many are permanent residents, but an approximately equal number are transient—relocating within the city, going from city to city, or spending part of the year in the city and part on the reservation. There is no known "typical" pattern of migration; tribal nations, families, and individuals differ according to their needs. A family may live in the city during the winter so the children can stay in school, then leave for the reservation in the summer. Construction workers are often busy in the cities during the warm months and leave in the winter. The pow-wow season and harvests also draw many urban Native Americans back to the reservations. In 1975, Jeanne Guillemin pointed out in *Urban Renegades* that the young Micmac women of Boston often preferred to return to their kin in the Canadian Maritime Provinces when it is time to give birth, where they could receive physical, emotional, and spiritual support and avoid the frightening aspects of the city, such as its clinics and hospitals. This pattern remains: The frequent moving to and from the reservation and within the city is one factor in the urban Native American's invisibility or elusiveness.

Urban Indian Identity. Another factor has been Native Americans' reluctance to identify themselves as Native Americans to non-Native Americans in the city. In 1976 the director of the American Indian Health Service in Chicago illustrated this problem with an anecdote. A young man had been playing baseball and had been hit hard by the bat. When he was taken to the emergency room, he removed all his turquoise beads, giving them to a friend to keep for him, and stuffed his long braids inside his baseball cap; he said, "Now the receptionist will think I'm a Mexican." His friend said they frequently tried to pass as Mexicans in order to be treated better.

The urban Indians' attempts to remain unidentified, coupled with the tremendous mobility of individuals and families, has in past years made it impossible for the U.S. Census to come close to an accurate count in the cities. In the 1990 U.S. Census, however, there was a huge increase in people identifying themselves as Native Americans, Eskimos, and Aleuts, and there was yet another significant increase in the 2000 Census. These increases cannot be completely explained by actual population growth, so there has been much speculation regarding what has made so many more Native Americans willing to be identified. Some cynical observers insist that the motive must be monetary: to obtain funds and services that are due Native Americans under the law. One thing that scholars studying Native American culture have learned over the decades, however, is that Native Americans usually cannot be coaxed to take a particular course of action because of the promise of money. Most Native Americans living in cities do not receive federal funds or services of any kind, because of distrust of Indian or non-Indian agencies and a preference for finding survival strategies among one another.

In the past, most sociological studies have focused on the atypical urban Native American—the one most visible, "lying in the gutter," cut off from kin. It is important to learn how most urban Native Americans (neither the upper middle-class professionals nor the indigent) have found their way in this foreign environment, maintaining strong kin relationships and networks and not necessarily assimilating. Native Americans have arrived in cities all over the United States for many reasons; work opportunities and education are the most commonly cited. Guillemin pointed to another very important reason in her chapter "The City as Adventure." For the Micmac of Canada, she noted, going to Boston was seen as extending one's tribal boundaries. While trying to survive in this environment, young Micmacs learn much about coping with conditions as they meet them in the South End, a settling ground for immigrants from all over the world. Their risk taking and networking are important parts of a young urban Native American's education. Flexibility is seen as one key to their tribal nation's survival. While it is often assumed that cities temper and neutralize (if not actually melt) the unique cultures of their residents, in this case a native people is claiming the city as their own and using it for their own purposes—to strengthen themselves as members of an Indian nation as well as to survive and enjoy themselves. Some cities, such as Chicago, operate high-quality schools for Native American children as further insurance against their losing precious traditions and ways of thinking.

Pan-Indianism. In several respects, the increase in the nation's urban-based Native American population can be seen as the basis for broad, non-tribal movements of the 1970's and later. In 1978, the American Indian Movement (AIM) organized the Longest Walk—a five-month trek from Alcatraz Island in San Francisco

Many urban Indians participated in The Longest Walk—a protest march that began in San Francisco in 1978 and ended five months later in Washington, D.C. *(Library of Congress)*

Bay to Washington, D.C., in which many urban Indians as well as others participated. This watershed event brought many formerly isolated Native Americans together and built a foundation for self-respect, self-actualization, political activism, and later economic improvements such as the gaming movement of the late 1980's and 1990's, which has done much to improve economic conditions on the reservation. Although controversial for its tendency to lump many tribes and nations into one group, this Pan-Indianism has provided a social and political connection for many formerly isolated Native Americans, advancing their interests in a way that would be impracticable if not impossible for individual nations or tribal groups.

Roberta Fiske-Rusciano

Sources for Further Study

Fixico, Donald Lee. *The Urban Experience in America*. Albuquerque: University of New Mexico Press, 2000.

Guillemin, Jeanne. *Urban Renegades*. New York: Columbia University Press, 1975.

LaGrand, James B. *Indian Metropolis: Native Americans in Chicago, 1945-75*. Urbana: University of Illinois Press, 2002.

Lobo, Susan, and Kurt Peters, eds. *American Indians and the Urban Experience*. Walnut Creek, Calif.: AltaMira Press, 2001.

Spade, Watt, and Willard Walker. "Relocation." In *The Way: An Anthology of American Indian Life*, edited by Shirley Hill Witt and Stan Steiner. New York: Alfred A. Knopf, 1972.

Waldman, Carl. *Atlas of the North American Indian*. Rev. ed. New York: Facts on File, 2000.

Weibel-Orlando, Joan. *Indian Country, L.A.: Maintaining Ethnic Community in Complex Society*. Rev. ed. Urbana: University of Illinois Press, 1999.

See also: Alcoholism; Demography; Employment and unemployment; Gambling; Pan-Indianism; Relocation.

Visions and Vision Quests

Tribes affected: Pantribal
Significance: *In the vision quest, an individual fasts in a secluded place, seeking knowledge or help from the spiritual world.*

The vision quest is a ritual conducted traditionally by men, but occasionally by women, seeking spiritual help. The vision quest is a personal experience. In an isolated place—sometimes a secluded place away from the village, sometimes a confined space such as a pit—a man fasts, avoiding food and water, commonly for a period of four days. The man humbles himself before the Great Mystery and seeks health or help for himself or his family. For example, a man might seek the courage needed to undergo a Sun Dance, seek protection before going to war, or pray for the health of a sick relative. He might go on a vision quest in thanksgiving because a great gift has been bestowed, or he might simply seek help in providing food and shelter for his family. Afterward, a holy man interprets the dream or spiritual instruction that has been received during the fast. Personal visions are kept in confidence.

"Vision question" is an American term for the process. Nicholas Black Elk called it "to go out lamenting," a translation of the Sioux word *hanbleceya*. *Hanbleceya* has also been translated as "crying for a dream," or "night journey."

To understand the purpose of a vision quest, the spiritual difference between "being called" and "having a calling" must first be understood. Among Indian nations it was not uncommon for young men, usually before they reached puberty, to have a profound religious experience in the form of a vision. The vision or dream involved one or more of the archetypal spirit masks of the tribe. A spiritual teacher would instruct a young man on how to use his visionary experience for the good of the people, since spiritual gifts were useless if not shared. The process of instruction about how to use the spiritual knowledge invariably involved fasting and sacrifice, the experience that in modern times has become known as the vision quest.

Whether men only or both men and women can seek visions is particular to each tribe. The fasting experience of the Arapaho involves teams of men and women chosen by elders, and it is so sacred to that culture that sharing the experience with non-Arapahos is out of the question. Plains, Eastern Woodland, Southeast, Great Southwest, and Northwest Coast cultures trained their medicine people in very different ways, but in each case fasting and personal sacrifice were involved.

Traditionally, vision quests commonly resulted in instructions on how to use power from the spiritual world in the course of conducting tribal rituals and ceremonies, dreams of where to find curative herbs for the health of the people, or dreams of animals— these animals might help the seeker feed his family, help a warrior in battle, or help a scout in pursuit of the enemy. Animal visions often gave the seeker a song which would call that animal helper in the future.

Nearly all tribes shared the belief that anyone could have a personal, unique religious experience, one which was also sent for the good of all the people. Those with similar visions would form dream societies that might be dedicated to healing or to dancing— even sacred clown societies were formed. Spiritual gifts humble the gifted; in humility the power is enhanced. Thomas Mails's *Fools Crow: Wisdom and Power* (1989) discusses Fools Crow becoming a "hollow bone" through which spiritual power flowed.

Today, if a man or a woman chooses to undertake a night journey to discover his or her calling or purpose in life, the person will usually present a gift and a cultural instrument of prayer (Plains tribes use a stone pipe) to a respected holy person and ask for guidance and help in the undertaking. A purification rite is performed in a sweatlodge preceding the quest. The seeker is then taken to an isolated place by the holy man. The faster is told to stay in that place "no matter what happens" until the holy man returns. The vision circle in which the seekers stays is often a pit, but it does not have to be. When a pit is not used, prayer flags (colored cloth symbolizing the four directions, with tobacco offerings bundled into them and tobacco ties attached to a string) create a circle around the seeker. As described in *Black Elk Speaks* (1932): "Within the circle thus formed, two paths are created, one running north and south, the other east and west. The seeker walks these paths, praying and weeping."

Finally, it should be noted that in recent years the vision quest has become widely known (as well as widely misunderstood) and commercialized; commercialization of vision questing disregards the original purpose of the rite: the channeling of spiritual healing or instructional power through an individual (a humble servant) to then be shared for the good of the people.

Glenn J. Schiffman

Sources for Further Study

Brown, Joseph Epes, ed. *The Sacred Pipe: Black Elk's Account of the Seven Rites of the Oglala Sioux*. Norman: University of Oklahoma Press, 1989.

Mails, Thomas E. *Fools Crow: Wisdom and Power*. Tulsa, Okla.: Live Oak Press, 1989.

See also: Ethnophilosophy and Worldview; Guardian Spirits; Puberty and Initiation Rites; Religion; Rites of Passage; Totems.

Walam Olum

Tribe affected: Lenni Lenape
Significance: *The creation story and pre-contact history of the Lenni Lenape nation is told in this set of verses.*

The Walam Olum is a long set of verses keyed to mnemonic drawings and preserved as the creation myth and traditional history of the Lenni Lenape, or Delaware, people, who formerly lived on the East Coast in the present state of Delaware. The poem begins with the creation of the world by the great creator, Manitou; it is a peaceful paradise in which men and animals live harmoniously. An evil snake threatens this paradise, but the world is saved through the efforts of Nanabush the trickster/creator, who shapes the present world on the back of a great turtle. Following these events is an account of migration from a land of wind and snow to a land with milder climate where technology emerges. The remaining verses recite clan origins and the list of chiefs up to the first encounter with Europeans.

The present text of the Walam Olum derives from a manuscript written down in the early part of the nineteenth century by an unknown scribe who was apparently not fluent in Delaware; it was first printed by Daniel Brinton in *The Lenape and Their Legends* (1885). Delaware is an Algonquian language, and themes and characters such as the earth-supporting turtle and the character of Nanabush are familiar from other Algonquian traditions.

Helen Jaskoski

See also: Tricksters.

Wampum

Tribes affected: Widespread but not pantribal
Significance: *Native Americans used wampum to record the lives of significant people, tribal laws and events, and treaties or alliances.*

The historical literature points out that the term "wampum" is not an Indian one. Instead, wampum was coined from New England settlers who shortened an Algonquin term, *Wampumpeag*, meaning a string of white beads. In the Seneca language, it is called *Otekoa*, a name for a small freshwater spiral shell. Wampum has been described as finely embroidered belts or strings, many with glass beads that were typically cylindrically shaped, about one-fourth of an inch long and half that in diameter. The original bead, before glass ones were introduced, was purported to be a round clam shell (called *quahog*) that was traditionally drilled by hand, using stone or reed drills, before iron drill bits came from Europeans. Porcupine quills and animal whiskers were also traditionally used, and the Mohawks claim that even eagle feathers were earlier evident in wampum.

The first to use wampum were the coastal Indians along the Atlantic seaboard and the New England indigenous peoples. The Long Island Indians were especially noted for their skill in manufacturing wampum, which took a lot of labor and patience in a time-consuming process. The belts and strings could be of varying length and width, depending on their representative purpose. Five- to ten-foot lengths of wampum could be made in one day. Wampum strings were made from bark or leather, and later beaver skins and painted sticks were utilized.

The native nations primarily used wampum for commercial relations, often symbolizing a ritualization of reciprocity. It was only later that the belts were made for ornamentation or adornment to wear as jewelry, which eventually led them to be viewed as craft art showpieces for exhibition. A wampum myth is that the term is synonymous with "Indian money"—the traditional Indian societies never used it as currency. It was actually American colonialists who were the first to initiate its use as money. The Dutch, in 1627, were the first to produce counterfeit wampum.

Wampum was originally used for documentation and record-keeping of significant events and agreements, such as treaties between two sociopolitical entities, as well as seals of friendship. They were also viewed as certificates of authority and credentials that guaranteed a message or promise. They were thought of as ritual ratification when accompanying treaties or alliances, which may have involved emigration, a prisoner's ransom, or the extradition of a criminal. The Iroquois used wampum for both official communication and religious purposes. According to their oral history, it was introduced to the Eastern Woodland nations by Hiawatha at the time of the founding of the League of the Five Nations.

The Iroquois Council meetings were recorded with wampum, and there were Wampum Keepers who kept the records among the Onondaga Nation. At special councils, these recordkeepers would recite the message or law that went with a particular wampum to a gathering of the people. It is also said that the Great Orator first in-

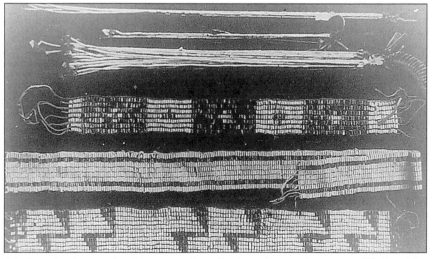

A belt and string made of wampum from the late nineteenth century. *(National Archives)*

troduced wampum to the Mohawks to bring binding peace among disagreeing parties, and to take the place of the shedding of blood.

Each people among the Iroquois traditionally had a unique design of wampum that was to represent their respective nation. It is also said that traditionally every chief of the confederacy and every clan mother had a designated wampum as a certificate of his or her esteemed office. Wampum could also be named for an individual important to the confederacy or a particular membership group among the people of the nations. Some of the most well-known wampum belts are named after significant events in tribal history.

Even though there are still a few native individuals who act as guardians of certain wampum belts and strings, most of those that have not been lost are found in glass-enclosed showcases in U.S. museums. A very few non-Indians may even have one or two in their own private possession as collector's items, but this is unusual. The traditional meaning and use of wampum has been denigrated by American law and policy. Its mnemonic significance is still a powerful one of unity and hope for the future among those native nations who still honor its sacred symbolism, if not its secular use in rituals of ratification and reciprocity.

M. A. Jaimes

Sources for Further Study

Beauchamp, W. M. "Wampum Used in Council and As Currency." *American Antiquarian* 20, no. 1 (January/February, 1931): 1-13.

Fenton, W. N. "The New York State Wampum Collection: The Case for the Integrity of Cultural Treasures." *Proceedings of the American Philosophical Society* 115, no. 6 (December, 1983): 437-461.

Tehanetorens. *Wampum Belts*. Reprint. Ohsweken, Ontario: Iroqrafts, 1983.

See also: Money; Oral Literatures; Oratory; Pictographs; Shells and Shellwork.

War Bonnets

Tribes affected: Apache of Oklahoma, Arapaho, Arikara, Assiniboine, Atsina, Blackfoot, Cheyenne, Comanche, Cree, Crow, Flathead, Fox, Hidatsa, Iowa, Jicarilla Apache, Kansa (Kaw), Kiowa, Lipan Apache, Mandan, Missouri, Nez Perce, Omaha, Osage, Oto, Pawnee, Ponca, Sarsi, Sauk, Shoshone, Sioux, Ute, Wichita

Significance: *In Plains societies, a war bonnet was one of the most valued articles that a warrior could own.*

Plains culture centered on the hunt and war, making conflict an integral part of western Indian society. The war bonnet was one way warriors recorded their achievements in battle. Two types of bonnets characterized those headdresses designed for battle: the golden eagle-feathered headdress and the split-horned bonnet.

The golden eagle-feathered bonnet was fashioned by placing twenty-eight to thirty-six eagle tail feathers into a circular skullcap base made of buffalo hide. The different cone shapes formed by the arrangement of the feathers were often an indication of the tribe to which the owner belonged. The tail of the bonnet, also made from buffalo hide, hung from the cap to the ground and was decorated with approximately thirty eagle tail feathers. The feathers were attached by their quills with rawhide and flannel cloth. Fixed to these feathers with glue and white clay were horse hair and eagle feathers. The size of these war bonnets was considerable; however, they could be rolled and folded into a diameter of eight inches, then reopened to achieve their perfect shape.

Every part of the eagle-feathered headdress had special meaning that was understood by the tribe members, including the tubular form of the Cheyenne and Blackfoot war bonnets. The feathers standing straight up from the skullcap were radiating shafts of light that symbolized the universe and brought enlightenment to the wearer from the One Above. Red, the sacred color, was the most commonly used dye on feathers, used to indicate the owner's accomplishments in battle.

The second type of war bonnet, the split-horned headdress, held the highest position in the warrior society. Only a few of the highest-ranking leaders in each band were given the right to wear the split-horned bonnet. This headdress was constructed with a buffalo hide and a tail cut into two lengths. The short tail still had the buffalo fur on it and hung to the middle back of the warrior, while the long tail was decorated with eagle wing, hawk, or owl feathers placed at right angles. The bison horns, after being hollowed out to reduce their weight, were attached to the skullcap. Items placed on the skullcap often marked significant moments in the warrior's life. These items might include sea shells, clusters of split or whole feathers, braided and dyed horse tails, beaded headbands, white ermine skins, and felt fringe. All split-horned war bonnets also possessed a long plume, the Sun Dance plume, which extended twenty-four inches from the peak of the bonnet.

A man might make four to five bonnets in his lifetime, each one a little different from the others. The war bonnets, though not worn into battle until the outcome was assured, were always worn in religious gatherings. Periodically, the headdresses were blessed in ceremonial dances performed by honored women selected to wear the bonnet during the dance. A war bonnet, which might bring three horses if bartered, was one of the most valued articles that a warrior could own.

Jennifer Rivers

See also: Dress and Adornment; Feathers and Featherwork; Headdresses; Warfare and Conflict.

Warfare and Conflict

Tribes affected: Pantribal

Significance: *The causes and modes of Indian warfare before contact with Europeans reflected the social values and religious beliefs of the various Indian cultures; the arrival of Europeans modified and intensified Indian warfare.*

Warfare was endemic among the Indian peoples of North America before European contact. War was most emphasized and most frequent in the Northeast, Southeast, and Great Plains culture areas. It was much less emphasized in the Great Basin, Plateau, and California culture areas and among many of the peoples of the Southwest area. In many places there were traditional alliances, and individual tribes often had traditional enemies with whom war was more or less constant. The practices and motives discussed below applied—with specific cultural variations—throughout North America.

Economic Causes of War. Before the arrival of Europeans, there seem to have been few economic reasons for waging war. Traditional subsistence economies offered little incentive to attack neighbors and few effective means for occupying and exploiting a neighbor's lands. There were examples, however, of a tribe yielding part of its territory because of repeated raids by a neighbor. Another exception, found especially in the Northeast, occurred when a powerful tribe forced a weaker one to acknowledge its client status and pay an annual tribute. The two were then allies with reciprocal responsibilities, but one tribe was dominant. The Pequot, for example, forced a number of weaker tribes to become tributaries. In the Northeast in the early seventeenth century, tribute came to be paid in wampum. There were other exceptions to the weakness of economic motives in aboriginal warfare, such as the raids of Athapaskan-speaking hunter-gatherers on the settled Pueblo peoples of the Southwest after the Athapaskans arrived there about 1500 C.E.

Mourning War. In eastern North America and in the Great Plains, the most common form of warfare has been labeled "mourning war" by historians. Mourning war resulted from grief over the death of a family member. Usually, but not always, the lost loved one had been slain by an enemy. Among the Iroquois of the Northeast, such grief was expected to be extreme, even temporarily incapacitating, and it could only be assuaged by securing an enemy life in retaliation. Such revenge was also necessary to quiet the angry spirit of the slain. It was a moral duty, therefore, to join in such a raid. The family of the deceased, especially the women, would urge kinsmen to join a raiding party. To refuse would be to risk the charge of cowardice. A raiding party would be organized under the leadership of a recognized warrior or war chief; with the appropriate rituals performed, the party would set out for an enemy village. Typically, there were a number of nations with whom a tribe considered itself always at war. Such a war party might be very small (a half-dozen men or even fewer), or it might number a hundred or more. In either case, its aim was to kill a few of the enemy—or, even better, to take prisoners—and to return with no casualties of its own. Such raids had no purpose other than to inflict a few deaths and thereby relieve the grief of suffering kinsmen. These raids, the most common mode of aboriginal warfare, had no economic motive.

Adoption of Captives. A captive brought in by a raiding party would belong to the warrior who had taken him (or her), typically by being first to lay hands on the victim. An adult male captive would be required to "run the gauntlet"—when blows would be rained on him by the assembled people, who in this way acted out their rage. The successful warrior would then make a grieving friend or relative a present of the prisoner. The recipient would decide the captive's fate: If adopted, the prisoner would become a member of the family, taking the place of a lost son, husband, daughter, or other family member. Raiding for prisoners was a widely practiced means of restoring families and of maintaining numbers in tribal groups experiencing population decline. In time, hundreds of non-Indian captives were adopted in this way, and the accounts that some of them wrote ("captivity narratives") are a fascinating historical source. Captives rejected as unsuitable for adoption were usually killed—often tortured to death by burning—thereby appeasing the spirits of the grieving. These torture rituals, probably most elaborate among the Iroquois and Huron, were religious ceremonies as well, with the prisoners being dedicated to the god of war.

Public War. The raiding parties that characterized mourning war were typically organized and carried out without reference to or permission from any village or tribal council or authority. There was sometimes a "higher" form of war, however, in which tribal chiefs in council, or sachems and their councils, made decisions for or against war that involved an entire people. Participation in such a larger war was left to individual decision, however. There was no compulsion, largely because participation in war was so bound up with religion and personal magic.

Warfare, Religion, and Magic. A prisoner burned by the Iroquois was dedicated to Aireskoi, their god of war, and great care was taken to keep the prisoner alive through the night-long burning with firebrands so that he might be taken outdoors at dawn and placed on a special raised platform. When the first sliver of the sun appeared, the charred but still living victim was killed by a blow. Then the body was butchered and boiled in a kettle, and the flesh was shared in a community-wide feast. If no human enemies had been sacrificed for a time, the Iroquois might sacrifice a bear to Aireskoi, with apologies.

Before joining a war party, a warrior would devote much care to purification rituals in order to strengthen his personal magic or "medicine." If the warrior felt doubts about his medicine, or if his preparation rituals were inadvertently spoiled, it was understood that he was to abandon the project. Village shamans would perform augury rituals to divine the raid's prospects, and unfavorable signs would produce its cancellation. Each warrior had a personal medicine pouch or bundle with sacred objects connected with his tutelary spirit. Among some peoples, such as the Cherokees, Chickasaws, and Creeks of the Southeast, the leader of a war party carried on his back a special wooden box, about a foot wide by a foot-and-a-half high, filled with sacred objects of proven power. Pre-raid and post-raid war rituals, in which the entire village participated, served to strengthen group solidarity.

War Honors and Personal Status. War was so important in the cultures of many American Indian societies that success in war was the principal means of attaining personal esteem and status. As a result, war trophies and war honors had a special significance in many cultures. The best-known example is the taking and displaying of scalps. Most historians agree that scalping—the removal of the skin and attached hair from the top of the head—was widely practiced in pre-contact North America. Jacques Cartier reported the custom along the St. Lawrence River in 1535, and members of the Hernando de Soto expedition (1539-1543) reported it in the Southeast at almost the same time. While each tribal group had its own particular customs, the curing and preserving of enemy scalps for display on certain ceremonial occasions was a widely practiced custom. In such ceremonies, the warrior was permitted to recite his war exploits, while other warriors or elders affirmed them. Among many peoples of eastern North America, it was the practice for men to wear their own hair in a special "scalplock," with the rest of the head shaved.

In the Southeast culture area, the winning of war names and titles was of fundamental importance. Among the Creek, for example, a warrior winning recognition would be given a traditional war name owned by his clan ("Crazy Snake" was one) in an impressive ceremony. In the Chickasaw ceremony in which war names were conferred, the recipients wore red moccasins and other special adornments. Creek warriors were ranked in three grades: warriors, big warriors, and war chiefs. Promotion through these ranks depended on war exploits, especially the number of scalps taken. Before taking scalps (and being recognized as a warrior) a Creek continued to do the menial work required of boys.

Among the Plains tribes, although scalps were taken, they did not have the importance as war honors that scalps had in the Northeast and Southeast. Among Plains Indians, the "coup" (from the French for "a blow") was more important. A warrior "counted coup" by touching an enemy with his hand or with a "coup stick." Many Plains warriors carried a specially decorated coup stick to be used to "strike coup." This was a light wand, not a weapon. Among the Cheyenne, it was striped like a barber's pole. To touch the person of an enemy during battle, as opposed to shooting him with a bow or gun, was to demonstrate one's fearlessness. Killing an enemy, therefore, unless it involved touching him, was less honored than counting coup. To be the second, third, or even the fourth to touch an enemy carried merit in a recognized scale of honors. The Cheyenne allowed three men to count coup on the same enemy, with the first to touch him accorded the greatest merit. The enemy need not even be alive; to be the first to touch the body of a fallen enemy also conferred honor. Other war honors were earned by taking something from the enemy in battle, such as a shield, a gun, or a horse. Capturing horses from an enemy camp by stealth, especially a horse picketed near its owner's tipi, was another feat conferring honor. These graded war honors both emphasized personal courage and encouraged military aggression in the form of raiding.

War honors were recognized and publicized in a number of ways. In war dances before and after a raid, the entire band or village celebrated such achievements. A warrior's exploits could be painted on his tipi cover. He recited his deeds on special occasions, and many Plains tribes used a special symbolism in the construction of feather headdresses or war bonnets. An Assiniboine wore an eagle feather for each slain enemy. As in eastern North America, the winning of war honors and the quieting of the grief of mourners were the principal motives of aboriginal warfare on the Plains.

European American Influences on Warfare. The arrival of European fur traders and colonists began to modify Indian warfare patterns in the early seventeenth century, because European guns were deadlier than aboriginal bows and warclubs. Even in the early seventeenth century, muskets had a much longer effective killing range than did bows, so that a group armed with muskets could inflict heavy losses on an enemy armed with bows. Indians quickly recognized the advantages of the new weapons (and the superiority of steel knives, hatchets, and arrowpoints) and exerted themselves to obtain them. This was imperative, because warriors armed with traditional weapons were vulnerable not only to European soldiers but also to Indian enemies equipped with European weapons. Almost the only way to obtain these weapons was through the fur trade.

The fur trade, and in the Southeast the deerskin trade, had ramifications that extended ever more deeply into eastern North America, intensifying warfare and providing new economic motives for it. Some of the most spectacular and best-documented effects occurred in the wars of the Iroquois, especially with their traditional enemies, the Huron.

By the 1620's the Iroquois were obtaining guns in significant numbers at the Dutch trading post of Fort Orange (Albany, New York), near the junction of the Hudson and Mohawk rivers. The beaver, which provided the bulk of the pelts in the trade, were trapped out by about 1640 in the home territories of the Iroquois nations. Their scarcity started the Beaver Wars. By the 1640's, to obtain furs, the Iroquois were raiding far to the north to intercept Algonquian and Montagnais hunters as they were carrying their catch to market, as well as raiding the villages of their neighbors—Hurons, Eries, Neutrals, Petuns, and Susquehannocks—to drive them out and win their hunting territories. Within a few years, the Iroquois were raiding into Ohio and as far west as Illinois. The scale of these attacks, especially the number of deaths produced, eclipsed that of traditional warfare. In these same years, a series of severe epidemics sharply reduced the populations of Iroquois villages, bringing an even greater need for captives to maintain numbers. This intensified warfare cost more lives, necessitating more raids for captives. The Huron Confederacy and the Erie, Neutral, and Petun nations were destroyed, and entire villages of the defeated were adopted as Iroquois. By the end of the seventeenth century the Iroquois themselves acknowledged defeat.

Although the eruption of the Iroquois was the most extreme example of the European American impact on Indian warfare, the effect was felt everywhere. On the Plains, the arrival of the horse (and later, the gun) had profound consequences. As Plains Indians became mounted, economic motives for warfare appeared. Capturing horses became the most common reason for raids.

Bert M. Mutersbaugh

Sources for Further Study

Axtell, James, and William C. Sturtevant. "The Unkindest Cut: Or, Who Invented Scalping?" *William and Mary Quarterly*, 3d ser., 37 (July, 1980): 451-472. An excellent scholarly inquiry into a tradition that has been seen as a stereotype of Indian culture.

Ewers, John C. "Intertribal Warfare as the Precursor of Indian-White Warfare on the Northern Great Plains." *Western Historical Quarterly* 6 (October, 1975): 397-410. A look at pre-contact war among various Indian nations.

Hudson, Charles. *The Southeastern Indians*. Knoxville: University of Tennessee Press, 1976. A thorough examination of the Southeast nations and warfare in social and political terms.

Richter, Daniel K. *The Ordeal of the Longhouse: The Peoples of the Iroquois League in the Era of European Colonization*. Chapel Hill: University of North Carolina Press, 1992. A study of traditional warfare and how it was influenced by the arrival of Europeans.

_____. "War and Culture: The Iroquois Experience." *William and Mary Quarterly*, 3d ser., 40 (October, 1983): 528-559. A brief treatment of the Iroquois reasons for and approach to warfare.

Smith, Marian W. "The War Complex of the Plains Indians." *Proceedings of the American Philosophical Society* 78 (1937): 425-461. Discusses the culture of and motives for warfare of the Plains tribes.

Taylor, Colin F. *Native American Hunting and Fighting Skills*. The Lyons Press, 2003. A survey of Native American warfare and battle tactics.

Trigger, Bruce G. *The Children of the Aataentsic: A History of the Huron People to 1660.* 2 vols. Montreal: McGill-Queen's University Press, 1976. An examination of the social and political worlds of traditional warfare and the effects of European contact.

Wallace, Anthony F. C. *Death and Rebirth of the Seneca.* New York: Alfred A. Knopf, 1973. A study of the mental world of the Iroquois people, carrying their history into the period after their defeat.

See also: Adoption; Bragskins; Captivity and Captivity Narratives; Ethnophilosophy and Worldview; Scalps and Scalping; Slavery; War Bonnets; Weapons.

Wattle and Daub

Tribes affected: Primarily tribes in the Southeast
Significance: *Wattle and daub dwellings provided effective shelter in the relatively mild environmental conditions of the Southeast.*

Wattle and daub

The term "wattle and daub" refers to a type of construction that, with variations, was widely used for dwellings in North America, especially in the Southeast. Wattle and daub construction involves a pole framework around which is interwoven a latticework of branches, twigs, or vines (the wattle). The construction is then covered with clay or mud plaster (the daub). The typical wattle and daub dwelling of the Southeast was roughly rectangular in shape and had a thatched roof with a smoke hole. The ancient "jacal" construction which preceded true masonry techniques in the Southwest was similar to wattle and daub; in jacal construction, stone slabs, held in place with adobe, were placed against the bottoms of walls.

See also: Architecture: Southeast; Chickee.

Weapons

Tribes affected: Pantribal
Significance: *The demands of daily living, such as hunting and warfare with other tribes and white settlers, required a variety of weapons.*

American Indian life required weapons for hunting game and, in many cases, for fighting with other tribes (and eventually with white settlers and soldiers). Accordingly, a variety of weapons were developed.

Bow and Arrow. This weapon preceded the arrival of whites in North America. Indian archers were skilled marksmen, and they developed a variety of bows and arrows with a deadly combination of accuracy and power. For example, chain-mail armor worn by the soldiers of the Spanish explorer Hernando de Soto could be pierced by an arrow at 150 paces. Even soldiers wearing plate armor could be felled by arrows through the eyes, mouth, or throat. In less than four years, de Soto lost 250 troops and 150 horses to the bow and arrow. Silent and quickly reloaded, the bow and arrow was universally used by North American Indians for centuries.

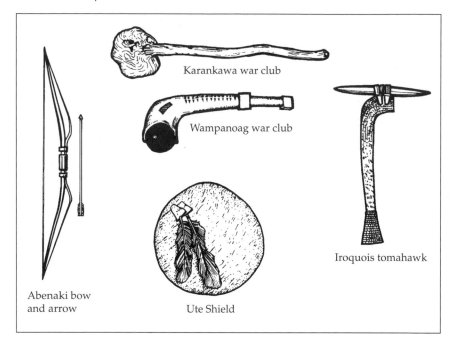

Karankawa war club

Wampanoag war club

Iroquois tomahawk

Abenaki bow and arrow

Ute Shield

Crossbow. It is highly likely that Indians borrowed the crossbow from whites, as the earliest French and Spanish explorers had them. They were used by some eastern tribes (Cherokees, Potawatomis), but it is not known when they first came into use. The crossbow had a gun-shaped grooved stock in which the arrow was placed. The bow was mounted at a right angle at the stock's forward end, and the bowstring was released by a trigger device.

Although very powerful and accurate, the crossbow never attained the popularity and universal use of the bow and arrow—possibly because it was more difficult to carry and slower to reload or because it was developed at about the same time that the bow and arrow began to be supplanted by firearms.

Tomahawk and Lance. The tomahawk was commonly used by the Algonquian tribes of the eastern United States during combat at close quarters. It was made of wood and consisted of a stem or handle about 3 feet long and a head which was a round ball or solid knob of wood. Where the stem pierced the head, a point projected forward which could be thrust like a lance. When the Indians were taught the use of iron and steel, the wooden tomahawk gave way to metal hatchets.

The lance was a long pole to whose end was attached a warhead made of chipped stone, not unlike an arrowhead. It was widely distributed among American Indians and developed into a number of varieties depending on the environment and type of animal hunted. For example, the Inuits developed the greatest variety, in response to an environment characterized by numerous animal forms. The Plains Indians made more extensive use of the lance as a weapon of war than other tribes did, because it adapted well to use from the horse.

Blowgun and Dagger. The blowgun was used by a few tribes, including the Cherokee, Choctaw, and Iroquois, solely for hunting small game—not for war. It was a hollow tube from 6 to 10 feet in length made from plant material such as cane or walnut. Darts, ranging in length from 15 to 26 inches, were placed in the end of the blowgun and expelled with a quick, sharp breath. This was a versatile weapon: Highly accurate at fairly short distances, it could also propel a dart more than a hundred yards.

The dagger was a sharp-pointed instrument used to stab and thrust at close range. Originally made of stone or bone, later versions were of copper, iron, or steel.

Rifle. Muskets were obtained from whites as early as the 1600's by eastern tribes, primarily through fur trading. The Indians became accomplished marksmen and also built their own forges and engaged in gunsmithing. Firearms spread west and were utilized by many tribes, often with great advantage to the tribes who used them first. For example, the Chippewa became the first in their region to receive firearms from white traders, which enabled them to drive the Sioux from the woodlands in the late 1600's.

The rifle was used at first as a supplement to native weapons rather than as a replacement for them. The bow and arrow was cheap and readily available, and its rapid rate of fire made it an excellent weapon. It was not until the development of the repeating rifle that native weapons gave way significantly to firearms.

Laurence Miller

Source for Further Study

Taylor, Colin F. *Native American Weapons*. Norman: University of Oklahoma Press, 2001.

See also: Bows, Arrows, and Quivers; Guns; Lances and Spears; Tomahawks; Tools; Warfare and Conflict.

Weaving

Tribes affected: Pantribal but especially the Navajo
Significance: *Textiles were made and used by the American Indian for everyday life as well as for trade and gift giving; the best-known and most prolific weavers were the Navajo.*

Weaving is the creation of a textile by means of a mechanical device called a loom. Vertical yarns (the "warp") and horizontal (the "weft") are interlaced in a variety of patterns to produce goods such as blankets, cloth, and rugs. Weaving—a very old art, preceded historically by basketry and finger weaving—progressed as different types of looms were developed and put to use.

Pre-contact Textiles. Before Europeans arrived in the Americas, the native populations made fabrics from cotton, milkweed, yucca fiber, bark fiber, strips of fur, twine, and hair. Textiles had utilitarian purposes heavily influenced by regional and climatic considerations. They were generally soft, two-dimensional items, but by 500 C.E. the Anasazi of the Southwest were making woven footwear and bags. By 700, the Anasazi probably had a simple upright loom.

By the time Europeans arrived, weaving was technically quite advanced, having slowly progressed from plaiting, braiding, and finger weaving. Three basic types of loom were in use: elementary one-beam looms for use with unstretched warp yarns, two-beam looms that used stretched warp (the first true loom), and the combination loom on which the warp was stretched over a roller loom. The latter variety, used in the area around Puget Sound, Washington, was a considerable advancement over the simpler methods, producing more even, finished, and wider pieces in less time.

In the early years, color was usually rubbed or painted onto the finished woven piece. Eventually, the fibers were dyed first and then woven. Textiles were decorated with embroidery, applique and beadwork. Beads were sometimes woven into the work.

European Influence. By the nineteenth century, the influence of Europeans had been felt. The settlers brought new materials, such as commercial dyes, and new styles and design concepts to the American Indian weaver—as well as different markets. Spanish settlers and missionaries introduced sheep in the sixteenth and seventeenth centuries, adding wool to the fiber content in blankets and rugs. The use of Shroud cloth (made in Shroud, England, in the early seventeenth century) became widespread except in the Southwest, replacing the majority of native weaving by the mid-eighteenth century.

Regional Centers. While weaving was practiced at some level throughout American Indian culture, some prominent practitioners can be identified. These were the Indians of the Southwest and Great Lakes region, the Tlingit of Alaska, and the Salish of the Puget Sound area.

The Pueblo are known to have been weavers since around 800 C.E., and the Navajo—known for high-quality blankets and rugs—since around 1700. The Great Lakes area was known for the weaving of flat, rectangular wool bags, and the Tlingit weavers of southeastern Alaska produced the prized Chilkat blanket. The Salish of the Northwest Coast area were known for using mountain goat and dog hair to make blankets.

Weavers of the Pueblo culture wove blankets and articles of clothing of cotton; after the Spanish introduced sheep into the area, they began to use wool. In Central America, Mexican serapes and blankets were made in Saltillo and Oaxaca.

Little is known about prehistoric weaving of the Tlingit people, largely because of the ill effects of their climate on the preservation of goods and materials, but it is believed that the Chilkat blankets they made are evidence of the survival of a very old primitive craft. These blankets were produced on a simple "suspension" or "bar" loom using cedar-bark fibers and mountain-goat wool. Each took from six months to a year to complete. Design motifs—all of which were symmetrically balanced and intricately patterned—featured totemic animals, family crests and natural forms in black, white,

A Navajo woman engaged in the art of weaving circa 1930. *(Museum of New Mexico)*

yellow, and green. Blankets were five-sided and fringed on two or three of the five sides. The Tlingit were also known for making ceremonial dance skirts and robes.

In the Eastern Woodlands areas, Indians made twined medicine bags, storage bags and woven belts with beadwork. In the Plains region, where leather and beadwork were more prevalent than weaving, woven mats were used to cover medicine bundles and as altar cloths for displaying objects. The Cherokee were very active weavers who used the English loom and allowed their weaving to be influenced by social and artistic forces outside their tribal group.

The best-known textiles were produced by Navajo women who made blankets, rugs, clothing, and other household items. They would use a simple loom made of two straight poles hung between two trees or a backstrap loom which had one end attached to a wall or tree and the other anchored at the weaver's waist. On these looms they produced narrow lengths of cloth used for headbands, belts, and sashes.

The development of Navajo weaving was connected to the introduction of sheep-raising. At first, the Navajo used undyed natural wool in white, black, and brown. After 1800, dyed bayeta cloth imported from Spain and England to Mexico made its way into their work; they unravelled the cloth and rewove the yarns into their own designs. Experimentation with dyes and a variety of weaves began about this time as well, although they seldom used more than five colors in addition to black, white, and undyed wool. Designs were simple, using the repetition of a few elements on a plain or striped background. The Chief's Blanket, also popular with the Plains Indians, was considered the best product of the Navajo.

By the mid-1800's, during what is known as the Classic period of Navajo weaving, Navajo weavings were the most valuable product of the Southwest. After 1925, however, because of increased commercialization, the level of quality dropped. More recently there has been a rise in quality with smaller quantities of higher-quality goods generally being produced.

Social Aspects. Social forces exerted an influence in the design and use of woven items. Textiles were highly valued not only for their beauty and utility but also because they represented an interweaving, so to speak, of social, religious, historic, and economic forces. Traditional ceremonial and mythological symbols particular to the tribe were made a part of the design. A variety of statements about social position or wealth, such as the wearing of the Chief's Blanket or Chilkat robe, could be made. Textiles were also used in gift giving, courtship, and intertribal trade as well as commerce with whites, for whom the blanket represented a standard of currency.

Diane C. Van Noord

Sources for Further Study

Bennett, Noèl, Tiana Bighorse. *Navajo Weaving Way: The Path from Fleece to Rug.* Loveland, Colo.: Interweave Press, 1997.

Conn, Richard. *Native American Art in the Denver Art Museum.* Denver: Denver Art Museum, 1979.

Coulter, Lane, ed. *Navajo Saddle Blankets: Textiles to Ride in the American West.* Santa Fe: Museum of New Mexico Press, 2002.

Dockstader, Frederick J. *Weaving Arts of the North American Indian.* New York: Thomas Y. Crowell, 1978.

Kapoun, Robert W. *Language of the Robe.* Salt Lake City, Utah: Peregrine Smith Books, 1992.

LaFarge, Oliver, et al. *Introduction to American Indian Art.* Glorieta, N.Mex.: Rio Grande Press, 1973.

Rodee, Marian E. *Weaving of the Southwest.* Westchester, Pa.: Schiffer, 1987.

Zolbrod, Paul, and Roseann Willink. *Weaving a World: Textiles and the Navajo Way of Seeing.* Santa Fe: University of New Mexico Press, 1996.

See also: Arts and Crafts: Plateau; Arts and Crafts: Southwest; Blankets; Chilkat Blankets; Cotton; Star Quilts.

Weirs and Traps

Tribes affected: Pantribal
Significance: *Ingenious traps were used throughout North America for capturing fish and animals.*

Hunting and fishing were labor-intensive activities, but various inventions permitted the capture of animals with less time and effort. All Indian tribes, including agriculturalists, used these devices both before and after contact with Europeans. Their variety in native North America was tremendous, but they can be divided into three classes: enclosing, arresting, and killing devices.

Enclosing devices prevented an animal—who was unharmed—from escaping. Pits, camouflaged with leaf-covered mats and dug into game trails; and wicker fences on mudflats adjoining estuaries, forming enclosures ("weirs") to trap fish as high tides receded, are examples of enclosing devices.

Arresting devices went one step further, grabbing or entangling an animal. Nets, set between trees to catch birds, or under water to catch fish and aquatic mammals, are one form of this device. Another is the snare, which trapped an animal's leg in a noose. The Montagnais used an ingenious spiked-wheel trap, a tethered hoop of wood with flexible, sharp rods pointing inward like spokes but not quite meeting. A caribou would step into such a trap and be unable to escape.

Killing devices incorporated some means of killing the prey, as when a weight was released by a trigger tripped by the animal (a deadfall). The Tanaina used a complicated torsion trap in which a striker would be held under tension from twisted rawhide until an animal tripped a trigger, releasing the trap on itself. An ingenious, if rather gruesome, killing device used by the Inuit was a sharpened strip of whale baleen, bent double, encased in animal fat and frozen. Left in a place frequented by bears or wolves, it would be swallowed whole by one of these predators and then suddenly spring open after thawing in the animal's stomach, killing it from within.

An artist's depiction of Native Americans using nets, traps, and spears to fish in late nineteenth century North Carolina. *(National Archives)*

Indian traps often were cleverly designed to catch only game of a predetermined size. The mesh size of fish nets, for example, was determined by the size of the desired catch, since smaller fish could swim through the mesh and larger fish could not insert their heads far enough to become snagged at the gills. Among the Indians of the Atlantic Coast, mesh gauges were used in making nets so that the desired mesh size would be maintained throughout.

Most traps have left few remains that can be studied, so it is difficult to estimate when traps came into use in North America. Net weights, however, indicate that birds or fish probably were netted in most of eastern North America by 3500 B.C.E. Weirs leave distinctive remains, and the Boylston Street Fishweir under the streets of Boston dates from as early as 2500 B.C.E.; other less well-dated weirs may have predated these by as much as three thousand years.

The European fur trade stimulated Indian fur-trapping, and traditional trap technology was inadequate to the task. The older methods gave way to the use of efficient European iron traps.

Russell J. Barber

See also: Fish and Fishing; Hunting and Gathering; Subsistence; Trade.

Whales and Whaling

Tribes affected: Clallam, Inuit, Makah, Nootka, Quileute, Quinault

Significance: *Whales provided a primary source of food, grease, and oil for personal use and trade; whales and whaling also fostered a sense of solidarity and provided the basis for religious and magic rituals.*

The coastal dwelling Inuit (Eskimo) of the Arctic culture area depended exclusively on animals as their food source for much of their history. The spring whale migration was an important source of food and oil, especially in the western region. A successful hunt marked the beginning of a good year and reaffirmed the interrelationship between the two worlds, animal and Inuit. An unsuccessful hunt was inauspicious; it meant further expenditures of energy and time hunting other sea mammals—and the possibility of starvation if the effort failed.

The whale was an integral part of tribal life in the Northwest Coast culture area as well. The Makah, Nootka, Quileute, and

Quinault embarked on expeditions to kill humpback, finback, and California gray whale, as they moved up the Olympic peninsula in the spring on their way to summer in the Arctic. The Clallam, on the other hand, hunted whales only if they entered their inland waters. Other tribes, such as the Chinook and Salish, only took dead whales that drifted to shore.

Whaling expeditions were suffused with specialized knowledge, ritual, and ceremony. The Inuit knew the various whale migration routes and schedules in minute detail, and they developed a system to describe the whales themselves in great detail. Magical charms were placed in the whaling boat, which was then launched by ritually selected women who danced and dispensed gifts. The crew sang magic songs to weaken the whale and entice it to the surface. The captain and owner, or *umialik*, exerted religious and economic authority. When the whale was brought to shore the head was severed in order to release the spirit of the whale. The boat owner's wife, herself a type of priestess, would then offer the

Twentieth century Eskimos harpoon a whale in Point Barrow, Alaska. *(National Archives)*

head a cup of water and thank it for coming, after which the spirit was urged to return to the land of living whales and report how well it had been treated. For the Inuit, who lack a true village-based community, whaling helped to impart a sense of community solidarity.

Among Northwest Coast tribes the harpooner generally owned the boat and equipment and commanded the appropriate magic to ensure success; magical powers were imputed to the harpooner to explain his extraordinary strength and skills. Songs were sung to bring the whale near, to make it gentle when harpooned, and to bring it safely to shore. The harpooner's share of blubber (whale fat) was placed on display and decorated with feathers to please the whale's spirit; it was believed that otherwise the harpooner might not live to kill another. The ritual ended with the giveaway feast, which was also an occasion for the harpooner to present gifts (usually whale oil) to the tribe and to honor the whales so that they would return the following year.

The depletion of whale populations, their international protection, the movement of tribal members to inland urban cities, and the development of other economies have all reduced the importance of whales and whaling in contemporary tribal life.

Laurence Miller

See also: Fish and Fishing.

White Buffalo Society

Tribes affected: Hidatsa, Mandan
Significance: *The purpose of the all-female White Buffalo Society was to entice buffalo herds to come near the village.*

The function of the White Buffalo Society, the highest order among women's societies of the Mandan and Hidatsa tribes, was to entice the buffalo herds to come near the village. It was especially used during times of want, when hunting efforts had not proved successful and further measures were deemed necessary. The idea was that if the buffalo were mimicked, they would draw near to the hunters.

This society was an age society with collective purchase: When prospective members were of a certain age, they would buy the right to join the group from the oldest members, whose time it was to leave the group. This purchase provided for the rights to use and practice certain dances, songs, and regalia of the society.

White Buffalo Society members imitated a herd of buffalo. They grouped together in a sort of loose huddle and mimicked the steps and movements of the buffalo with dances and gestures. Each member wore a cap topped with a fan of hawk feathers. The cap itself was high and round, made from the prized skin of an albino buffalo. As they performed their ceremony, the women carried dry branches with tufts of eagle down fastened to the ends of the branches.

Ruffin Stirling

See also: Buffalo; Gender Relations and Roles; Societies: Non-kin-based; Women's Societies.

White Deerskin Dance

Tribe affected: Yurok
Significance: *This world-renewal ceremony celebrates the continuing cycles of life.*

The White Deerskin Dance, performed during the fall, lasts from twelve to sixteen days. While essentially a reenactment of the Yurok creation story, it is much more than a retelling: The dance itself is thought to put the world back in order. The ceremony is designed to correct temporary flaws in the relationship of the human community to the natural world and thus to enable the seasonal cycles to continue properly. At the center of the story is the life cycle of the salmon, the main source of sustenance along the rivers of the Yurok homeland.

The name "White Deerskin Dance" was given to this ceremony by non-Indian people and is something of a misnomer. "White" refers to specially prepared deerskins, decorated with feathers, shells, and other materials, that are held up on poles by the dancers during the exoteric portion of the ceremony. The skins are not always white in color.

White, for the Yurok, represents not only a color but also a concept of something pure and clear. It also refers to a tradition of an ancient race of people, called "white" or "clear," who embodied the highest virtues and nobility.

Helen Jaskoski

See also: Dances and Dancing; Salmon.

Wickiup

Tribes affected: Apache, Paiute, Ute, other Great Basin tribes
Significance: *The wickiup, a dome-shaped structure, was widely used in the Great Basin culture area.*

"Wickiup" is the popular name for a dome-shaped dwelling made of a circular framework of poles bent over and tied together at the top and covered with brush, bark, animal skins, or earth. The name appears to have origins in the Algonquian languages, where the word *Wikiyapi* can mean house, dwelling, or lodge.

The wickiup was used by the mobile hunter-gatherers of the Great Basin culture area—the Apache, Ute, and Paiute in particular—as a temporary residence while moving from area to area in search of food. This type of housing could accommodate from one to several people.

In some cases, an elongated and arched entry, made of the same poles and brush as the domed portion of the structure, was added to form a shaded porch under which people could sit during the

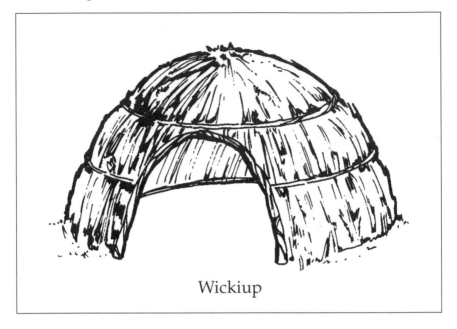

Wickiup

heat of the day while eating, talking, or sleeping. When local food supplies were used up, the wickiup was simply abandoned as people moved on to other areas.

Michael W. Simpson

See also: Architecture: Great Basin; Grass House.

Wigwam

Tribes affected: Northeast tribes
Significance: *The wigwam was a type of dwelling used by tribes in the Northeast.*

Wigwam is an Algonquian word for a house type that was used throughout the Northeast. The wigwam was an oval or round structure of light poles whose lower ends were stuck in the ground and whose upper ends were bent over and lashed together in the shape of a hoop. Lighter horizontal poles were lashed to the uprights to give the framework strength. Over this frame large sheets of bark (or, sometimes, mats woven of reeds) were lashed, overlapping like shingles. In one end was a door; a small hole in the roof let out smoke. Daniel Gookin described seventeenth century New England wigwams:

> The best sort of their houses are covered very neatly, tight and warm, with bark of trees. . . . These houses they make . . . some twenty, some forty feet long, and broad. Some I have seen sixty or a hundred feet long, and thirty feet broad. . . . In the greater houses they make two, three, or four fires, at a distance from one another.

Gookin said he "found them as warm as the best English houses." One or two nuclear families lived in the small wigwams; several shared the larger ones.

Bert M. Mutersbaugh

See also: Architecture: Northeast; Architecture: Subarctic.

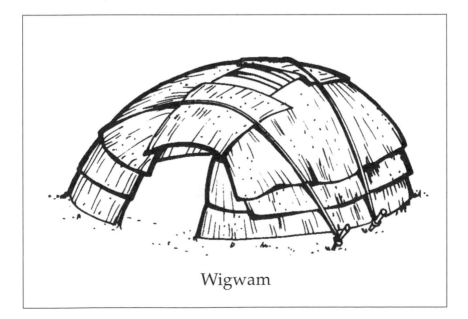

Wigwam

Wild Rice

Tribes affected: Menominee, Ojibwa, Winnebago, other tribes of
the Upper Mississippi Valley and Great Lakes regions

Significance: *Wild rice, an abundant grain that requires no agricultural effort, was gathered for food by various tribes of north-central North America.*

Wild rice grows along the shores of rivers, streams, and lakes from New Brunswick to Manitoba and southward as far as Massachusetts and Nebraska. It is found in greatest abundance around the Great Lakes and in the upper Mississippi Valley, where it forms dense stands covering extensive areas. It is believed that all occurrences outside this area are historic plantings by humans. Most wild rice is of the species *Zizania aquatica*; common names include Indian rice, Canadian rice, water oats, water rice, tuscarora, manomin, and folle avoine.

Wild rice is an annual grass that grows to several feet above water level. It produces several thousand rice grains per plant, each long and black with a starchy core. These are attached to the stem by a very brittle connection, and even a slight breeze can detach the grains and drop them into the water, where they germinate to produce the next generation.

Indian harvesting took advantage of this brittle attachment. The most common method was to glide a canoe into a stand of wild rice as gently as possible and then bend the stems delicately over the canoe and shake them gently, with the ripe grain simply falling into the canoe. Since individual grains mature at different rates, one stand might be visited several times over the two-week ripening period in late summer. An alternate harvesting method involved bundling several stems together with twine while the grains were immature, then returning at maturity and shearing off the entire bundle for threshing on land. Women used distinctive bundle patterns to designate their rights to particular bundles. Either technique permitted enough seeds to escape to ensure a good growth the following year.

After harvesting, the grain was dried in its hulls and could be stored effectively in baskets for a year. Small portions were hulled as needed by heating the grain gently until it split the hull, when it could then be winnowed in baskets. Wild rice was—and is—cooked exclusively by boiling.

It is not known when wild rice was first exploited by Indians. Some hunting-gathering tribes, especially in Wisconsin and Minnesota, depended so strongly on wild rice that they stored large quantities of it and, in the process, became virtually sedentary. Others, especially in more northerly areas, used it as an adjunct to other foods in a seasonal pattern.

In modern times, wild rice has been an important cash crop on some Indian reservations. There, harvesting and sale have been restricted to bona fide members of the tribe using the traditional canoe-harvesting method. Planting and mechanical harvesting of wild rice by commercial concerns, particularly in California, has increased production and lowered prices since the 1980's—adversely affecting the economy of wild-rice producers in the traditional heartland.

Russell J. Barber

Source for Further Study
Vennum, Thomas, Jr. *Wild Rice and the Ojibway People*. St. Paul: Minnesota Historical Society Press, 1988.

See also: Hunting and Gathering; Subsistence.

Windigo

Tribes affected: Cree, Montagnais, Naskapi, Ojibwa (Chippewa)
Significance: *A legendary cannibalistic Algonquian giant, the Windigo personifies the unrelenting forces of winter and starvation that can drive a person to antisocial acts of violence.*

One of a category of mythic beings found in Northern Algonquian mythology and folklore, the Windigo is usually visualized as an emaciated, filthy, bestial creature of prodigious strength and size that roams the snow-covered boreal forests, seeking to assuage its insatiable hunger for human flesh. Thunderous roars, terrifying whistles, and strange, sparkling lights can all herald its approach, leaving its victim paralyzed with fear. Particularly powerful shamans, however, can defeat a Windigo in "spiritual" combat, whereas native therapists can treat humans in the throes of Windigo transformation—a metamorphosis induced by anthropophagous acts, sorcery, or a vision encounter with a Windigo spirit—through the application of large doses of hot grease, intended to "melt" the patient's icy heart before he or she completely passes from a human state. Windigo symptomatology described in native and non-native oral and documentary accounts have led some anthropologists to hypothesize the existence of a differentiated "windigo psychosis," a rare, psychopathological disorder of the northern Algonquians.

Joseph C. Jastrzembski

See also: Ethnophilosophy and Worldview; Religion.

Wintercounts

Tribes affected: Dakota and Lakota Sioux
Significance: *Wintercounts were pictorial records kept by bands of the Lakota and Dakota to record the most important event of each year. The events recorded form a chronology and are an organized way to preserve band history. Originally, wintercounts were recorded on hide—deer, elk, or buffalo—and in later years, as these materials became scarcer, wintercounts were kept on cloth or paper.*

Many tribes in the Americas kept some picture records on rock, cave walls, ivory, bone, birch bark, and so on. Wintercounts, however, refer specifically to the records kept by the Lakota and Dakota bands to document their history. One man in each band was selected as the keeper of the wintercount, and he was responsible for consulting with the headmen in the tribe; together they decided on some event or phenomenon to represent for the year. Among the Dakota and Lakota people their year extended from winter to winter, and so wintercounts span two calendar years according to the Gregorian calendar (the dominant calendar in the West).

The keeper of the wintercount was the official band historian, and he was expected to recite the details of each year so that the band had a sense of history. Generally, all adult band members could retell the history of their people. Artistic skill was not a prerequisite for keepers of the wintercount. Keepers of the wintercounts were well-respected men who performed an important cultural obligation to preserve their band history.

The chosen event was represented symbolically, often in a few shorthand strokes. Drawings were terse and served as mnemonic devices for band history. Because wintercounts were individualized records of events intended to reflect and preserve cultural and band history, they varied from group to group. A wintercount kept by a Yanktonais Dakota named Lone Dog depicted a human shape with spots all over to represent the year 1801-1802. This was denoted as "The Winter When Many Died of Smallpox." In another drawing on this wintercount, 1833-1834 is "The Winter When the Stars Fell," and it memorialized a meteor shower that was observed all over the United States on November 12, 1833.

Wintercounts kept on hide often began in the center and then spiraled outward. The keeper of the wintercount would use a porous bone or fibrous piece of wood as a painting tool. Generally, the image was drawn in black outline and then filled in with colored pigments. In order to make paint, a beaver tail was boiled to make glue, which was then mixed with ground clays or plant juices. In later years, when wintercounts began to be recorded on cloth and paper, band historians often used crayons, colored pencils, or watercolors.

Carole A. Barrett

Source for Further Study

Cheney, Roberta Carkeek. *Sioux Wintercount: 131 Years of Dakota History, 1796-1926.* Interpreted by Kills Two. Happy Camp, Calif.: Naturegraph, 1998.

See also: Bragskins; Petroglyphs; Pictographs.

Witchcraft and Sorcery

Tribes affected: Pantribal
Significance: *Witchcraft provided a means, although largely a socially unacceptable one, of dealing with offenses that could not be corrected in other ways.*

The use of witchcraft and sorcery, although considered deviant, was common among American Indians, and it operated along with religion in providing an understanding of everyday life. Within a community, witchcraft was often employed by someone, usually male, who believed that a wrong had been committed against him, especially when that wrong could not be redressed through other socially sanctioned means. A disaffected person would seek the satisfaction that would come with harming or even causing the death of the transgressor. Witchcraft was usually condemned in native cultures, and suspected witches or sorcerers could be killed by members of the community for the offense. It is notable that among the Pueblo, men considered overly ambitious for political power were automatically suspected of witchcraft. In some cultures, datura, or jimson weed, was used as a tonic to determine who was guilty of witchcraft.

Among the Navajo, one who was accused of witchcraft and captured was pressured to confess. If no confession was forthcoming, the accused was executed. If there was a confession, it was believed that the witch would soon die of the same witchcraft he was practicing on his victim.

Witches were seen in some communities as part of a long-term aberrant subculture, with apprentice witches learning their art from an older relative, and employing complicated rituals of membership. Less serious were sorcerers, whose spells were carried out less violently and without all the ritual trappings. Witchcraft directed at a rival community was also considered possible, and along with revenge for deaths, desire for captives, misappropriation of hunting land or other resources, it was considered an appropriate reason for competing groups to go to war. When social constraints such as the need for community harmony or preserving the established leadership structure prevented individuals in native communities from achieving what they perceived as justice, they might resort to witchcraft.

Thomas P. Carroll

See also: Ethnophilosophy and Worldview; Religion; Religious Specialists; Social Control.

Women

Tribes affected: Pantribal

Significance: *Women have held more central and more powerful roles within Indian communities than outsiders have often realized, although in many cases their power was diminished after tribal contact with Europeans.*

The lives of Indian women have been as varied as those of any women. Not only have their experiences differed greatly among regions and tribes (and among individuals within those groups), but also Indian women's lives have undergone significant changes historically, both before and after colonization.

Perhaps the most useful generalization one can make about Indian women is that they have often been overlooked and misunderstood by non-Indians. In popular films and novels, when included at all, Indian women typically have been depicted as more passive and less important than Indian men. Indian women have also often been missing from studies authored by historians and social scientists.

The few American Indian women who have gained widespread attention among non-Indians quite often have been those thought to have come to the aid of settlers. Probably the most famous of such women is Pocahontas, who popular legend has credited with saving the life of Captain John Smith and assisting the settlers of the Jamestown colony. In visual images of the colonial era, Pocahontas was used to embody the New World—imagined as a welcoming, feminine, and fertile body. Other women remembered by non-Indians for their aid to whites include Sacajawea of the Shoshone, Winema of the Modoc, and Nancy Ward of the Cherokee—women whose lives were much more complex than one might guess from their popular reputations as charitable maidens and princesses.

Also not very well known is the fact that Indian women were often the most determined to resist European influence. Seventeenth century Huron women, for example, proved far more difficult than Huron men for Jesuit missionaries to convert to Christianity.

One of the main reasons the Huron women gave for their resistance was that they could not imagine how they could agree to make a lifetime commitment of marriage. Many Huron women rightly suspected that the missionaries were offering women the possibility of salvation in exchange for less freedom and control over their lives than they had previously enjoyed.

Economic and Social Contributions. Early European and European American accounts of Indians frequently characterized Indian women as subservient drudges, as poor "squaws" who were abused by Indian men. Such characterizations should be understood in relation to the expectation of many European Americans, especially prevalent during the nineteenth century, that in their own societies virtuous women were incapable of and demeaned by physically demanding labor, particularly labor performed outdoors. When European Americans observed native women vigorously hauling firewood, planting and harvesting crops, or tanning hides, they erroneously inferred that Indian women occupied a lowly position in society. Outside observers frequently failed to recognize that women often took great pride in their work and acquired significant respect within their communities as a result of it. Moreover, the work of Indian men was often less visible from the perspective of a village or camp, if, as was often the case, it focused on hunting.

The specific tasks performed by men and women varied considerably among tribes, and there were exceptions to the typical patterns—in many Plains societies, for example, there were women who departed from the norm and became known as warriors, hunting big game and leading war parties. In general, however, women tended to have greater responsibilities than men in caring for children and preparing food. Among some groups, such as the Iroquois tribes, women not only prepared food, but were responsible for farming, fishing, and gathering wild plant products valued for medicinal as well as nutritional purposes; many Indian women also maintained the right to distribute any food, even that procured by men.

Throughout Indian history, Indian women have gained great admiration and personal satisfaction from producing and designing objects; in pre-contact societies, much of women's everyday labor involved creative, artistic abilities. In the Southwest, for example, many women were highly skilled potters, who made wares valued for their aesthetic and religious importance as well as for their practical usefulness. Especially among Plains Indians, many women took great pride in decorating leather and designing clothing. In many areas, women wove extraordinarily beautiful and functional baskets. Although today Indian women have much less often produced objects such as pots and baskets for use within their own communities, many Indian women have established successful careers as artists; two of the most renowned include Hopi potter Nampeyo and San Ildefonso potter María Martínez. In parts of the Southwest, pottery and basketry, still made by women more often than men, currently provide significant sources of income for Indian communities as well as a sense of continuity, with designs and techniques handed down among generations of women. Many modern native women have also developed artistic skills in fields not typically associated with Indian people—including oil painting, photography, and performing arts such as ballet.

In interpreting early written accounts of Indian women's labor, in addition to considering the possible biases of outside observers, it is useful to consider how perceptions of Indian women as hapless drudges might reflect how women's lives may already have been transformed by interactions with Europeans. For example, during periods when Indian people were trading vast quantities of furs and skins to Europeans, the workloads of many native women increased dramatically. Furthermore, social changes brought about by increased warfare, famine, dependence on trade, and disease epidemics often had a negative influence on the position women occupied within their communities. The social problems endemic to many Indian communities have added to women's domestic and economic responsibilities; many Indian women rear families single-handedly. Some researchers have suggested, however, that

Indian women's great responsibilities for home and family, while difficult, have also been an important source of strength, stability, and determination.

Religion, Healing, Myth, and Storytelling. Among many Indian communities, past and present, women have been as likely as men to serve as spiritual leaders and doctors. Women have been powerful members of religious societies—some composed of women only, others including both women and men—within tribal communities. Many Indian communities have also held their most powerful and sacred ceremonies centering around female rites of passage, such as a girl's first menstruation. Yet even when indigenous religious practices might appear to be more men's affairs than women's, beliefs about power, deities, and the nature of the universe have tended to emphasize and venerate women. Among Pueblo people in the Southwest, for example, even though women have been excluded from many of the most significant religious activities, the most important deities are female. Many Southwestern Indian people tell sacred stories of female creators and teachers, such as Thought Woman, Changing Woman, Salt Woman, or Spider Woman. Lakota people tell of Falling Star, who on earth became White Buffalo Calf Woman and gave the Lakotas their sacred ceremonies. Similar stories of divine female beings can be found throughout native North America; such beliefs contrast sharply with Christian notions of a single, all-powerful, male creator.

Nevertheless, in many cases Indian women have responded enthusiastically to Christianity, often blending Christian traditions with indigenous ones. They also have taken up powerful positions in many religious revitalization movements that combine Christianity and indigenous beliefs and practices. Among California Indians, for example, women have been among the most prominent leaders in the Bole Maru movement, frequently serving as "Dreamers," a role with political as well as spiritual dimensions. Women have also held important roles within the Native American Church.

In addition to occupying specialized roles within religious systems, Indian women have an ancient history of passing down knowledge and values as storytellers and as family and community historians. Many Indian women continue to be especially revered for their formal and informal storytelling. Some have incorporated oral traditions into written literature; writing for Indian and non-Indian audiences, Native women—including Louise Erdrich, Leslie Marmon Silko, and Joy Harjo—have become renowned novelists and poets. Others, such as Ella Cara Deloria and Beatrice Medicine, have made significant contributions to anthropology and history.

Politics and Policies. In precolonial societies, Indian women usually had their own particular ways of exerting political authority. Among the Iroquois, for example, women did not serve on the Council of Elders, but the men who served were appointed and could always be deposed by Iroquois matrons. In Cherokee council meetings, women tended to observe rather then actively contribute, voicing their opinions outside of the public forum. Occasionally, women departed from the usual political roles and occupied leadership positions typically taken by men. In many societies, women's authority was strengthened by matrilineal and matrilocal kinship systems, in which property and land-use rights were inherited through women and which required a man to live with his wife's family after marriage. Kinship and politics were often inseparable, and women often retained the right to arrange marriages for their children; divorces typically could be initiated by men or women.

During the colonial and early reservation periods, the political authority of Indian women was undermined in a number of important ways. Missionary and government agents tended to encourage patrilineal systems of naming and inheritance and often did not recognize the ways in which women had previously influenced political appointments and decisions. For example, in contrast to the way that many Indian Communities traced inheritance and identity through mothers, the Canadian Indian Act of 1876 denied an official native identity to native women and their children who married men from outside their band; native men who married non-native women, however, suffered no similar loss of identity or recognition.

In the late nineteenth and early twentieth centuries, Indian women in the United States and Canada were subject to federal education policies designed to train native women as domestic servants and housekeepers. Among tribes where women had once carried out all the farming, government programs attempted to teach men to farm, while women were trained in such domestic skills as cooking and sewing.

Despite such misguided policies, many Indian women emerged in this period as influential proponents of Indian rights and policy reform. These women included Sarah Winnemucca, who worked as a scout and interpreter for the U.S. Army in the 1870's before writing a book and giving lectures to audiences around the country urging public support for her people, the Northern Paiutes. In the early twentieth century, Gertrude Simmons Bonnin wrote books and articles based on her experiences as a Sioux and devoted much research, writing, and public speaking to issues important to Indian people throughout the United States. Other influential women of this period include writer and administrator Ruth Muskrat Bronson, anthropologist Ella Cara Deloria, and physician Susan La Flesche Picotte.

In the 1960's and 1970's, many women took part in Indian-related activism, such as the Trail of Broken Treaties, the standoff with the FBI at Wounded Knee, and the occupation of Alcatraz. Although women tended to be less prominent than men in such activities, many women who took part in them went on to become especially influential leaders. One such woman was Wilma Mankiller, who in 1985 became the chief of the Cherokee Nation. Increasingly, native women are being elected to tribal councils and are filling other politically important roles as policymakers, judges, and lawyers.

Indian women leaders have been most concerned with issues that pertain to both men and women in Indian communities. Their identities as Indian people—or as members of particular Indian communities—have tended to take precedence over identities as women. Since the 1970's, however, native women have begun to organize politically around concerns specifically identified with Indian women—including their representation in tribal politics, problems with domestic violence, health care, and access to legal services. The Women of All Red Nations (WARN) was formed in 1978; many other native women's organizations have been formed since, both national and local.

Although the polar stereotypes of Pocahontas and lowly squaw continue to survive in non-Indian thinking, they have been continually challenged by Indian women. The stereotypes have also been challenged by a growing body of scholarship and writing, which increasingly is being produced by Indian women themselves.

Molly H. Mullin

Sources for Further Study

Albers, Patricia, and Beatrice Medicine, eds. *The Hidden Half: Studies of Plains Indian Women*. Washington, D.C.: University Press of America, 1983. A volume of essays offering diverse perspectives on Plains women. The essays cover topics such as women's work, the persistent biases of outside observers, and historical changes in Plains Indian women's lives.

Allen, Paula Gunn, ed. *Spider Woman's Granddaughters: Traditional Tales and Contemporary Writing by Native North American Women*. New York: Fawcett Columbine, 1989. An anthology of works written and told by native women. Informative introduction by Allen, who has written widely on native women's literature.

Anderson, Karen L. *Chain Her by One Foot: The Subjugation of Women in Seventeenth-Century New France*. New York: Routledge, 1991. A study of how Huron and Montagnais women responded to Europeans, particularly Jesuit missionaries, and how religious conversion involved dramatic changes in beliefs about women.

Bataille, Gretchen M., and Kathleen Mullen. *American Indian Women: A Guide to Research*. New York: Garland, 1991. An extensive annotated bibliography of writing and films pertaining to North American Indian women, including more than 1,500 citations.

Bataille, Gretchen M., and Kathleen Mullen Sands. *American Indian Women: Telling Their Lives*. Lincoln: University of Nebraska Press, 1984. Much can be learned about native women's lives from their autobiographies, but it is useful to know something about the context in which these autobiographies were produced. This guide to native women's autobiographical narratives includes an annotated bibliography.

Deloria, Ella Cara. *Waterlily*. Lincoln: University of Nebraska Press, 1988. A fictional portrayal of nineteenth century Sioux women. Written in the 1930's by a Sioux historian and anthropologist who devoted her career to combatting popular stereotypes of Indians.

Devens, Carol. *Countering Colonization: Native American Women and the Great Lakes Missions, 1630-1900*. Berkeley: University of California Press, 1992. A study of the diverse ways in which women among the Ojibwa, Cree, and other tribes of the Great Lakes region responded to and were affected by colonization.

Katz, Jane, ed. *I Am the Fire of Time: Voices of Native American Women*. New York: Dutton, 1977. A wide-ranging collection of material, including songs, prayers, and essays, from various tribes and historical periods.

Powers, Marla N. *Oglala Women: Myth, Ritual, and Reality*. Chicago: University of Chicago Press, 1986. A study of Oglala Sioux women, past and present, illustrated with black-and-white photographs. Emphasizes the central role of women in Sioux myth and cosmology and women's perspectives on the important changes in their lives.

Underhill, Ruth M. *Papago Woman*. 1936. Reprint. New York: Holt, Rinehart and Winston, 1979. The life story of a Papago (Tohono O'odham) woman with particular skills as a healer, born in 1845. Includes songs, stories, and descriptions of tribal life.

See also: Gender Relations and Roles; Kinship and Social Organization; Marriage and Divorce; Stereotypes; Women's Societies.

Women's Societies

Tribes affected: Pantribal

Significance: *Societies for both men and women were important organizations that created a sense of tribal identity, instilling a sense of allegiance beyond the bonds of family. Members of societies had obligations to each other, strict rules for membership, and an obligation to work for benefit of their people. Indian women's societies were of three major types: craft, religious, and those connected to warfare.*

The origins of all Indian societies lay in the dream or vision of a founder, and this often contained information on the number of members allowed, rules for participation, goals of the society, ceremonial clothing, and rituals. Almost all societies had a medicine bundle, which contained objects to remind members of the sacred origins of the founder's vision. Women's societies generally were one of three types: craft guilds, religious groups, and war-related societies.

Craft Guilds. Craft guilds involved the most women. These societies recognized women who were especially gifted in the arts of the tribe, such as tanning, painting robes, designing and applying quillwork or beadwork patterns, making baby carriers, and manufacturing moccasins. These non-kin-based societies were considered as important as the men's societies. Members of the craft guild taught their art to other women, and the most talented students were invited into the society. Each craft society sponsored an annual feast at which their members' handiwork was displayed, and in this way the women's work was exalted.

Religious Societies. Women's religious societies had fewer members and different rules for participation. To become a member of a religious society, a woman had to have a very strong vision that led her to understand how she could work for the welfare of the people by performing rituals to ensure healing, plentiful crops, or a successful hunt. Women who performed as healers had extensive knowledge of roots and herbs; they generally specialized in illnesses of women and children and assisted in childbirth. Because women, in their roles as wives and mothers, were often associated with bounty, women's religious societies often conducted the ceremonies that would ensure abundant crops or attract game closer to the village. In some tribes, women's religious societies sponsored important rituals. For instance, among the Blackfeet the Women's Fasting Society was responsible for initiating the Sun Dance. In other tribes, women's religious societies reenacted the sacred stories of origin. Women in religious societies gave generously of their time and knowledge and sought to maintain blessings for their people.

War Societies. Women's war societies functioned in various ways. Generally these groups were adjuncts to the men's warrior societies. It was relatively common for wives to accompany their husbands to war in order to cook for them and sing songs of encouragement. Though there are accounts of women who fought alongside the men or sought to avenge the death of their husbands on the battlefield, such activity was relatively rare. Women's war society members also took a lead role in celebrating the return of the men from battle and in comforting the widows and mothers of the slain, roles that continue into the present day in many tribes. The modern versions of these societies arrange feasts and celebrations to greet returning veterans, lead honor dances at pow-wows, comfort relatives if a soldier is killed.

Carole A. Barrett

See also: Medicine and Modes of Curing: Pre-contact; Military Societies; Societies: Non-kin-based; White Buffalo Society; Women.

Zapotec Civilization

Significance: *Their early urban culture thrived and flourished at Monte Albán, influencing later generations of central Mexico.*

Five hundred years before the Christian era, the Zapotec peoples of the mountains and valleys of central Mexico—the modern state of Oaxaca—laid foundations for a brilliant culture that reached its height between 700 and 900 C.E. Because the Zapotec had no written language (although they devised hieroglyphs), knowledge of their civilization depends entirely upon the discoveries and analyses of archaeologists and cultural anthropologists. The work of these experts ranges from studies of historic Mesoamerican farming, religion, political organization, and ecology to science, mining, metalworking, trade, and systematic archaeological reconstructions of the great urban site at Monte Albán, as well as lesser sites at Mitla, Etla, Tlacolula, and in the Zimatlán valleys.

Such evidence suggests that by the time Zapotec culture appears in the historical record, about 500 B.C.E., it was already characterized by increasing social and political complexity marked by communities of villages and temple centers. Between the opening of the Christian era and 500 C.E., the Zapotecs had developed a regional political state that reached its cultural apogee at the great urban center at Monte Albán between two hundred and four hundred years later, even as Aztec expansion, military unrest, and large-scale migrations had begun to affect it adversely. Between the years 900 and 1520, the heart of Zapotec civilization shifted from Monte Albán to Mitla, as Aztec military expansion and attempts to incorporate the Zapotecs into an Aztec confederation marked a decline that was completed by the Spanish conquest of Mexico.

Zapotec origins are unknown, although the Zapotecs probably lived side by side with other central Mexican cultures during what archaeologists designate as the region's archaic, or Middle Formative and Late Formative, eras. The Zapotecs themselves ascribed their origins to their ancestors' birth directly from rocks, trees, and jaguars in a mythic past. From the earliest available records, they appear to have been a sedentary farming people, predisposed to living in communities and urban centers and committed to substantial trading activities involving products of their mines, as well as sophisticated, high-quality copper and gold work. Although much of Oaxaca consists of eroded mountains that were unsuitable for agriculture, the valleys of its central section were fertile, subtropical, and frost-free, and thus helped develop the Zapotecs' penchant for urban living.

Like other peoples of Mexico's central plateau, the Zapotecs broke the soil with digging sticks, planted corn, beans, tomatoes, and chili peppers, and supplemented their diets with fish and game. During the Formative era, they irrigated their fields with pots and canals. Having learned metalworking from cultures to their south, they not only were among the first Mesoamericans to work in metals but also soon exceeded all others except the Maya in their *repoussé* work, the quality of their bas-relief stonework (learned from the Olmecs to the south), and their gold, silver, and

Area of the Zapotecs

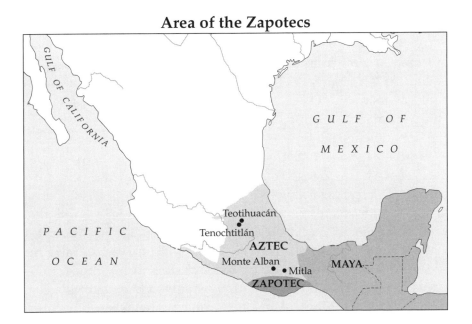

turquoise jewelry. Trade in these manufactures was facilitated by the Zapotecs' locational advantage in the paths of people moving north and south through Mesoamerica, as well as people traveling from the Pacific coast to the Gulf of Mexico.

The lives of the Zapotecs were dominated by religion. They worshiped a number of gods, the most important of which was Cosijo, the god of lightning and rain. Their affairs were partially ruled over by a hierarchy of priests; therefore, their political establishment functioned as a centralized theocracy, although it seems that power never was concentrated in the hands of a single individual. Power was divided between a monarch, who probably represented the army along with other worldly interests, and a high priest whose authority may have been greater than that of the king. Zapotecs also had developed an elaborate cult of the dead; accordingly, they were devoted to the worship of their ancestors, whom they believed inhabited an idyllic underworld. Their scientific achievements, which experts have ranked as equal to those of the Maya, related closely to their religious beliefs. Their ritual calendar, or *tonalpohuali*, consisted of 260 days, but they also were familiar with the solar calendar—evidence indicates that this had been true since before the Christian era.

At its height, between 700 and 900 c.e., Zapotec culture was epitomized by its capital, Monte Albán, the origins of which preceded the Christian era. The Zapotecs' first capital had been located at Teotitlán del Valle in the Tlacolula Valley. By the time a shift was made to Monte Albán—reasons for which are unclear— the Zapotecs had evolved an advanced culture comparable to others in the central highlands. Scholars estimate that between 600 and 200 b.c.e., the transformation of Monte Albán was under way and its superb plaza four hundred meters above the valley had begun taking shape. Toward the end of this Middle Formative period, Monte Albán had become the site of religious structures notable among archaeologists for their beautiful carved and inscribed columns and decorated bases that showed Olmec influences. After a transitional period, during which some of the earlier structures on Monte Albán were covered by newer buildings, the Zapotec culture that was centered there became one of the most influential—both politically and culturally—in Mesoamerica. Several scholars have described Monte Albán's Great Plaza as one of the most splendid civic spaces created by humankind, as well as the most beautiful in Mesoamerica. In conformity with the religious values that informed their construction, the score of impressive structures running along the mountaintop on a rough north-south axis close off views of the valleys below, heightening the feeling of completion and enclosure. When occupied, these structures—one of them an astronomical observatory—were painted but, unlike elsewhere in Mesoamerican cultures, they featured little decoration, although what little there was, was elegant. Their builders relied on the contrasting effects of sunlight and shadow to emphasize their meaning. It was from this mountaintop that Zapotec merchants and metal workers extended their commercial route, including the turquoise trade, across thousands of miles, from central Mexico as far northward as the Colorado Basin.

After 900 C.E., Monte Albán began to decline, and the focus of Zapotec civilization shifted to Mitla, now a well-researched ruin. Monte Albán remained occupied until the Spanish conquest that was carried into Oaxaca in 1521 by Francisco de Orozco. Mitla became a significant religious center as well as a necropolis, serving as the burial place of kings and the Zapotecs' chief priests during the years when the Zapotecs struggled to remain independent of the expanding Aztec confederation and then confronted the Spaniards. Neither Monte Albán nor Mitla was fortified, relying instead on the reputation of their great religious authority to dissuade potential enemies. Archaeological investigation of both Monte Albán and Mitla continues, as Monte Albán alone covered more than forty square kilometers and embraced a substantial population spread beyond its immediate precincts throughout nearby valleys.

Clifton K. Yearley

Sources for Further Study

Chinas, Beverly. *The Isthmus Zapotecs.* 2d ed. Fort Worth, Tex.: Harcourt Brace Jovanovich, 1992. Chinas, a specialist on Zapotec women, focuses on their traditional matrilineal roles, which cast light on lingering Monte Albán influences.

Coe, Michael D., and Rex Koontz. *Mexico: From the Olmecs to the Aztecs*. 5th ed. New York: Thames & Hudson, 2002. An exhaustive introduction to Mexico's early history and peoples.

Flannery, Kent V., and Joyce Marcus, eds. *The Cloud People: Divergent Evolution of the Zapotec and Mixtec Civilizations*. New York: Academic Press, 1983. A comparison of the development of two major Mesoamerican cultures.

Hardoy, Jorge E. *Pre-Columbian Cities*. Translated by Judith Thorne. New York: Walker, 1973. Excellent synthesis of extant knowledge from archaeologists and cultural historians about Zapotec cities during their formation.

Kearney, Michael. *The Winds of Ixtepeji*. New York: Holt, Rinehart and Winston, 1972. Deals with modern Zapotec society in one town; also reveals myths and folkways that trace back to the Zapotecs' earliest origins.

Marcus, Joyce, and Kent V. Flannery. *Zapotec Civilization: How Urban Society Evolved in Mexico's Oaxaca Valley*. New York: Thames and Hudson, 1996. An analysis of the development of the Zapotec civilization and the growth of Monte Albán.

Wiley, Gordon, and Jeremy A. Sabloff. *A History of American Archaeology*. London: Thames and Hudson, 1974. Includes numerous comments about archaeologists who studied the Zapotecs, what they discovered, and how they proceeded to design and classify chronologies that fit evidence about the ancient Zapotecs.

Wolf, Eric. *Sons of the Shaking Earth*. Chicago: University of Chicago Press, 1966. A historical-archaeological study of the peoples of Mexico and Guatemala and their cultures, which places the evolution of the Zapotecs in context.

See also: Culture Areas; Gold and Goldworking; Metalwork; Religion; Silverworking; Trade; Turquoise.

Educational Institutions and Programs

The following is a select list of institutions with various types of American Indian studies programs. Tribally controlled colleges are included in the section headed "American Indian Higher Education Consortium (AIHEC) Member Institutions." "Canadian Institutions" are covered in the final section.   —H.J.M.

U.S. UNIVERSITIES AND COLLEGES

Alaska, University of
Fairbanks
Native studies program. Major and minor. Alaska Native Language Center, established in 1972, conducts research and publishes story collections, histories, geographies, dictionaries, and grammars.

Arizona, University of
Tucson
American Indian studies program. M.A. in American studies. Courses in Hopi and Tohono O'odham languages.

Arizona State University
Tempe
American Indian studies program offering a B.S. Emphasis on issues related to American Indian sovereignty, theory and application of American Indian law, economic development, cultures, languages, arts, and education. Associated with Center for Indian Education, which publishes the *Journal of American Indian Education*. First such center in the United States, established in 1959.

Augsburg College
Minneapolis, Minn.
American Indian Support Program.

Bacone College
Muskogee, Okla.
Founded as Indian University in 1880. The college has a special
mission to serve American Indian students.

Bemidji State University
Bemidji, Minn.
Indian Studies Department. Major and minor. Minor in Ojibwa
language.

Black Hills State College
Spearfish, S.Dak.
Minor in American Indian studies.

California, University of
Berkeley
Native American Studies Program offers a B.A. major and an Ph.D.
in ethnic studies with a concentration in Native American studies. Classes focus on the historical, literary, and cultural analysis
of Native American cultures as well as present-day legal and
social circumstances of Native American communities. Course
topics include Native American oral and written literary traditions, Native American law, tribal governments, Native American women, and reservation economic development.

California, University of
Davis
Native American Studies Department. Major.

California, University of
Irvine
Native American Studies Program offers an interdisciplinary minor with courses in history, sociology, ecology, history, and other humanities and social sciences.

California, University of
Los Angeles
American Indian Studies Center offers a B.A. major and minor in American Indian studies; an M.A. in American Indian studies; a J.D./M.A. in law and American Indian studies. Program focuses on four areas: history and law; expressive arts; social relations; and literature, folklore, and language. Publishes *American Indian Culture and Research Journal.*

California, University of
Riverside
Native American Studies Program offers a B.A. in Native American studies; minor in Native American studies; B.A. in ethnic studies with emphasis in Native American studies; Ph.D. in Native American history, and a major or minor Ph.D. fields. Course offerings include Indian histories of California, Southwest, and Northwest; history of disease among Americans Indians; American Indian oral and written literatures; Ojibwa history, resistance and survival movements, and strategies.

California State University
Chico
Minor in Native American studies.

California State University
Fresno
Courses in American Indian studies.

California State University
Long Beach
American Indian Studies Program. Minor, certificate, and concentration.

California State University
Sacramento
Major and minor in Native American studies.

Colgate College
Hamilton, N.Y.
Native American Studies Program offers major and minor concentrations. Takes a comparative and historical orientation to North, Central, and South America, focusing on the integrity and richness of traditional American Indian cultures as well as the reciprocal effects of colonization.

Colorado, University of
Boulder
American Indian Studies Program offers a B.A and minor in ethnic studies. Class topics include American Indian religious traditions, the history of tribal governments, American Indian women's experience, Native American and environmental ethics, Marxism and Native Americans, and portrayals of Indians in motion pictures.

Connecticut, University of
Storrs
Native American Studies Program. An interdisciplinary course of study offering a B.A. that focuses on Native American social studies, history, art, and literature.

Cornell University

Ithaca, N.Y.

American Indian Program offers both undergraduate and graduate minors. Program focuses on the unique heritage and perspectives of North American Indians, issues of sovereignty, and the contemporary importance of American Indian environmental concepts and values. Publishes the American Indian studies journal *Akwe:kon*.

Dakota Wesleyan University

Mitchell, S.Dak.

Major and minor in American Indian studies. Offers course in Lakota language.

Dartmouth College

Hanover, N.H.

Native American Studies Department (founded 1972) offers B.A. Includes classes on histories and cultures of North American Indians, American Indian religious systems, American Indian law and federal Indian policy, American Indian languages, and American Indian literature. Sponsors annual symposium on Native American subjects. Dartmouth was founded in 1769 to educate Indians using money raised in Great Britain by Samson Occom, a Mohegan.

Five College, Inc.

Amherst, Mass.

Native American studies consortium with courses offered on five campuses, including University of Massachusetts, Amherst College, Hampshire College, Smith College, and Mount Holyoke College, in different fields of study. Classes focus on issues affecting the history and current conditions of indigenous peoples.

Fort Lewis College
Durango, Colo.

Offers B.A. in Southwest studies. Courses include Navajo language. Free tuition for all American Indians and Alaska Natives.

Hampton University
Hampton, Va.

American Indian Educational Opportunities Program. Hampton Normal and Agricultural Institute first accepted Indian students in 1878.

Harvard University
Cambridge, Mass.

Harvard's Native American Program prepares American Indians to fill leadership positions in schools and school systems. Part of Harvard's original 1636 charter was to Christianize Indians.

Haskell Indian Nations University
Lawrence, Kans.

Founded as an Indian boarding school in 1884, Haskell became Haskell Indian Junior College in 1970 and was renamed again in 1993, the same year that a four-year teacher education program was added. Haskell is the only university operated directly by the U.S. Department of the Interior's Bureau of Indian Affairs (BIA).

Humboldt State University
Arcata, Calif.

Offers B.A. and M.A. in Native American studies. Indian Teacher and Education Personnel Program. Natural Resource, Science, and Engineering Program.

Illinois, University of
Chicago
Native American Studies Program. Minor in Native American studies.

Iowa, University of
Iowa City
American Indian and Native Studies Programs offer undergraduate and graduate minors with certificates in American Indian and Native studies. Program is interdisciplinary, including classes in American Indian histories, cultures, languages, political and social organizations, economies, and contemporary political and legal questions.

Iowa State University
Ames
American Indian Studies Program offers minor in American Indian studies. Class topics include American Indian literature, anthropology, history of Prairies-Plains, and contemporary issues.

Kansas, University of
Lawrence
Center for Indigenous Nations Studies offers an M.A. in indigenous nations studies. Among the program's goals are to train graduate students to understand the complexities of Native peoples of the hemisphere, to prepare them for academic teaching and research, and to prepare candidates to assume leadership and policy-making roles in indigenous communities and in state, national, and international institutions and organizations

Maine, University of
Orono

Native American Studies offers an interdisciplinary academic program with a minor in Native American studies. The goal of the program is to educate students concerning indigenous perspectives on their traditions and self-determination.

Massachusetts, University of
Amherst

Native American Studies Program offers approximately twenty courses in anthropology, history, geosciences, legal studies, English, Afro-American studies, linguistics, and STPEC (social thought and political economy). Students may also take courses offered by the Five Colleges consortium.

Minnesota, University of
Duluth

Duluth American Indian Teacher Training Program and a variety of other programs that serve Indian students.

Minnesota, University of
Twin Cities, Minneapolis

American Indian Studies Program offers major and minor. Courses in Ojibwa and Dakota languages.

Montana, University of
Missoula

Native American studies with a B.A major and minor. An interdisciplinary holistic and humanistic program that focuses on the diversity and continued evolution of American Indian cultures, histories, and experiences.

Montana State University
Billings

Minor in Native American studies.

Montana State University

Bozeman

Center for Native American Studies offers M.A. in Native American studies, B.A. minor in Native American studies. An interdisciplinary program that provides students opportunities for independent study, seminars, internships, and courses in special topics.

Morehead State University

Morehead, Minn.

Minor in American Indian studies.

NAES (Native American Educational Services) College

Chicago, Ill.

Offers a degree in tribal administration and has campuses on the Fort Peck Reservation in Montana, the Menominee Reservation in Wisconsin, Chicago, and Minneapolis.

Nebraska, University of

Lincoln

Native American Studies Program offers a B.A. major or minor. Courses include Native American anthropology, ethnography, history, and literature with emphasis on Northern Plains.

New Mexico, University of

Albuquerque

Native American Studies Center offers B.A., M.A., and Ph.D. Classes in education and communication; expressive arts and technology; governance, law, and economics; health and environment; history, politics, and ethics; language and literature; science, religion, and philosophy; societies and cultures. The University of New Mexico was the first in the United States to offer an American Indian studies Ph.D. program.

New York, State University of
Buffalo

Program in Indigenous Studies offers B.A. in American studies with a concentration in indigenous and Native American studies; M.A. and Ph.D. in American studies with a concentration in indigenous and Native American studies. Courses included Indians and film, American Indian law, indigenous women, introduction to Native American history, mythology, contemporary problems of American Indians, indigenous health and healing, Native American literature.

New York, State University of
New Paltz

Native American Studies Program offers B.A. with minor in North American Indian studies. Courses include North American ethnology, archaeology of Mesoamerica, and archaeology of New York State.

North Carolina, University of
Pembroke

American Indian Studies Program offers B.A. major, minor, or concentration. Classes on North and Latin American Indian history and culture; American Indian religions, art, and literature; American Indian women; and American Indians and film.

North Dakota, University of
Grand Forks

Indian Studies Department offers B.A. major and minor. Indians into Medicine (INMED) program serves pre-med and medical students.

North Dakota State University
Fargo

Native American Pharmacy Program.

Northeastern State University
Tahlequah, Okla.
Native American Studies Program offers major and minor. Has Center for Tribal Studies. Located on the site of the former Cherokee Female Seminary.

Northern Arizona University
Flagstaff
Four Corners Intertribal Science and Mathematics Summer Program, Native American Forestry Program, and Indian Education Program. Courses in Navajo language.

Northern Kentucky University
Highland Heights
Native American Studies Program offers minor in Native American studies. Classes include North and Mesoamerican Indians, Plains Indian history, North and South American archaeology, and modern American Indians.

Northern State University
Aberdeen, S.Dak.
American Indian studies minor.

Oklahoma, University of
Norman
Native American studies program offers B.A. major and minor. Students select relevant courses from different departments, including anthropology, history, geography, English, communications, music, and fine arts, to fulfill degree requirements. Publishes *American Indian Quarterly*. American Indian Institute houses Native American Research Information Service.

Oklahoma, University of
Oklahoma City
Native American Center of Excellence program dedicated to increasing the number of Native American physicians.

Pembroke State University

Pembroke, N.C.

Department of American Indian Studies offers major and minor. Founded in 1887 as the Croatan Normal School to serve the Lumbee Indians of North Carolina.

Pennsylvania State University

University Park

American Indian Leadership Program offers M.A. and Ph.D.

Prescott College

Prescott, Ariz.

Center for Indian Bilingual Teacher Training.

St. Scholastica, College of

Duluth, Minn.

Department of American Indian Studies offers minor.

San Diego State University

San Diego, Calif.

Department of Indian Studies offers minor with a B.A. in another field. Program includes classes on American Indian heritage, American Indian oral literature, American Indian poetry and fiction, federal Indian law, American Indian languages (survey), Native American educational issues, and media images of American Indians.

San Francisco State University

San Francisco, Calif.

Department of American Indian Studies offers a minor in American Indian studies; can constitute part of a special major or be an emphasis of an M.A. in ethnic studies. Program stresses a multidisciplinary appreciation for the historic and contemporary diversity of American Indian tribes and tribal lifeways.

Santa Fe at Albuquerque, College of
Albuquerque, N.Mex.
Sponsored Summer Institute of Linguistics for Native Americans (SILNA) in 1994.

South Dakota, University of
Vermillion
American Indian Studies Program offers B.A. major, double major, and minor. Curriculum includes anthropology; Lakota language, thought, and culture; American Indian law; American Indian literature; American Indian history; history of American Indian education; American Indian government.

South Dakota State University
Brookings
American Indian Studies Program. This interdisciplinary program offers a minor and includes classes in anthropology, English, geography, history, languages (Lakota), philosophy, political science, religion, and sociology that deal with American Indian topics and issues.

Stanford University
Stanford, Calif.
Native American Cultural Center/The American Indian, Alaska Native and Native Hawaiian Program. Primary mission is to meet the needs of the students by recognizing the variables that exist within the Native American community and creating programs that assist them in successfully addressing the factors that influence degree progress and completion.

Tulsa, University of
Tulsa, Okla.
Native American Law Center offers certification in American Indian law as part of a J.D. program. Curriculum includes nine specialized Indian law courses and the opportunity for students to help tribal members as part of a Center-run clinic.

Washington, University of
Seattle
American Indian Studies Center offers B.A. (individual studies). Program includes courses on American Indian history, ethnology, religions, federal Indian policy, Navajo language, folklore, contemporary literature, and museology, with special attention given to Western and Northwest Coast tribes. School of Medicine's Native American Center for Excellence promotes medical careers for Indian students.

Washington State University
Pullman
Offers B.A. in comparative American cultures. Minor in Native American studies.

Wisconsin, University of
Eau Claire
American Indian Studies Program grants B.A. major and minor in American Indian studies. Also offers graduate studies in American Indian history and literature.

Wisconsin, University of
Madison
American Indian Studies Program offers a certificate in American Indian studies. Includes classes in anthropology, sociology, social work, history, archaeology, history, law, and literature.

Wisconsin, University of
Milwaukee
American Indian Studies Program offers an interdisciplinary degree option.

Wyoming, University of
Laramie
American Indian Studies Program offers minor. Interdisciplinary
approach includes classes in anthropology, sociology, history,
literature, and geography.

AMERICAN INDIAN HIGHER EDUCATION CONSORTIUM (AIHEC) MEMBER INSTITUTIONS

American Indian Arts, Institute of
Santa Fe, N.Mex.
Associate's degree.

American Indian Higher Education Consortium (AIHEC)
Washington, D.C.
Represents thirty-one Indian-controlled colleges in the United
States and Canada. Collects data on tribal colleges and sponsors
Tribal College: Journal of American Indian Higher Education.

Bay Mills Community College
Brimley, Minn.
Associate's degree.

Blackfeet Community College
Browning, Mont.
Associate's degree.

Cankdeska Cikana (Little Hoop) Community College
Fort Totten, N.Dak.
Associate's degree.

Chief Dull Knife College
Lame Deer, Mont.
Associate's degree.

College of the Menominee Nation
Keshena, Wis.
Associate's degree.

Crownpoint Institute of Technology
Crownpoint, N.Mex.
Associate's degree.

Diné College
Tsaile, Ariz.
Associate's degree.

D-Q University
Davis, Calif.
Associate's degree.

Fond du Lac Tribal and Community College
Cloquet, Minn.
Associate's degree.

Fort Belknap College
Harlem, Mont.
Associate's degree.

Fort Berthold Community College
New Town, Mont.
Associate's degree.

Fort Peck Community College
Poplar, Mont.
Associate's degree.

Haskell Indian Nations University
Lawrence, Kans.
Associate's and bachelor's degrees.

Keweenaw Bay Ojibwa Community College
Baraga, Minn.
Associate's degree.

Lac Courte Oreilles Ojibwa Community College
Hayward, Wis.
Associate's degree.

Leech Lake Tribal College
Cass Lake, Minn.
Associate's degree.

Little Big Horn College
Crow Agency, Mont.
Associate's degree.

Little Priest Tribal College
Winnebago, Nebr.
Associate's degree.

Nebraska Indian Community College
Macy, Nebr.
Associate's degree.

Northwest Indian College
Bellingham, Wash.
Associate's degree.

Oglala Lakota College
Kyle, S.Dak.
Associate's, bachelor's, and master's degrees.

Saginaw Chippewa Tribal College
Mount Pleasant, Minn.
Associate's degree.

Salish Kootenai College
Pablo, Mont.
Associate's and bachelor's degrees.

Sinte Gleska University
Rosebud, S.Dak.
Associate's, bachelor's, and master's degrees.

Sisseton Wahpeton Community College
Sisseton, S.Dak.
Associate's degree.

Si Tanka/Huron University
Eagle Butte, S.Dak.
Associate's degree.

Sitting Bull College
Fort Yates, N.Dak.
Associate's degree.

Southwestern Indian Polytechnic Institute
Albuquerque, N.Mex.
Associate's degree.

Stone Child College
Box Elder, Mont.
Associate's degree.

Tohono O'odham Community College
Sells, Ariz.
Associate's degree.

Turtle Mountain Community College
Belcourt, N.Dak.
Associate's degree.

United Tribes Technical College
Bismarck, N.Dak.
Associate's degree.

White Earth Tribal and Community College
Mahnomen, Minn.
Associate's degree.

OTHER U.S. EDUCATIONAL INSTITUTIONS AND PROGRAMS

Akwesasne Freedom School
Rooseveltown, N.Y.
Alternative elementary school provides a bilingual Mohawk-English curriculum.

American Indian Graduate Center
Albuquerque, N.Mex.
National nonprofit organization founded in 1969 to enhance the cultural and economic well-being of American Indian graduate students.

American Indian Higher Education Consortium (AIHEC)
Washington, D.C.
Represents thirty-one Indian-controlled colleges in the United States and Canada. Collects data on tribal colleges and sponsors *Tribal College: Journal of American Indian Higher Education*.

American Indian Science and Engineering Society
Boulder, Colo.
Sponsors various programs to encourage Indian students to major in the sciences and engineering. Publishes *Winds of Change* magazine.

American Indian Studies Research Institute
Bloomington, Ind.

Established at Indiana University to in 1985 to serve as an interdisciplinary research center for projects concerning Indian peoples of the Americas. Provides the institutional structure necessary to carry out research and educational projects funded by outside sources.

Arizona Department of Education, Indian Education Office
Phoenix

Offers support for general education, from literacy programs to higher education, and publishes educational material about Arizona Indians.

Blue Quills Native Education Centre
St. Paul, Alta.

Formerly Blue Quills Residential School, the Centre was opened under local control in 1970 to serve students from seven different bands. Offers Cree language courses. Started postsecondary extension courses in 1975.

California Department of Education, American Indian Education Office
Sacramento

Publishes a handbook on American Indians for educators.

Chemewa Indian School
Salem, Oreg.

An off-reservation boarding high school founded in 1880 and sponsored by the Bureau of Indian Affairs.

D'Arcy McNickle Center for the History of the American Indian, Newberry Library
Chicago, Ill.

Sponsors programs to promote the study of American Indian history.

Denver Indian Center, Circle of Learning Pre-K Program
Denver, Colo.
Culturally based preschool classes, home-based instruction, and parent education services for Indian families.

ERIC Clearinghouse on Rural Education and Small Schools (ERIC/CRESS)
Charleston, W.Va.
Federal education clearinghouse serving American Indian education. Publishes digests and monographs on American Indian education.

Flandreau Indian School
Flandreau, S.Dak.
An off-reservation boarding high school established in 1893 and supported by the Bureau of Indian Affairs.

Greyhills Academy
Tuba City, Ariz.
A high school with a model song, dance, and drama program, funded by the Bureau of Indian Affairs.

Heard Museum
Phoenix, Ariz.
Sponsors a variety of educational outreach programs focusing on the American Indian.

Heart of the Earth Survival School
Minneapolis, Minn.
Alternative school serving urban Indian students.

Institute of American Indian Arts

Santa Fe, N.Mex.

Government-chartered postsecondary school serving the entire United States. Founded in 1962 and chartered by the U.S. government in 1988. Serves more than two hundred students from seventy different tribes.

Mt. Edgecumbe High School

Sitka, Alaska

State-operated magnet boarding school serving Alaska's Native and non-Native population.

National Indian Education Association (NIEA)

Washington, D.C.

Founded in 1970, NIEA lobbies Congress on legislation affecting Indian education, sponsors annual state and national Indian education workshops, and recognizes outstanding Indian educators at its conferences.

National Museum of the American Indian

Washington, D.C.

Cultural Resources Center houses library, archives.

Native American Language Issues (NALI)

Choctaw, Okla.

Promotes the maintenance and renewal of American Indian languages through annual conferences and legislative activity.

Navajo Area School Board Association

Window Rock, Ariz.

Works with members at schools operated by the Bureau of Indian Affairs.

Navajo Ceremonial Art, Museum of
Santa Fe, N.Mex.
Collection and educational materials focus on traditional Navajo religion.

Navajo Division of Education
Window Rock, Ariz.
Sponsors Navajo tribal scholarships, research on Navajo education, Navajo North Central Accreditation Association, and a variety of other programs.

Navajo Nation Public School Boards Association
Window Rock, Ariz.
Works with members in public schools serving Navajo students.

Navajo Preparatory Academy
Farmington, N.Mex.
High school funded by the Bureau of Indian Affairs to train Navajo leaders.

Northwest Indian Head Start Coalition
Fort Washakie, Wyo.
Works to improve Indian Head Start programs.

Office of Indian Education, U.S. Department of Education
Washington, D.C.
Administers programs funded through the Indian Education Act. Programs include educational personnel development, educational services, formula grant, Indian fellowship, Indian gifted and talented pilot, and Indian-controlled schools enrichment. Six regional Indian education technical assistance centers serve the various regions of the United States.

Office of Indian Education Programs (OIEP), Bureau of Indian Affairs, U.S. Department of the Interior

Washington, D.C.

Administers Bureau of Indian Affairs (BIA) schools and BIA-funded schools. Maintains twenty-five offices throughout the United States. The 185 elementary and secondary schools funded by the federal government teach 50,000 students from birth through grade 12. Also operates two colleges and funds twenty-five colleges operated by tribes and tribal organizations. OIEP programs include adult education, bilingual education, Close Up (grades nine through twelve civic education), effective schools, exceptional education, family and child education, higher education grants, Johnson O'Malley funding (assistance to public schools for the education of Indian children), junior achievement, National Indian School Board Association, Principals Leadership Academy, Sandia and Los Alamos National Laboratories (providing training to teachers in math and science), science and math summer workshops, showcase of excellence (showcasing outstanding boarding school programs), Solo Parent (for single-parent high school students), Special Higher Education Grants (funds for Indian students to pursue graduate degrees), summer law, and Whole Language Summer Workshop.

Peach Springs School District

Peach Springs, Ariz.

Hualapai Bilingual Academic Excellence Program. Publishes a variety of Hualapai curriculum materials.

Piegan Institute

Browning, Mont.

Founded in 1887 to increase the number of Blackfeet speakers and knowledge of Blackfeet culture. Operates the Nizipuhwahsin Blackfeet language immersion program for grades K-8; conducts seminars and conferences; and produces written, audio, and video materials on Blackfeet language and history.

Riverside Indian School
Anadarko, Okla.
Off-reservation boarding school sponsored by the Bureau of Indian Affairs, serving grades 2-12.

Rock Point Community School
Rock Point, Ariz.
A former boarding school of the Bureau of Indian Affairs, Rock Point became a locally controlled BIA-funded school in 1977. Rock Point pioneered English as a second language (ESL) and Navajo-English bilingual curricula.

Rough Rock Demonstration School
Chinle, Ariz.
First Indian-controlled school in modern times, founded in 1966. Rough Rock Press publishes a variety of Navajo curriculum materials.

San Juan School District
Blanding, Utah
Publishes Navajo curriculum material.

Santa Fe Indian School
Santa Fe, N.Mex.
Bureau of Indian Affairs boarding school opened in 1890, serving nineteen Pueblo tribes plus Navajo, Hopi, Mescalero Apache, and Jicarilla Apache students.

Sherman Indian High School
Riverside, Calif.
Bureau of Indian Affairs off-reservation boarding school founded in 1902.

Wahpeton Indian Boarding School
Wahpeton, N.Dak.
Bureau of Indian Affairs off-reservation boarding school serving grades 4-8.

Wingate High School
Fort Wingate, N.Mex.
Bureau of Indian Affairs boarding school serving Navajo and surrounding tribes.

CANADIAN INSTITUTIONS

Alberta, University of
Edmonton
School of Native Studies. B.A. in Native studies; combined degree program of B.A. (Native studies) and B.Ed. offers classes in First Nations issues and perspectives, economic development, Cree languages, Aboriginal government and political systems, patterns of land use, Native arts and oral traditions, Aboriginal health issues, Metis politics.

Brandon University
Brandon, Man.
Department of Native Studies. Has Native teacher training program and publishes *Canadian Journal of Native Studies*.

British Columbia, University of
Vancouver
First Nations House of Learning. Special programs for Native Canadian students. Publishes the *Canadian Journal of Native Education* in association with the University of Alberta, Edmonton.

Dene Standardization Project
Yellowknife, N.W.T.
Started in 1986 to develop a standardized writing system for northern Dene languages for use in schools and other areas of Dene life.

Department of Indian Affairs and Northern Development
Ottawa, Ont.
Funds First Nation schools throughout Canada.

Gabriel Dumont Institute of Native Studies and Applied Resesarch
Regina, Sask.
Promotes and publishes research on the Metis and Cree in Canada.

James Bay Cree School Board
James Bay, Que.
Manages Cree schools in Quebec since 1978.

Kahnawake Education Centre
Kahnawake, Que.
Offering Mohawk immersion classes since 1979 in primary grades and bilingual Mohawk-English classes in intermediate grades.

Kahnawake Survival School
Kahnawake, Que.
Since 1978, this high school has emphasized Mohawk history and culture.

Mi'kmawey School
Chapel Island, N.S.
A bilingual, bicultural school opened in 1981 to serve Mi'kmaq Indian children.

N'ungosuk Pre-school Project
West Bay, Ont.
Ojibwa preschool established in 1981.

Saskatchewan, University of
Saskatoon
Native Studies Department offers B.A. and M.A. Classes stress community-based experiences and histories of Canada's First Nations.

Saskatchewan Indian Federated College
Regina
Founded in 1976 in federation with the University of Regina.

Simon Fraser University
Vancouver, B.C.
Mount Currie Teacher Training program established in 1975 to train teachers for the Lil'wat Band.

Toronto, University of
Toronto, Ont.
Aboriginal Studies Program offers B.A. major and minor. Focuses on First Nations' cultures, histories, and languages, as well as their relationship with the Canadian government.

Festivals and Pow-Wows

A select calendar, not intended to be inclusive, of annual American Indian gatherings. —C.A.B.

JANUARY

Annual Native American Film
 Festival
Southwest Museum
Los Angeles, California

Evening Firelight Dance
San Ildefonso Pueblo
Santa Fe, New Mexico

Kachina Dances
Hopi Cultural Center
Second Mesa, Arizona

King's Day Celebration:
Buffalo, Deer, Eagle, and Elk
 Dances
All Pueblos in New Mexico

Mid-Winter Pow-wow
United Native American
 Cultural Center
Fort Devens, Massachusetts

New Year's Pow-wow
St. Francis, South Dakota

San Ildefonso Feast Day
San Ildefonso Pueblo
Santa Fe, New Mexico

Turtle Dance
Taos Pueblo, New Mexico

FEBRUARY

Candelaria Day Celebration
 Dances
Picuris Pueblo, New Mexico
San Felipe Pueblo, New Mexico

Deer Dances
San Juan Pueblo, New Mexico

First Americans in the Arts
 Awards
Beverly Hills, California

Grossmont College Pow-wow
El Cajon, California

Lincoln's Birthday Celebration
   Pow-wow
Warm Springs Tribal Council
Warm Springs, Oregon

Marin Indian Art Show
San Rafael, California

New Hampshire Intertribal
   Council Pow-wow
North Conway, New Hamp-
   shire

O'odham Tash Celebration
Tohono O'odham Nation
Sells, Arizona

Seminole Tribal Fair and Rodeo
Hollywood Reservation
Hollywood, Florida

MARCH

Agua Caliente Indian Market
Palm Springs, California

Denver March Pow-wow
Denver, Colorado

Easter Celebrations:
Basket and Corn Dances
All Pueblos in New Mexico

Epethes Pow-wow
Nez Perce Tribe
Lapwai, Idaho

Long Beach State Pow-wow
Long Beach, California

Mother Earth Awakens Pow-
   wow
Portland, Maine

Mul-Chu-Tha Community Fair
Gila River Indian Community
Sacaton, Arizona

Rug Auction and Trader's
   Trunk Show
Los Angeles, California

San Jose Feast Day
Laguna Pueblo
Laguna, New Mexico

Spring Crafts Fair
Sherman Indian High School
Riverside, California

Sugar Run Pow-wow
Laconia, New Hampshire

APRIL

All-Indian Days Pow-wow
Scottsdale Community
  College
Scottsdale, Arizona

Annual American Indian
  Days
Chico State University
Chico, California

Annual Intertribal Pow-wow
Sherman Indian High School
Riverside, California

Annual Pow-wow
Western Washington
  University
Bellingham, Washington

Annual South Umpqua
  Pow-wow
Myrtle Creek, Oregon

Annual Spring Pow-wow
University of Wyoming
Laramie, Wyoming

Arizona State University
  Pow-wow
Tempe, Arizona

Cocopah Festivities Day
Somerton, Arizona

Cupa Cultural Days
Pala, California

Fort McDowell Annual Spring
  Pow-wow
Fort McDowell, Arizona

Gathering of Nations Pow-
  wow
Albuquerque, New Mexico

Harvard University Annual
  Pow-wow
Cambridge, Massachusetts

Humboldt State University
  Pow-wow
Arcata, California

Institute of American Indian
  Arts Pow-wow
Santa Fe, New Mexico

Spring Pow-wow
Gulfport, Mississippi

Spring Roundup All-Indian
  Rodeo
White Mountain Apache
  Tribal Council
Whiteriver, Arizona

University of California,
Berkeley, Pow-wow
Berkeley, California

University of Washington
Pow-wow
Sandpoint Naval Air Station
Seattle, Washington

MAY

Abenaki Nation of Missisquoi
Swanton, Vermont

Annual First Peoples Cultural
Festival
Capilano Longhouse
North Vancouver, British
Columbia, Canada

Annual Intertribal Pow-wow
Trout Lake Community Centre
Victoria, British Columbia,
Canada

Chehalis Tribal Day
Celebration
Oakville, Washington

Choctaw Annual Rodeo
Jones Academy
Hartshorn, Oklahoma

Chumash Intertribal Pow-
wow
Thousand Oaks, California

Kenel Memorial Day
Wacipi Kenel, South Dakota

Louisiana Indian Heritage
Association Pow-wow
Folsom, Louisiana

Montana State University
Annual Pow-wow
Bozeman, Montana

Native Americans at
Dartmouth College
Hanover, New Hampshire

San Carlos Tribal Fair
San Carlos Apache Tribe
San Carlos, Arizona

San Felipe Pueblo Feast Day:
Corn Dance
San Felipe Pueblo

Santa Cruz Feast Day:
Blessing of the Fields and
Corn Dance
Taos Pueblo, New Mexico

Spring Pow-wow
Portland State University
Portland, Oregon

Stanford University Annual
Pow-wow
Palo Alto, California

Tse-Ho-Tso Intertribal
Pow-wow
Window Rick High School
Fort Defiance, Arizona

Tuscarora Nation of North
Carolina Pow-wow
Tribal Grounds
Maxton, North Carolina

University of Washington
Pow-wow
Seattle, Washington

JUNE

Badlands Celebration
Brockton, Montana

Bear Dance
Ute Mountain Ute Tribe
Towaoc, Colorado

Big Wind Pow-wow
Shoshone and Arapaho Tribes
Fort Washakie, Wyoming

Blessing of the Fields:
Corn Dance
TesuQue Pueblo, New Mexico

California Basketweavers
Gathering
Klamath, California

Cherokee Pow-wow
Eastern Band of Cherokee
Indians
Cherokee, North Carolina

Cheyenne-Arapaho
Pow-wow
Concho, Oklahoma

Comanche Dance
Santa Clara Pueblo, New
Mexico

Dokis First Nation Pow-wow
Honouring All Women
Dokis First Nation
Ontario, Canada

Hinkley Pow-wow
Hinkley, Minnesota

Honor the Firekeepers
Traditional Pow-wow
Lake Geneva, Wisconsin

Indian Fair
San Diego, California

Noongam Traditional Pow-
wow
Ottawa, Ontario, Canada

Osage Tribal Ceremonial
Dances
Pawhuska, Oklahoma

Potawatomi Pow-wow
Shawnee, Oklahoma

Red Rocks Arts and Crafts
Show
Jemez Pueblo, New
Mexico

Rogue Valley Pow-wow
Grants Pass, Oregon

San Antonio Feast Day:
Corn Dances
Sandia Pueblo, New
Mexico
Taos Pueblo, New Mexico

San Juan Feast Day
Taos Pueblo
Taos, New Mexico

San Pedro Feast Day:
Corn Dance
Santa Ana Pueblo, New Mexico

Shenandoah County Pow-wow
Mount Jackson, Virginia

Shoshone Indian Days Pow-
wow and Rodeo
Fort Washakie, Wyoming

Stommish Festival
Lummi Indian Tribe
Bellingham, Washington

Tecumseh Traditional Pow-
wow
Tecumseh, Michigan

Two Sisters Pow-wow
Lowell, Massachusetts

Warriors Memorial Pow-wow
Nez Perce Tribe
Lapwai, Idaho

Winds of the Northeast Pow-
wow
Olympia, Washington

JULY

Aabita Niibing (Midsummer) Pow-wow
Cass Lake, Minnesota

Annual All Nations Pow-wow
Big Bear City, California

Annual Bear River Pow-wow
Lac du Flambeau, Wisconsin

Annual Chumash Intertribal Pow-wow
Santa Ynez, California

Annual Competition Pow-wow
Norway House
Manitoba, Canada

Annual Homecoming Celebration
Winnebago, Nebraska

Annual Northern Cheyenne Fourth of July Pow-wow
Lame Deer, Montana

Annual Northern Ute Pow-wow and Rodeo
Fort Duchesne, Utah

Annual Taos Pueblo Pow-wow
Pow-wow Grounds
Taos, New Mexico

Arikara Celebration and Pow-wow
White Shield, North Dakota

Arlee Fourth of July Pow-wow
Pablo, Montana

Bahweting Homecoming Pow-wow and Spiritual Gathering
Sault Ste. Marie, Michigan

Bitterroot Valley All Nations Pow-wow
Hamilton, Montana

Carrefour des Nations
Wendake, Quebec, Canada

Coeur d'Alene Pow-wow
Plummer, Idaho

Eastern Woodland Intertribal Pow-wow
Lebanon, Maine

Emigrant Lake Pow-wow
Ashland, Oregon

Flagstaff Indian Days Celebration
Flagstaff, Arizona

Flandreau Santee Sioux Tribe
Traditional Wacipi
Flandreau, South Dakota

Harvest and Snake Dances
Nambe Pueblo
Picuris, New Mexico

Honouring Our Veterans
Kettle and Stony First Nation
Ontario, Canada

Jicarilla Apache Little Beaver
Roundup and Rodeo
Dulce, New Mexico

July Fourth Celebration Pow-
wow and Rodeo
Window Rock, Arizona

Kateri Circle Pow-wow
Lakewood, California

Mescalero Festival
Mescalero, New Mexico

Mihsihkinaahkwa Pow-wow
Columbia City, Indiana

Mississauga First Nation
Annual Pow-wow
Blind River, Ontario, Canada

Native American Festival
Redmond, Oregon

Nevada Indian Days Pow-
wow
Fallon, Nevada

North American Indian Days
Blackfeet Tribal Council
Browning, Montana

Ochiichagwe'Babigo'Ining
Traditional Pow-wow
Kenora, Ontario, Canada

Onion Lake Pow-wow
Onion Lake Reserve
Saskatchewan, Alberta, British
Columbia, Canada

Poundmaker-Nechi Pow-wow
St. Albert, Alberta, Canada

Quapaw Pow-wow
Quapaw, Oklahoma

Santa Ana Feast Day
Santa Ana Pueblo
Bernalillo, New Mexico

Santiago Feast Day Corn
Dance
Taos, New Mexico

Seafair Indian Days Pow-wow
Seattle, Washington

Shelburne Museum Intertribal
   Pow-wow
Shelburne, Vermont

Shoshone-Paiute Annual Pow-
   wow
Owyhee, Nevada

Sisseton-Wahpeton Pow-wow
Sisseton, South Dakota

Standing Tree Pow-wow
White Cloud, Michigan

Swan Lake First Nation
   Annual Pow-wow
Swan Lake, Manitoba, Canada

Three Rivers Indian Lodge
   Annual Pow-wow
Manteca, California

White Earth Pow-wow
White Earth, Minnesota

AUGUST

American Indian Exposition
Anadarko, Oklahoma

Annual Abegeweit Pow-wow
Panamure Island, Prince
   Edward Island, Canada

Annual Frank Liske Park
   Pow-wow
Concord, North Carolina

Annual Genaabaajing
   Traditional Pow-wow
Cutler, Ontario, Canada

Annual Indian Fair Days and
   Pow-wow
Sierra Mono, California

Annual Intertribal Indian
   Ceremonial
Church Rock, New Mexico

Annual Piegan Indian Days
Brocket, Alberta, Canada

Annual Southern California
   Indian Center Pow-wow
Costa Mesa, California

Annual Stockton Pow-wow
Stockton, California

Cherokee Nation Pow-wow
Tahlequah, Oklahoma

Cheyenne and Arapaho Labor
   Day Pow-wow
Colony Indian Park
Colony, Oklahoma

Cheyenne River Labor Day
   Pow-wow
Eagle Butte, South Dakota

Chief Seattle Days
Suquamish, Washington

Choctaw Annual Pow-wow
Arrowhead State Park
Canadian, Oklahoma

Crow Creek Sioux Tribe
   Annual Pow-wow
Fort Thompson, South Dakota

Crow Fair
Crow Agency, Montana

Fort Randall Pow-wow
Lake Andes, South Dakota

Ginoogaming First Nations
   Pow-wow
Longlac, Ontario, Canada

Hays Pow-wow
Hays, Montana

Indian Market, Basket,
   Butterfly, and Corn Dances
Santa Fe, New Mexico

Kalispel Pow-wow
Usk, Washington

Klamath Restoration
   Celebration
Chiloquin, Oregon

Land of the Menominee Pow-
   wow
Kenosha, Wisconsin

Lincoln Indian Club Pow-wow
Lincoln, Nebraska

Little Shell Pow-wow
New Town, North Dakota

Long Plain First Nation
   Celebration
Long Plain, Manitoba, Canada

Looking Glass Pow-wow
Lapwai, Idaho

Lower Brule Pow-wow
Lower Brule, South Dakota

Mihsihkinaahkwa Pow-wow
Columbian City, Indiana

Morning Star International
   Pow-wow
Litchfield, Maine

Native American Gathering
Williamston, North Carolina

Navajo Nation Fair
Window Rock, Arizona

Ni-Mi-Win Celebration
Duluth, Minnesota

Northern Arapaho Pow-wow
Arapaho, Wyoming

Numi'Pu Council Pow-wow
Mount Pleasant, Utah

Oglala Nation Pow-wow and
Rodeo
Pine Ridge, South Dakota

Ottawa Pow-wow
Miami, Oklahoma

Pioneer Days Traditional
Pow-wow
Wetaskawin, Alberta, Canada

Ponca Indian Fair and
Pow-wow
Ponca City, Oklahoma

Rapid River Traditional
Anishnabeg Pow-wow
Rapid River, Michigan

Rocky Boys Pow-wow
Box Elder, Montana

Rosebud Fair and Rodeo
Rosebud, South Dakota

Saco River Intertribal
Pow-wow
Kearsarge, New Hampshire

San Antonio Feast Day Laguna
Pueblo, New Mexico

San Augustin Feast Day Isleta
Pueblo, New Mexico

San Lorenzo Sunset Vespers
and Feast Day Picuris
Pueblo Picuris, Pueblo, New
Mexico

Santa Clara Pueblo Feast Day
Santa Clara Pueblo, New
Mexico

Santo Domingo Pueblo Feast
Day, Corn Dance
Santo Domingo Pueblo, New
Mexico

SEPTEMBER

American Indian Days
Woodson Terrace, Missouri

Arkansas Trail of Tears Annual
Pow-wow
De Queen, Arkansas

Bishop Paiute Tribe Annual
Handgame Tournament
Bishop, California

Corn Dance
San Ildefonso Pueblo, New
Mexico

Everything Is Sacred Pow-
wow Gathering
Thousand Oaks, California

Fall Spirit Festival
Harrisville, Pennsylvania

First People's House
McGill University
Montreal, Quebec, Canada

Four Winds Annual Pow-wow
Killeen, Texas

Honouring Our Children
Pow-wow
Midland, Ontario, Canada

Kickapoo Pow-wow
Horton, Kansas

Narragansett Nation:
Great Swamp Massacre
Kingston, Rhode Island

**Nativity of the Blessed Virgin
Mary Feast Day:**
Harvest and Social Dances
Laguna Pueblo, New Mexico

Nooksack Days Pow-wow
Deming, Washington

Northern Plains Tribal Arts
Show and Pow-wow
Sioux Falls, South Dakota

Saint Augustine Feast Day and
Harvest Dance
Isleta Pueblo, New Mexico

Saint Elizabeth Feast Day:
Harvest and Social Dances
Laguna Pueblo, New Mexico

San Estevan Feast Day
Harvest Dance
Acoma Pueblo, New Mexico

San Geronimo Feast Day:
Buffalo, Comanche, Corn
    Dances, Trade Fair
Taos, New Mexico

San Jose Feast Day:
Buffalo, Corn, Eagle, Harvest,
    and Social Dances
Old Laguna Pueblo, New
    Mexico

Santa Ynez Pow-wow
Santa Ynez, California

Semiahmoo First Nation
    Pow-wow
White Rock, British Columbia,
    Canada

Shoshone Indian Fair
Fort Washakie, Wyoming

Shoshone-Bannock Indian
    Festival and Rodeo
Fort Hall, Idaho

Siksika Fair
Siksika, Alberta, Canada

Siletz Indian Pow-wow
Siletz, Oregon

Snake Dance
Hopi Cultural Center
Second Mesa, Arizona

Southern Ute Fair and Pow-
    wow
Ignacio, Colorado

Spirit of the North Celebration
Mahnomen, Minnesota

Spokane Tribal Fair and Pow-
    wow
Wellpinit, Washington

Standing Rock Pow-wow
Fort Yates, North Dakota

Stone Lake Fiesta
Dulce, New Mexico

Sycuan Pow-wow
Sycuan, California

Thunder Mountain Lenape
    Nation Native American
    Festival
Saltsburg, Pennsylvania

Trail of Tears Pow-wow
Hopkinsville, Kentucky

Turtle Mountain Labor Day
    Pow-wow
Belcourt, North Dakota

Tusumbia Pow-wow
Tuscumbia, Alabama

Tyendinaga Mohawk
   Traditional Pow-wow
Deseronto, Ontario, Canada

United Tribes International
   Pow-wow
Bismarck, North Dakota

Wadopana Traditional
   Celebration
Wolf Point, Montana

Washagamis Bay Traditional
   Pow-wow
Kenora, Ontario

Wichita Tribal Pow-wow
Anadarko, Oklahoma

OCTOBER

American Indian Pow-wow
Honolulu, Hawaii

American Indian Society of
   Washington, D.C.
Urbana, Maryland

Annual Canadian Thanks-
   giving Pow-wow
Mt. Currie, British Columbia,
   Canada

Apache Days
Globe, Arizona

Black Hills Pow-wow and
   Art Market
Rapid City, South Dakota

Boiling Springs Indian Expo
Woodward, Okalahoma

Cherokee Fall Festival
Cherokee Nation of Oklahoma
Tahlequah, Oklahoma

Cherokees of Georgia
   Gathering and Pow-wow
Tribal Grounds
St. George, Georgia

Chickasaw Nation Annual
   Day
Chickasaw Nation of
   Oklahoma, Oklahoma

Corn Festival
Tunkahannock, Pennsylvania

Drums on the Pocomoke
Pocomoke, Maryland

Fall Arts Fiesta
Jemez Pueblo, New Mexico

Four Nations Pow-wow
Nez Perce Tribe
Lapwai, Idaho

Four Winds Cherokee Tribe
   Pow-wow
DeRider, Louisiana

Healing of All Nations
   Accohannock Indian Tribe
Fall Festival and Pauwau
Marion Station, Maryland

Honoring the Grandmothers
Cedartown, Georgia

Hopi Tuhisma Arts and Craft
   Market
Kykotsmovi, Arizona

Indio Pow-wow
Indio, California

Lakeland Community College
   Pow-wow
Kirtland, Ohio

Northern Lights Thanksgiving
   Pow-wow
Prince Albert, Saskatchewan

Northern Navajo Fair
Shiprock, Arizona

Pkanyket/Wampanoag
   Federation Pow-wow
Pawtucket, Rhode Island

Pow-wow and Fall Festival
Nashville, Tennesee

**Saint Margaret Mary's
Feast Day:**
Harvest and Social Dances
Laguna Pueblo, New Mexico

San Francisco Feast Day:
Corn or Elk Dance
Nambe Pueblo, New Mexico

San Manuel Pow-wow
California State University
San Bernardino, California

NOVEMBER

American Indian Film Festival
Palace of Fine Arts
San Francisco, California

Federation of Old Plimouth
    Indian Tribes

Annual First People Cultural
    Festival
Plymouth, Massachusetts

Poarch Band of Creeks Pow-
    wow
Atmore, Alabama

Red Mountain Eagle Pow-
    wow
Scottsdale, Arizona

San Diego Feast Day
Jemez Pueblo, New Mexico
Tesuque Pueblo, New Mexico

Veterans Day Pow-wow
Nespelem Community Center
Nespelem, Washington

Veterans Day Pow-wow
Owyhee, Nevada

Veterans Day Rodeo
San Carlos, Arizona

Walatowa Winter Arts and
    Crafts Show
Jemez Pueblo, New Mexico

DECEMBER

Annual All-Indian Rodeo
Colorado River Reservation
Parker, Arizona

Christmas Dances
Laguna Pueblo, New Mexico
San Felipe Pueblo, New Mexico
Santa Ana Pueblo, New Mexico
Tesuque Pueblo, New Mexico
Zia Pueblo, New Mexico

Christmas Pow-wow
Portland State University
Portland, Oregon

Christmas Pow-wow
Umatilla Reservation
Pendleton, Oregon

Harvest Dance
Laguna Pueblo, New Mexico

Los Matachinas Dance
Pojoaque Pueblo, New Mexico

Los Matachines
Picuris Pueblo, New Mexico

Los Matachines and Pine
   Torch Procession
San Juan Pueblo, New Mexico
Taos Pueblo, New Mexico

Matachina Dance
San Ildefonso Pueblo, New
   Mexico

Palms Band Mission Indians
   December Pow-wow
Indio, California

Shalako
Zuni Pueblo
Zuni, New Mexico

Walatowa Winter Arts and
   Crafts Show
Jemez Pueblo, New Mexico

Glossary

Adobe: Unfired brick, usually made of clay and dried in the sun; a structure made with such bricks.

Allotment: U.S. government policy, officially put into effect in 1887, of dividing tribal lands into individually owned parcels, or allotments. The hope of the government and various reformers was that Indians would become typical "American" small farmers and would assimilate into European American society, but the policy ultimately failed.

Amerind: A contraction of "American" and "Indian" that is most often used to refer to pre-Columbian settlers of the Americas, with the exception of Eskimos.

Amulet: An object or artifact that is worn to ward off evil and danger, such as from witchcraft and spirits.

Artifact: Any object found in the context of an archaeological site that was once used by humans; examples include tools, weapons, articles of clothing, and works of art.

Assimilation: The process through which a minority cultural group becomes absorbed into the dominant cultural group. Federal policies toward American Indians have historically bounced back and forth regarding whether attempting to force or coerce Indians to assimilate into mainstream American society is an appropriate policy.

Atlatl: A notched stick used to throw spears, darts, or harpoons.

Band: A tribal subunit, often an extended family; also, in modern Canada, a community of Indians registered under the Indian Act ("status Indians" as opposed to "non-status Indians").

Beadwork: The use of beads (most often of glass) for decorating clothing, bags, and other items; it largely replaced quillwork after trade with Europeans began.

Bear: A common character in stories, a powerful ally in healing that is also admired for its hunting skill.

Bear Dance: A ceremonial dance of medicine societies in many tribes to foster curing or to ask for a long life.

Berdache: Reversal of sex roles, including cross-dressing and assumption of the other sex's occupations. Most North American cultures traditionally accommodated the practice, which is not necessarily homosexual in nature (from the French for "male prostitute").

Bola: A hunting weapon, made of two or more thongs with weights on the end that are attached to a longer thong; when thrown, a bola wraps around the prey's legs or wings, immobilizing it.

Buffalo: A key animal in most midwestern and Great Plains cultures, the buffalo, as a guardian spirit, bestows game on humankind, governs fertility in women, protects unmarried women, mediates in love, rewards the generous, and chastens the stingy.

Bungling host: A common character type in stories throughout North America, marked by his failure to obtain food even when imitating other animals' methods.

Bureau of Indian Affairs (BIA): The U.S. agency established as part of the Department of the Interior in 1824 to manage Indian issues; responsible for overseeing reservation and trust lands and providing Indian education.

Cacique: A prince, chief, or boss; a political system that centers power in such a figure.

Calumet: A sacred pipe; a tobacco pipe made of a reed stem, clay or stone bowl, and feather or carved ornamentation.

Cannibals: Among the most pervasive characters in Indian myths, often in the form of monsters or grotesque humans.

Clairvoyance: Seeing into the future, a belief upon which many cultures relied to diagnose disease or for other purposes.

Clan: A social unit defined by a common lineage from either the female side (matrilineal) or male side (patrilineal).

Clown: In Pueblo cultures, clowns, often acting in ceremonial troupes, entertain by joking or by satirizing individuals or features of society, especially by mocking, burlesquing, displaying backwards or inverse behavior, and simulating gluttony or sexual behavior.

Corn: In mythologies and rituals of corn-growing cultures, corn, often personified as a woman, symbolizes fertility and medicine.

Coup: In some Plains cultures, particularly the Sioux, the points earned during battle for striking or touching an enemy or other acts of bravery; coup increased a warrior's honor and prestige (from the French for "a blow").

Coyote: Among the most common characters in North American myths and story traditions, coyote is the supreme trickster; always male, curious, and imitative, he is sometimes said to be responsible for unpleasant features of culture or life in general.

Cradleboard: A carrier for infants, most often made of wood and leather and worn on the back.

Creation: Although few creation stories start with a cosmic void, as does the creation story in Genesis, most American Indian cultures have stories explaining the beginning of the world and the origin of people, social institutions, animals, plants, and phenomena such as famine and death.

Cremation: A funeral at which the body of the dead person is burned.

Crest: Among Northwest Coast tribes, an artifact made of copper that represents important lineages; ownership of a crest confers prestige.

Crow: An important character in myths, sometimes a trickster.

Culture area: A region in which the indigenous population is more similar than dissimilar; environment, language, physical type, and cultural adaptation are considerations in making such a classification.

Culture hero: A figure in legend or myth who magically performed a feat or taught humans something that inaugurated a distinctive element of culture or feature of nature.

Dance: Dance is an inseparable expression of much Indian ritual, from large-scale public ceremonies (often involving special religious societies) to private rites. Dances can be passed from one generation to the next or invented, usually based upon a vision.

Datura: Jimsonweed, a psychoactive plant whose roots and leaves are used as medicine and whose roots induce visions.

Deer: A common story character, usually female and portrayed as a wife, mother, or sister.

Dialect: A group's distinctive variations in the pronunciation, grammar, and vocabulary of a language; although noticeably different, a dialect can be understood by other groups speaking the same language.

Dirty boy: A common story figure throughout North America; he appears dirty or crippled and is shunned or mistreated, although actually he is a powerful and handsome young man who lavishly rewards those who treat him kindly.

Dog: A significant spirit in myths who is responsible for friendship, faithfulness, and other powers.

Dreams: In Indian belief systems, dreams are portals to the spirit world; they can lead to illness, but they can also heal and initiate new belief systems, rituals, or stories.

Drum: A shamanistic ritual aid of great power; drumming, like dancing, is a central element in many Indian rituals and celebrations.

Eagle: A frequent figure in myth and ritual who possesses great power in hunting and war.

Earth diver: A type of creation tale common in North America: A primal animal scoops up soil from the bottom of a world-covering sea and fashions the first land from it.

Earthlodge: A large dome-shaped building with a log frame covered by branches and packed with mud.

Endogamy: The practice or custom of marrying within a particular group to which one belongs, such as a clan.

Eskimo: A generic term for the Inuit and Yupik peoples of northernmost Alaska and Canada. Its derivation and meaning are debated, but it probably derived from a Montagnais (eastern Canada) word via Basque whalers, and then was adapted into French and English.

Ethnocentrism: The tendency to judge other people's behavior and values on the basis of one's own culture, which is usually considered superior.

Ethnography: The detailed descriptive study of a particular society and its culture.

Exogamy: The practice or custom of marrying outside a particular group to which one belongs, such as a clan.

False face: An English term for the wooden masks and masking ceremonies used to promote healing among the Iroquois.

Fasting: Abstinence from food, especially in preparation for or as part of a ritual.

Federally recognized tribe: A tribe that has official government-to-government relations with the U.S. government and that is eligible for services the government provides to American Indians.

Fetish: An artifact, often a small carved bird or animal, used in rituals and believed to possess power.

Flaking: A technique for shaping stone, such as flint, chert, or obsidian, into tools by removing chips.

Gambler: A colorful human or animal character that appears frequently in stories, sometimes as a cannibal.

Gaming sticks: Sticks of wood, reed, cane, or horn used for gambling.

Ghost Dance: There was a Ghost Dance of 1870 that involved Great Basin and California tribes as well as one in 1890 that affected the Great Basin and Plains. Both were religious revitalization movements based upon the expected return of the dead, who would drive out white people and establish a paradise.

Ghosts: Stories about spirits, the return of the dead, and beings that help the dead pervade North American cultures; ghosts are sometimes honored with feasts.

Giants: Present in myths in a great variety of forms and specializing in stealing children and wives, although some are helpful.

Girls' puberty rites: The introduction to womanhood upon menarche or soon after often involved seclusion, during which girls learned the responsibilities and privileges of their new status and became eligible for marriage.

Giveaways: Practiced in many cultures, the distribution of one's possessions to members of the community was sometimes a ritual in itself and sometimes part of a larger ritual; examples include the Lakota White Buffalo Ceremony, the Crow Aasshke, the Blackfoot Grass Dance, and, the most widely known, the potlatch of the Pacific Northwest.

Gorget: A small breastplate worn suspended from the neck as adornment or rank insignia.

Grandmother: A common story character, a solitary old woman who advises a hero about killing monsters, using magic, and escaping dangers.

Grass Dance: In the Plains, a strenuous competitive men's social dance involving much leaping and bending by dancers who wear large amounts of grass tied to belts.

Guardian spirits: Across the northern Plains, young men, and sometimes young women, undertake quests for personal visions by fasting in isolation; the power they gain by the experience assumes the form of a being who can later be called on for help.

Healing: A primary goal of rituals, because illness, often considered a disorder of society or the world, may be corrected by community involvement.

Hogan: A Navajo hut made of wood, sod, mud, or branches.

Human-animal transformations: Shape-changing, from animal to human or vice versa, occurs for a variety of reasons, often evil, in myths and stories.

Igloo: An Eskimo dome-shaped hut made of blocks of compacted snow.

Initiation: A trial of endurance or isolation required for entrance into some societies or a new stage of life.

Jerky: Sun-dried meat strips.

Joking relationships: Teasing and sexual jokes exchanged between people of the opposite sex in some, but not all, family roles, such as between brothers-in-law and sisters-in-law.

Jugglers: Male or female shamans in the Great Lakes and Northeast areas who defanged snakes to display their power over death (from the French *jongleur*).

Kachina: In Pueblo and Southwest cultures, a masked figure or doll representing mediators between the human and spirit worlds.

Keeper: The caretaker of a sacred object who also conducts the rituals and ceremonies pertaining to the object.

Kinnikinnik: The term, of Delaware origin, for a mixture of sumac leaves, the inner bark of dogwood or willow, and other materials smoked in pipes in place of tobacco or mixed with it.

Kiva: In Southwest cultures, most notably Pueblo cultures, a partly subterranean ceremonial council chamber, either circular or rectangular, with an altar.

Kokopelli: In Southwest art, the Humpbacked Flute Player, who appears widely in rock art and ancient pottery and has been revived as a motif in modern pottery and jewelry decoration.

Koshare: Clowns wearing horned headdresses and black-and-white stripes in the Pueblo culture.

Labret: A stone, shell, or bone ornament inserted through the lip.

Lacrosse: A hockey-like field game in which opposing teams try to send a small ball into goals using a hooked stick (from the French *crosse*).

Land cession: Land that Indian tribes gave to Europeans or the United States government as part of a treaty.

Leister: A three-pronged fishing harpoon used by Arctic peoples.

Longhouse: An Iroquoian dwelling in which several family units within an extended family reside; also, a public building for councils or other meetings.

Makai: In the Southwest, medicine men who concern themselves with crops, war, and weather.

Manifest Destiny: A widespread feeling among European Americans, especially in the nineteenth century, that it was the inevitable destiny and right of the United States to stretch from the Atlantic to the Pacific; used to justify seizing Indian lands.

Manioc: A tropical plant, also called cassava, that is a staple of Caribbean Indians; now used to make tapioca.

Manitou: Any of a group of Algonquian spirits and supernatural forces inhabiting all living and inanimate things.

Mano and metate: A set of upper and lower millstones used to grind corn and other grains.

Matrilineal: Any social organization which bases descent or heritage on the female members.

Matrilocal: Any social organization in which husbands move into their wives' households.

Medicine: A term denoting the power in persons, spirits, objects, and activities that can be used for healing, divination, control of nature, or sorcery.

Medicine bundle: A bag or wrapping containing feathers, herbs, stones, animal parts, scalps, pipes, or other objects with special powers or significance.

Metis: The French word for people of mixed blood, specifically those descended from white fur traders who lived with and married Indians; the term is primarily used in Canada, which has a large Metis population.

Military society: A society or club of warriors with special rituals and clothing; most prevalent in Plains cultures.

Moccasin: A soft shoe made of deerskin or other leather.

Moiety: Either of two classes or halves of a tribal group.

Mukluk: A soft Inuit boot made of sealskin.

Native American Church: A pantribal system of rites and celebrations centered on the vision-instilling powers of peyote; officially established in 1918.

Nomadic: A way of life in which people periodically move from one location to another, usually in search of food.

Orenda: An Iroquoian spiritual power or force inherent in all objects; one can communicate with orenda through song.

Paddling: A decorative technique for pottery in which a flat or curved paddle is pressed against the wet clay before firing.

Paleo-Indian: The prehistoric stone age ancestors of modern Indians.

Paleontology: The study of ancient life forms and fossils.

Papoose: The Algonquian word for an infant.

Parfleche: Rawhide with the hair removed, used in garments.

Patrilineal: Any social organization which bases descent or heritage on the male members.

Patrilocal: Any social organization in which wives move into their husbands' households.

Pemmican: Lean meat pounded and mixed with melted fat, forming a paste that is shaped into cakes and flavored with berries.

Petroglyph: A prehistoric carving or inscription on rock.

Peyote: A small cactus, *Lophophora williamsii*, or the buttonlike structures of the cactus that induce hallucinations.

Pictograph: A prehistoric drawing or painting, often depicting an important event.

Pipestone: A hard red clay or soft stone used to make tobacco pipes.

Pit house: A prehistoric dwelling dug into the ground and generally roofed with tree limbs and mud.

Plaiting: A basket or cloth weaving technique in which two different elements cross each other for a checkerboard appearance.

Potlatch: A Northwest Coast (particularly Nootka) feast in which gifts are given to guests in order to increase the host's prestige.

Power: A central concept in Indian religious systems; a spiritual force that gives meaning to, and some measure of control of, life.

Pow-wow: A ceremony, celebration, council, or conference that includes dance contests, group dancing, and giveaways.

Prayerstick: In the Pueblo culture, a piece of ornamental stone or wood to which is attached a feather or streamer imbued with prayer; it is stuck into the ground so that the streamer can wave in the wind and broadcast the prayer.

Pre-Columbian: All human culture and history in the Americas before Christopher Columbus's voyage of exploration in 1492.

Pueblo: A communal village in the Southwest; also, when capitalized, the cultures that built them (from the Spanish for "town").

Quetzalcóatl: The Toltec and Aztec god of the morning and evening star and patron of priests, represented as a plumed or feathered serpent.

Quilling: Particularly prevalent in the Plains, the art of using dyed porcupine quills, softened in the mouth, to decorate clothing.

Rabbit stick: A curved wooden stick about 70 centimeters long used in rabbit hunts, and possibly as a weapon, in the Southwest.

Radiocarbon dating: The measurement of a substance's age based upon the decay of carbon 14, a radioactive isotope.

Rattles: Percussion instruments fastened to arms, legs, or the waist or held in the hand and used to accompany dancing and singing; individual rattles may have special meaning for a ritual.

Relocation: The U.S. government policy of the 1950's according to which rural Indians were encouraged to move to urban areas to find employment.

Removal: The U.S. government policy of the 1830's-1850's according to which eastern Indians were "removed" to lands west of the Mississippi; the Trail of Tears was the most infamous event of the removal era.

Reservation: An area of land set aside for exclusive Indian use by treaty with the United States government; in the initial reservation era, tribes were forced to live on their assigned reservations.

Revitalization movement: Any of various attempts to restore Indian cultural features lost after contact with Europeans.

Roach: A hairpiece worn on the head as adornment.

Sachem: The overall leader or chief of a Algonquian tribe.

Sagamore: An Algonquian chief subordinate to a sachem.

Scalping: Flaying the skin and hair from an enemy's head as part of coup.

Seine: A fishing net that hangs from the surface of the water on floats and is anchored with weights on the bottom.

Shaking Tent Ceremony: A nighttime conjuring ritual, held in a small hut or tent, in which a conjurer who has been bound sings and beats a drum until spirits release him; thereafter, the spirits divulge information about people or events, which the conjurer translates to his employers.

Shaman: A priest or priest-doctor who consults spirits or magical powers in order to guide or cure others.

Singer: The English term for a Navajo *hataalii*, who conducts rituals and preserves religious lore.

Six Nations: The six tribes—Mohawk, Oneida, Onondaga, Cayuga, Seneca, and Tuscarora—that make up the Iroquois Confederacy.

Snakes: Frequent characters in stories and myths; live snakes are used in some rituals.

Song duel: An opportunity to resolve conflicts among tribal members by ritual exchange of humorous songs; each singer praises himself and makes fun of his opponent's faults.

Sovereignty: Complete national independence; the issue of the sovereignty of Indian tribes or nations has been a perennial problem in Indian-white relations. Under U.S. law, tribes are considered to have distinct but "dependent" governments.

Spirits: Invisible, named entities with distinctive personalities who can influence the human world.

Status Indians: In Canada, Indians who are officially entitled, according to the Indian Act, to be registered by the Department of Indian Affairs and Northern Development.

Storyteller: A highly esteemed person who, from memory, narrates traditional stories, legends, or myths, often as part of a ritual.

Subsistence round: A recurrent migration pattern, usually annual, based on the changing availability of various food sources.

Sun Dance: A yearly summer dance held by many Plains Indians that lasts for three or four days and is considered fundamental to participants' spiritual health.

Sweatlodge: A structure, usually dome-shaped, for sweating, a rite of purification through exposure to heat generated by a fire or by steam from water poured over hot rocks.

Taboo: A restriction or prohibition for reasons of religion or custom.

Thunderbird: In stories, a large bird (or flock) that produces thunder by flapping its wings and personifies thunder.

Tipi: A tent formed of bark, mats, skins, or canvas on a cone-shaped pole frame (also spelled "tepee").

Toboggan: A light sleigh made of thin planks of wood curved at one end.

Tomahawk: An ax, made of a shaft about 60 to 90 centimeters long and a sharpened stone, metal, or horn head, used as a weapon and as a tool in agriculture.

Totem: The term, from an Algonquian word, for a hereditary mark, emblem, or badge of a clan or tribe that takes the image of an animal or other natural object having spiritual powers.

Travois: A sled that consists of a wooden A-frame covered with planks or webbing; pulled by a dog or horse.

Treaty: A formal agreement, pact, or contract jointly agreed upon by a tribe and the United States or Canadian government (or, earlier, by a tribe and a European government).

Tribe: A general term, first applied to Indian societies by Europeans, for a variety of Indian sociopolitical organizations; among the considerations for tribal identity are common ancestry, language, and culture.

Trickster: A widespread type of story character whose principal qualities include cleverness, deception, buffoonish behavior, and misdirection.

Trust lands: Indian lands not classified as reservations that are protected by federal or state governments.

Tule: A bulrush (*Scirpus lacustris* or *Scirpus tatora*) often used as a construction material.

Turquoise: A green-blue semiprecious gem used in Great Basin and Southwest jewelry.

Two-hearts: A common expression denoting a liar or witch.

Underworld: A mythological realm below the earth's surface; frequently it is the place from which the first humans appeared or in which the dead live.

Usufruct: A situation in which a group has access to certain land and its resources, based on a history of usage; no one "owns" the land.

Vision: A direct communication with the realm of spirits.

Vision quest: The ritualized seeking of visions or dreams through self-deprivation, exposure, or hallucinogenic drugs during a rite of passage or other ritual.

Wakan Tanka: Literally, in Lakota Siouan, "the great mystery"; although often translated as "the great spirit," it stands collectively for the spiritual beings and powers in the Siouan belief system.

Walam Olum: The Delaware account of their origin and migrations, painted on sticks in red pictographs.

Wampum: Beads threaded into belts, bracelets, or collars that were used as messages and tribal records as well as ornamentation; the concept of wampum as money is largely a European superimposition.

War bonnet: A headdress containing feathers that symbolize achievements in battle.

Wattle and daub: A construction method that uses a pole frame interwoven with branches and surfaced with mud or plaster.

Weir: A fenced-in enclosure for trapping fish.

Wickiup: A temporary shelter made of grass or brush that was widely used in the Great Basin.

Wolf: An important character in stories and myths; associated with creation, war, and hunting.

Mediagraphy

Select films dealing with American Indians. Documentary films are listed first, followed by feature films. A selection of Web sites, sound recordings, and CD-ROMs follows the list of film and video treatments.

EDUCATIONAL AND DOCUMENTARY FILMS

Again, a Whole Person I Have Become
Color. 19 min. 16mm.
Shenandoah Film Productions (1982)
Stresses the importance of traditional Indian customs for Indian
   youth. Three tribal elders speak of the wisdom of the old ways;
   dances and ceremonies are portrayed. Will Sampson narrates.

Age of the Buffalo
Color. 14 min. 16mm.
National Film Board of Canada (1964)
Shows how the buffalo met the needs of the Indians for food, cloth-
   ing, shelter, and adventure, and how life changed when the buf-
   falo were gone.

The American Indian
Color. 62 min. VHS.
Library Distributors of America (1993)
Broad view of the origin and culture of American Indians; also ex-
   amines interactions between Indians and whites.

The American Indian: After the White Man Came
Color. 27 min. 16mm.
Handel Film Corporation (1972)
Extensive examination of American Indians since European dis-
   covery of the Americas. Moves to a discussion of the problems
   facing modern Indians.

The American Indian: Before the White Man
Color. 19 min. 16mm.
Handel Film Corporation (1972)
Comprehensive study of American Indians from the early migra-
tion routes to the development of the main tribes of North
America. Narrated by Iron Eyes Cody.

American Indian in Transition
Color. 22 min. 16mm.
Atlantis Productions (1976)
Presents an Indian point of view about land and heritage, narrated by an Indian mother who uses Indian chronicles and say-
ings. Provides a compassionate insight into Indian life and
thought.

American Indian Influence on the United States
Color. 20 min. 16mm.
Robert Davis Productions (1972)
Depicts the manner in which life in the United States has been influenced by the American Indian economically, sociologically,
philosophically, and culturally. Nine dances and ceremonies are
authentically portrayed. The graphics used in the film include
original Indian illustrations.

The American Indian Speaks
Color. 23 min. 16mm.
Encyclopedia Britannica Educational Corporation (1973)
Members of three Indian cultures state the position and attitudes
of American Indians in the twentieth century. Includes remem-
brances of the Trail of Tears and Wounded Knee.

The American Indian Struggle
Color. 29 min. VHS.
Kent State University (1981)
Examination of several important episodes that contributed to the
long history of conflict between American Indians and white
settlers. With Kent State University professors James Gidney
and Philip Weeks.

American Indians: A Brief History
Color. 22 min. 16mm.
National Geographic Society (1985)
Numerous examples of diverse Indian artistic and cultural traditions. Provides a history of the roots of conflict between the Indians and European settlers. Identifies several settlements and
tribes that existed before Columbus arrived in America.

American Indians as Seen by D. H. Lawrence
Color. 14 min. 16mm.
Lewin/Cort (1966)
At the D. H. Lawrence ranch near Taos, New Mexico, Lawrence's
wife, Frieda, speaks about his beliefs and thoughts. Aldous
Huxley presents selections from Lawrence's works.

The Americans: The Buffalo Story
Color. 28 min. 16mm.
O'Laughlin Company (1971)
The great usefulness of the buffalo to the Plains Indians is detailed;
it furnished them with food, clothing, and shelter. Buffalo
masks convey the spirit of the annual Spring Buffalo Dance.

The Americans: Chief Black Hawk
Color. 23 min. 16mm.
O'Laughlin Company (1971)
Chief White Eagle explains the meaning and logic of sign language and various war paint designs. The story of Black Hawk, war chief of the Sauk Indians, follows, dramatized by paintings and sound effects.

The Americans: Chief Crazy Horse
Color. 26 min. 16mm.
O'Laughlin Company (1971)
Beginning with the Bering Strait migration theory of Indian prehistory, Chief White Eagle moves into a description of Indian cultural evolution, including introduction of horses. Crazy Horse, brilliant leader and military strategist of the Sioux, is profiled.

The Americans: Chief Joseph
Color. 23 min. 16mm.
O'Laughlin Company (1971)
After describing the kinds of horses that Indians used for various purposes and how these horses were trained, Chief White Eagle tells the story of Chief Joseph and the Nez Perce.

The Americans: Geronimo
Color. 25 min. 16mm.
O'Laughlin Company (1971)
The Indians' closeness to nature and ability to forecast weather are discussed. Geronimo is profiled.

America's Great Indian Leaders
Color. 65 min. VHS.
Questar (1994)
Examines the lives and contributions of Crazy Horse, Chief Joseph, Geronimo, and Quanah Parker, who emerged to protect their people and culture.

America's Great Indian Nations
Color. 65 min. VHS.
Questar (1995)
Profiles six of the most powerful tribes in American history: the Iroquois, Seminoles, Shawnee, Navajo, Cheyenne, and Lakota Sioux.

America's Indians
Six-part series.
Color. 13 min. each. VHS.
Films for the Humanities & Sciences (1993)
The Indians Were There First
How North American Indians entered the Americas from Asia; various tribes and some of their characteristics.
When the White Man Came
Life among the major tribes before Europeans arrived.
The Bison Hunters
How the Indian became mythologized as the eastern United States became industrialized.
The Trail of Tears
The harm done by explorers and pioneers.
The Warpath
How pioneers moving westward ignored treaties reserving land for Indians.
The Death of the Bison
The many Native American issues that remain unresolved.

Ann of the Wolf Clan
Color. 60 min. VHS.
Rainbow TV Works; Great Plains Instructional TV, University of Nebraska (1982)
Young, middle class Indian girl receives the gift of her Cherokee heritage from her great-grandmother while spending a summer on the reservation.

Apache

Color. 30 min. VHS.

Schlessinger Video Productions (1993)

Examines the history, changing fortunes, and current situation of the Apache tribe. Includes a discussion of their crafts. For grades 5-10.

Apache Indian

Black and white. 11 min. 16mm.

Cort (1943)

Shows the life, ceremonies, and industries of the Apaches. The beauty of their native territory forms the setting for the tribal functions and ceremonies, including a puberty ceremony and devil dance.

The Apache Indian (Revised version)

Color. 11 min. 16mm. VHS.

Cort (1975)

Acquaints young viewers with the life, culture, and traditions of the Apache of Arizona. Emphasizes the problems that modern living has caused and the Apaches' struggle for education, health care, and economic opportunity.

Arrow to the Sun

Color. 22 min. 16mm.

Texture (1973)

Animated film by Gerald McDermott that illustrates a tale from the Acoma Pueblo of the Southwest. A boy's search for his father leads him to a dazzling voyage on an arrow to the sun.

The Ballad of Crowfoot
Color/black and white. 11 min. 16mm. VHS.
National Film Board of Canada/McGraw-Hill (1968)
Documents the events and problems that characterized the relationship between whites and Indians since whites arrived in the
Canadian West in the 1820's. Records Indian traditions and attitudes.

Before the White Man Came
Black and white. 50 min. Silent. 16mm
Northwestern Film Corp. (1921)
Filmed in the Bighorn Mountains of Montana and Wyoming in
1921. In an enactment by Indians, every effort was made to
present life as it was before the arrival of whites.

Behind the Masks
Color. 24 min. 16mm.
National Film Board of Canada (1973)
Study of the meaning and myths behind the masks of the tribes of
the Northwest Coast. Commentary and analysis by Claude
Levi-Strauss, noted French anthropologist.

Black Indians of New Orleans
Color. 33 min. 16mm.
Maurice M. Martinez (1976)
Depicts the activities of highly organized groups of African Americans with mixed Indian ancestry as they prepare for Mardi
Gras, with emphasis on their distinctive music, dancing, and
costumes.

Bones of Contention: Native American Archaeology
Color. 49 min. VHS
Films for the Humanities & Sciences (1998)
Examines the conflict between Native American groups and scientists, historians, and museum curators concerning the issue of the remains of more than 10,000 Native Americans unearthed at archaeological sites across the United States.

Boy of the Navajos
Color. 11 min. 16mm.
Cort (1975)
Shows the living habits and activities of a Navajo family in Arizona, with emphasis on the teenage son.

Boy of the Seminoles: Indians of the Everglades
Color/black and white. 11 min. 16mm.
Cort (1956)
Shows the living habits and activities of a teenage Seminole boy and his family in Florida.

The Broken Cord: Louise Erdrich and Michael Dorris
Color. 30 min. VHS.
PBS Video (1991)
Authors Louise Erdrich and the late Michael Dorris explain how traditions of spirit and memory weave through the lives of many Native Americans, and how alcoholism and despair have shattered so many other lives. The devastating effect of fetal alcohol syndrome on their adopted son, and on the Native American community as a whole, is also discussed. Hosted by Bill Moyers.

Broken Treaty at Battle Mountain
Color. 73 min. 16mm.
Cinnamon Production (1973)
The struggle of the Western Shoshone of Nevada to retain their culture and land is dramatically portrayed. The Shoshone struggle to keep 24 million acres of Nevada land originally promised to them by the U.S. government. Narrated by Robert Redford.

Catlin and the Indians
Color. 25 min. 16mm.
National Film Board of Canada/McGraw-Hill (1967)
Presents biographical material on George Catlin, historian and painter of Plains Indians. Includes paintings from the Smithsonian's Catlin collection.

Cherokee
Color. 26 min. 16mm.
British Broadcasting Corporation (1976)
Explores the dilemma the Cherokees face in preserving their traditions and captures the beauty of the pageants and ceremonies performed today. Includes scenes from a pageant play that recounts Cherokee history.

Cherokee
Color. 30 min. VHS.
Schlessinger Video Productions (1993)
Examines the history and current situation of the Cherokee people. Includes facts about the role of the U.S. government, debunks myths about Native Americans, explores their spiritual relationship with nature, and discusses the role of women in their societies. For grades 5-10.

Cheyenne

Color. 30 min. VHS.

Schlessinger Video Productions (1993)

Examines the history, changing fortunes, and current situation of the Cheyenne tribe. Includes facts about the role of the U.S. government, debunks myths about Native Americans, explores their spiritual relationship with nature, and discusses the role of women in their societies. For grades 5-10.

Children of the Eagle: A Tribute to American Indian Children

Color. 28 min. 16mm.

Oklahoma State University

Describes the American Indian family and contrasts contemporary family life with traditional Indian customs. Presents prenatal concerns, parenting behavior, and funeral rituals.

Circle of the Sun

Color. 30 min. 16mm. VHS.

National Film Board of Canada (1960)

Studies the way of life and ceremonial customs of the Blood Indians circa 1960. Pictures the Sun Dance camp and analyzes the feelings of the younger generation about the old Indian customs and the influences of whites.

Columbus Didn't Discover Us

Color. 24 min. VHS.

Turning Tide Productions (1992)

In preparation for the Columbus Quincentennial, 300 Native men and women came to the highlands of Ecuador to take part in the first Continental Conference of Indigenous Peoples. Features interviews with participants representing a wide spectrum of Indian nations from North, South, and Central America.

Comanche

Color. 30 min. VHS.

Schlessinger Video Productions (1993)

Portrayal of the Comanche tribe including their history, culture and way of life today. Challenges many prevalent myths and stereotypes. Examines the issue of the role of the U.S. government, debunks myths about Native Americans, explores their spiritual relationship with nature, and discusses the role of women in their societies. For grades 5-10.

Contrary Warriors

Color. 60 min. 16mm. VHS.

Rattlesnake Productions (1987)

The Crazy Dogs, one of the original Crow warrior societies, declared themselves "contrary warriors" and pledged to risk death when challenged by outsiders.

Corn Is Life

Color. 11 min. 16mm. VHS.

University of California Extension Media Center (1983)

Shows and explains traditional activities associated with corn that are still an important part of Hopi family and community life. Corn, a major cultural symbol, plays a central role in the life of every Hopi.

The Creek

Color. 30 min. VHS.

Schlessinger Video Productions (1993)

Examines the history and current situation of the Creek. Includes a discussion of their language, traditions, and crafts. For grades 5-10.

The Crow
Color. 30 min. VHS.
Schlessinger Video Productions (1993)
Examines the history and current situation of the Crow, a mobile
group of hunters who developed a strict code of conduct and a
deeply spiritual religion. For grades 5-10.

Crow Dog
Color. 57 min. 16mm.
Cinema Guild (1979)
Focuses on Leonard Crow Dog, spiritual leader of eighty-nine
American Indian tribes and a spokesman for many Indians who
wish to retain the beliefs and way of life of their forefathers.
Documents the politics and spiritual power of the American In-
dian Movement.

Cry of the Yurok
Color. 58 min. VHS.
Films for the Humanities & Sciences (1991)
Details the many problems of the Yurok tribe of California as they
struggle to survive encroachment of their lands. Some remain
on the reservation, others have moved to cities. All are caught in
a many-sided battle between the dominant white world and the
world of the Indian.

Custer at the Washita
Color. 26 min. 16mm. VHS.
McGraw-Hill (1966)
Account of the Battle of the Washita River, one of the few decisive
battles of the American Indian wars. It signaled the end of freedom for the Cheyenne and planted the seeds of Custer's defeat
at the Little Bighorn.

Dineh Nation: The Navajo Story
Color. 26 min. VHS.
Filmmakers Library (1991)
Focuses on the Navajo people who inhabit the Sovereign Dineh Indian Reservation which occupies parts of Arizona, New Mexico and Utah—an area rich in oil, coal, and uranium. The Navajo seek to preserve the land but outside forces are at work, strip mining the coal and polluting the water. Film emphasizes the spiritual essence of the Navajo people who consider Mother Earth to be sacred and forbid exploitation of her resources.

Discovering American Indian Music
Color. 24 min. 16mm. VHS.
Inform (1971)
Introduces the traditional customs, costumes, and dances associated with the music of eleven representative North American tribes, principally of the Plains and Southwest.

The Drummaker
Color. 37 min. 16mm.
Pennsylvania State University Psych Cinema Register (1978)
Presents William Bineshi Baker, Sr., an Ojibwa, one of the last of his people to perfect the art of drummaking. He discusses tradition and his frustration with those who will not take the time to follow it.

End of the Trail: The American Plains Indian
Black and white. 53 min. 16mm. VHS.
McGraw-Hill (1967)
Documents the growth and development of the Plains Indian culture, which culminate with the advent of whites. Illustrates many of the hostile acts committed by both sides.

Family Life of the Navajo Indians
Black and white. 31 min. Silent. 16mm.
New York University (1943)
Highlights some of the ways the Navajo child becomes an adult.

500 Nations
Eight-part series.
Color. 376 min. VHS.
Warner Home Video (1995)
An 8-part CBS television documentary exploring the history and
    culture of Native Americans. Episodes are:
The Ancestors: Early Cultures of North America
Mexico: The Rise and Fall of the Aztecs
Clash of Cultures: The People Who Met Columbus
Invasion of the Coast: The First English Settlements
Cauldron of War: Iroquois Democracy and the American Revolution
Removal: War and Exile in the East
Roads Across the Plains: Struggle for the West
Attack on Culture: I Will Fight No More Forever

Gatecliff: American Indian Rock Shelter
Color. 21 min. 16mm.
National Geographic Society (1973)
Team of amateur archaeologists led by Dr. David Hurst Thomas of
    the American Museum of Natural History dig in Gatecliff Rock
    Shelter in Nevada. Layer-by-layer examination reveals infor-
    mation on inhabitants of 5,000 years ago.

Geronimo and the Apache Resistance
Color. 60 min. VHS.
PBS Home Video (1990)
In 1886, the U.S. government mobilized five thousand men, one
    quarter of the entire U.S. Army, to capture Geronimo. This pro-
    file of Geronimo, believed by his people to have magical pow-
    ers, highlights the clash of cultures and the legacy of the battles
    of a century ago. (Part of the PBS series *The American Experi-
    ence*.)

Girl of the Navajos
Color. 15 min. 16mm.
Inform/Cort (1977)
Young Navajo girl recalls her feelings of fear and loneliness the
    first time she had to herd her family's sheep into the canyon
    alone. Returning to the canyon the following day, she becomes
    friends with another girl. Filmed on a Navajo reservation.

Giving Thanks: A Native American Good Morning Message
Color. 30 min. VHS.
Great Plains National TV Library (1996)
Based on the book by Chief Jake Swamp. Presents a Mohawk
    prayer celebrating the beauty, bounty and resources of the
    Earth. Part of the Reading Rainbow series hosted by LeVar
    Burton.

The Great Movie Massacre
Color. 28 min. 16mm.
United Indians of All Tribes Foundation (1979)
Explores the beginning of the "savage Indian" myth in popular
    American literature and entertainment, including wild west
    shows and early motion pictures. Will Sampson narrates. (Im-
    ages of Indians Series.)

The Great Plains Experience: The Lakota—One Nation on the Plains
Color. 30 min. 16mm. VHS.
University of Mid-America (1976)
Describes the movement of Indians onto the Great Plains and their
adaptation to the new environment, focusing on the Lakota in
the eighteenth century.

A History of Native Americans
Color. 30 min. VHS.
Schlessinger Video Productions (1993)
Examines the impact of European colonization on Native Ameri-
can tribes, including co-existence and trade, the struggles over
land ownership and the effects of European imports like guns,
horses, alcohol, religion and disease. Covers the policies of the
U.S. government, the forced removal of Indians in the Trail of
Tears, the Indian Removal Act and Indian boarding schools that
diluted tribal cultures and shared beliefs. For grades 5-10.

Home of the Brave
Color. 4 min. 16mm.
Pyramid Film and Video (1969)
The five-hundred-year story of a people is documented with great
precision in this four-minute encapsulation.

Hopi: Songs of the Fourth World
Color. 58 min. 16mm. VHS.
Newday (no date given)
Study of the Hopi that captures their spirituality and reveals their
integration of art and daily life. A farmer, religious elder, grandmother, painter, potter, and weaver speak about the preservation of the Hopi way.

Hopi Indian Arts and Crafts (Revised version)
Color. 10 min. 16mm.
Cort (1975)
Hopis are shown using their ancient tools and knowledge in basketweaving, potterymaking, silverworking, and weaving. Shows how methods of working are changing.

Hopi Indian Village Life
Color/Black and White. 11 min. 16mm.
Cort (1956)
Pictures the Hopi and their mode of living as it existed in the 1950's, emphasizing the changing character of Hopi life and work.

Hopi Kachinas
Color. 9 min. 16mm.
Inform (1961)
The Hopi kachina doll is intended primarily to teach Hopi children to see meaning in religious rituals and dances. Shows an artisan carving, assembling, and painting a doll; also shows Hopi life and dances.

Hopi Snake Dance
Black and White. 10 min. 16mm.
Inform (1951)
Presents the preparations of the dancers, handling of snakes, costumes, and part of a snake dance.

Hopis: Guardians of the Land
Color. 10 min. 16mm.
Inform (1972)
Hopi living on an Arizona reservation explains the tribal philosophy of seeking peace, brotherhood, and everlasting life by caring for all that is on the land. A nearby power plant and strip-mining operations threaten the union of people and land.

How Hollywood Wins the West
Color. 29 min. 16mm.
United Indians of All Tribes Foundation (1979)
Explores the concept of Manifest Destiny, which encouraged the
  taking of Indian lands that "nobody owned" by whites in the
  early nineteenth century.

How the West Was Lost
Color. 300 min. VHS.
Discovery Enterprises Group (1993)
Three-part Discovery Channel series exploring the history and culture of Native Americans. Documents the devastating effects of
  westward expansion on five Native American nations: the Navajo, Nez Perce, Apache, Cheyenne, and Lakota, through the
  recollection of their descendants, archival photographs, and
  historical documents.

How the West Was Lost II
Discovery Enterprises Group (1995)
Color. 350 min. VHS.
Four additional episodes of *How the West Was Lost* explore the Na-
  tive American experience during the eighteenth and nineteenth
  centuries. Chronicles the history of the Iroquois, Cherokee,
  Seminole, Dakota, Modoc, Ute, and the Indian Territory.

How to Trace Your Native American Heritage
Color. 30 min. VHS.
Rich-Heape Films (1998)
Guide to discovering one's Native American roots. Explains how
  to obtain tribal membership and official Native American status.

The Huron
Color. 30 min. VHS.
Schlessinger Video Productions (1993)
Profiles the Huron, who flourished in southern Ontario, Canada. Originally farmers and craftsmen, a small Huron community still survives in Canada, manufacturing goods for sale or trade while maintaining the Huron heritage. For grades 5-10.

I Will Fight No More Forever: The Story of Chief Joseph
Color. 106 min. 16mm. VHS.
Wolper Productions (1975)
How Chief Joseph led three hundred Nez Perce braves along with their women and children in the historic running battle against ten separate commands of the army in 1877.

In the White Man's Image
Color. 58 min. VHS.
PBS Video (1991)
Examines the experiment of federal government boarding schools for Indian children. Tells the story of the attempt to assimilate American Indians into white culture by educating them at special schools such as the Carlisle School for Indians. Founded by Richard Henry Pratt, this school and others like it attempted to wipe out all remnants of Indian culture. Narrated by Stacy Keach. Originally broadcast as an episode of the PBS television series *The American Experience*.

In Whose Honor?: American Indian Mascots in Sports
Color. 47 min. VHS.
New Day Films (1997)
Discussion of Chief Illinewek as the University of Illinois mascot and the effect the mascot has on Native American peoples. Examines the practice of using American Indian mascots and nicknames in sports.

Incident at Oglala
Color. 90 min. VHS, DVD.
Miramax (1992)
Reexamines the evidence in the 1975 murder case of two FBI
agents on the Pine Ridge Reservation. The conviction of Leon-
ard Peltier for the murders appears to be a travesty of justice.
Directed by Michael Apted; narrated by Robert Redford.

Indian Art of the Pueblo
Color. 13 min. 16mm.
Encyclopedia Britannica Educational Corporation (1976)
Introduces the arts and crafts of the Pueblo.

Indian Ceremonial Dances of the Southwest
Color. 11 min. 16mm.
Harold Ambrosch Film Productions (1954)
Presents a number of Southwest dances, accompanied by songs
and chants. Includes the Apache crown or devil dance, the
Laguna shield dance, and the Taos war dance.

Indian Crafts: Hopi, Navajo, and Iroquois
Color. 12 min. 16mm.
BFA Educational Media (1980)
Basketmaking, weaving, potterymaking, kachina carving, jewelry-
making, and mask carving.

Indian Heroes of America
Color. 17 min. 16mm.
Altana Films (1979)
Seven Indian personages are profiled, each representing an aspect
of history from the coming of whites to the final confrontations
in the late nineteenth century.

Indian Hunters
Black and white. 10 min. 16mm.
Inform (1948)
Shows two Indians seeking new hunting grounds for their band in
the wilds of northern Canada.

Indian Musical Instruments
Color. 14 min. 16mm.
University of Oklahoma
Shows big dance drums, rawhide drums, ring and straight beaters,
and other Indian musical instruments in the University of Okla-
homa museum.

The Indian Speaks
Color. 41 min. 16mm.
National Film Board of Canada (1970)
Presents Indians in parts of Canada who are concerned about pre-
serving what is left of their culture and restoring what is gone.

Indians: The Navajos
Color. 14 min. 16mm.
Hearst Metrotone News (1975)
Examines the winds of change that have been affecting the lives of
140,000 Navajos on the largest Indian reservation in the world.

Indians Among Us
Color. 46 min. VHS.
Discovery Communications (1992)
Focuses on the Indians of the American Southwest and how they
try to maintain their old traditions within a modern lifestyle.
Originally part of the television program *Roger Kennedy's Redis-
covering America*.

Into the Circle: An Introduction to Native American Powwows.
Color. 58 min. VHS.
Full Circle Communications (1992)
An introduction to Oklahoma powwows through excerpts of
   dances, songs and drumming sequences, interviews with tribal
   elders and participants, and historical photographs showing the
   ongoing evolution of the powwow. Narrated by J. R. Mathews.

Iroquois
Color. 30 min. VHS.
Schlessinger Video Productions (1993)
Portrayal of the Iroquois including their history, culture and way
   of life today. Challenges many still-prevalent myths and stereotypes. Examines the issue of the role of the U.S. government, debunks myths about Native Americans, explores their spiritual
   relationship with nature, and discusses the role of women in
   their societies. For grades 5-10.

Ishi, the Last Yahi
Color. 58 min. VHS.
Rattlesnake Productions (1993)
Distributed by Center for Media and Independent Learning,
   Berkeley, Calif.; Shanachie Entertainment, Newton, N.J.
Award-winning profile of Ishi, a California Indian who came out
   of hiding in 1911 and lived at the anthropology museum of the
   University of California at Berkeley until his death in 1916.

Late Woodland Village
Color. 20 min. 16mm.
University of Iowa AV Center (1974)
Excavations of the late Woodland Hartley Fort revealed details of
   life in a stockaded village of about 900 C.E.

Legend of Corn
Color. 26 min. 16mm.
Films for the Humanities & Sciences (1985)
An Ojibwa legend, dramatized by tribespeople, about how the
Great Manitou saved the tribe from starvation.

The Lenape
Color. 30 min. VHS.
Schlessinger Video Productions (1993)
Examines the history of the Lenape, who settled in the mid-Atlan-
tic region over 5,000 years ago. Today, the largest population of
the tribe now lives on part of the Cherokee Nation reservation.
For grades 5-10.

Life in the Woodlands Before the White Man Came
Color. 12 min. 16mm.
ACI Media (1976)
Dramatizes the daily life, ceremonies, and rituals of Woodlands In-
dians before whites arrived.

The Maya
Color. 30 min. VHS.
Schlessinger Video Productions (1993)
Examines the ancient civilization of the Maya, their temples, pal-
aces, and immense cities in Mexico's Yucatan Peninsula and
Guatemala. For grades 5-10.

The Maya: Temples, Tombs, and Time
Color. 53 min. VHS.
Questar (1995)
Breakthroughs in deciphering Maya glyphs and new archeological
discoveries help to provide a fresh look at the Maya, considered
to be one of the most advanced of the indigenous peoples of the
Americas.

Meet the Sioux Indian
Color. 11 min. 16mm.
Associated Film Artists (1949)
Portrays the nomadic life of the Sioux and shows how they ob-
tained, prepared, and preserved food, and made clothing.

The Menominee
Color. 30 min. VHS.
Schlessinger Video Productions (1993)
Examines the history of the Menominee, hunters and fishermen,
who lived in lodges along the upper peninsula of present day
Michigan. For grades 5-10.

Mesa Verde: Mystery of the Silent Cities
Color. 14 min. 16mm.
Encyclopedia Britannica Educational Corporation (1975)
Extensive aerial photography of the ruined cities and multiple-
family cliff dwellings of a thirteenth-century civilization. Nar-
rated by Jack Palance.

Mino-Bimadiziwin: The Good Life
Color. 60 min. VHS.
Deb Wallwork Productions (1998)
Examines the ancient Ojibwe tradition of wild rice harvesting still
practiced on Minnesota's White Earth Indian Reservation. An
in-depth portrait of a community whose people continue to live
off the land. Explores the themes of continuity and change in
Native American society at large.

Modern Chippewa Indians
Color. 11 min. 16mm.
Simmel-Miservey (1946)
Shows the life and work of the Chippewa Indians on the Red Lake
Reservation in Minnesota.

Momaday: Voice of the West
Color. 30 min. VHS.
PBS Home Video (1992)
Profiles Pulitzer prize-winning author, painter, poet and teacher,
N. Scott Momaday, who reads from his memoirs and published
works.

More Than Bows and Arrows
Color. 56 min. VHS.
Camera One Productions (1992)
Documents the contributions of American Indians to the develop-
ment of the United States and Canada. Deals with the role of the
American Indian in shaping various aspects of American cul-
ture, ranging from food and housing to our view of life. Nar-
rated by N. Scott Momaday.

Myths and Moundbuilders
Color. 60 min. VHS.
PBS Home Video (1990)
Examines the ancient Native American practice of mound build-
ing. Features archaeological excavations of mounds and exam-
ines pottery, jewelry, and other artifacts unearthed.

Nanook of the North
Black and white. Silent. VHS, DVD.
Pathé Exchange (1922)
This landmark of documentary filmmaking caused a sensation
when it was released. Robert Flaherty spent sixteen months in
the Arctic filming an Inuit family. Some events were enacted
specifically for the camera, but the portrait of Arctic life is generally realistic.

The Narragansett
Color. 30 min. VHS.
Schlessinger Video Productions (1993)
Profiles the southern Rhode Island tribe which was once the largest and most powerful of the Northeast, with ancestry dating back 11,000 years. For grades 5-10.

Native American Heritage
Color. 25 min. VHS.
Schlessinger Video Productions (1997)
Children are introduced to the history and culture of the diverse groups of Native Americans who first inhabited North America.

Native American Life
Color. 25 min. VHS.
Schlessinger Video Productions (1996)
Highlights of Native American history through the use of graphics and animations, live-action portrayals of historic figures, and stories told from a child's point of view. Narrated by Irene Bedard.

The Native Americans
Color. 264 min. VHS.
Turner Home Entertainment, (1994)
Six-part TBS television documentary exploring the history and culture of Native Americans. Series takes a regional look at Indians of the Northeast, Far West, Southeast, Southwest, and Plains. Examines the historical intrusion on Indian lands and the current effort by Native Americans to preserve their heritage. Features traditional as well as original music composed and performed for the series by Robbie Robertson and other Native American musicians. Narrated by Joy Harjo.

The Native Americans: How the West Was Lost
Color. 26 min. 16mm.
British Broadcasting Corporation (1976)
Highlights the life of the Plains Indians as it changed with the
westward movement of whites. Historical photographs and
drawings illustrate the Battle of Little Bighorn and the Wounded
Knee Massacre.

Natives of the Narrowland: The Unwritten History of the
First Cape Codders
Color. 35 min. VHS.
Documentary Educational Resources (1994)
Examines the history of the Wampanoag tribe of Cape Cod, Massa-
chusetts.

Navajo
Color. 30 min. VHS.
Schlessinger Video Productions (1993)
Examines the history, changing fortunes, and current situation of
the Navajo tribe. For grades 5-10.

Navajo: A People Between Two Worlds
Color. 20 min. 16mm.
Line Films (1958)
Study of the largest Indian tribe in the United States, including life
on the land and tribal government.

Navajo Night Dances
Color. 12 min. 16mm.
Lewin (1957)
Shows a Navajo family going to the Nine Day Healing Chant,
feasting, and watching the Arrow, Feather, and Fire Dance.

Navajo Talking Picture
Color. 40 min. VHS.
Women Make Movies (1986)
Documents the life of a grandmother on the Navajo Reservation in
   Lower Greasewood, Arizona.

Nez Perce: Portrait of a People
Color. 23 min. 16mm.
National Audio Visual Center (No date given)
Tells of the cultural heritage of the Nez Perce and shows how the
   Nez Perce National Historical Park has influenced and pre-
   served this culture.

North American Indian Legends
Color. 21 min. 16mm.
CBS (1973)
Dramatizes several Indian legends with special-effects photogra-
   phy to emphasize their mythical quality.

Northwest Indian Art
Color. 10 min. 16mm.
Lewin (1966)
Examples of the highly sophisticated art of Northwest Coast Indi-
   ans collected from six museums.

Now That the Buffalo's Gone
Color. 7 min. 16mm.
Pyramid Film and Video (1969)
Uses group and individual still-photograph portraits, combined
   with footage from old films, to emphasize the dignity of Indian
   culture.

Oneota Longhouse People
Color. 14 min. 16mm.
University of Iowa Audio Visual Center (1973)
Archaeological discoveries of longhouses in northwest Iowa. Including a reconstruction of a village and views of how life might have been lived at this site a thousand years ago.

Oren Lyons, the Faithkeeper
Color. 58 min. VHS.
Films for the Humanities & Sciences (1997)
Native American Chief Oren Lyons, a leader in the international environmental movement, talks with Bill Moyers about the ancient legends, prophecies, and wisdom that guide the Onondaga tribe. Lyons shares the spiritual basis of his environmentalism—a vision of the degradation of the earth that was revealed to the Onondaga nation in 1799.

Paddle to the Sea
Color. 25 min. 16mm.
National Film Board of Canada (1967)
The story of a small, hand-carved Indian and a canoe, both called "paddle to the sea." From a book of the same name by Holling C. Holling.

Painting with Sand: A Navajo Ceremony
Color. 11 min. 16mm.
Encyclopedia Britannica Educational Corporation (1949)
Portrays the traditional sand painting and healing rite as performed by a Navajo medicine man for his ailing son.

People of the Buffalo
Color. 14 min. 16mm.
National Film Board of Canada (1969)
Depicts the dependence of western Indians on the buffalo for food, shelter, and clothing. Shows how the coming of whites and subsequent slaughter of the buffalo herds changed the lifestyle of the Indians.

The Place of the Falling Waters
Color. 90 min. VHS.
Montana Public Television (1991)
Relates the complex and volatile relationship between the people of the Confederated Salish and Koontenai Tribes and a major hydroelectric dam situated within the Flathead Indian Reservation. Covers history of tribal society and culture before the dam's construction, the construction of the Kerr Dam in the 1930's and its impact on the reservation, and the hopes and dilemmas of the Salish and Kootenai people as they prepare to take over the dam during the next three decades.

Pocahontas: Her True Story
Color. 50 min. VHS.
A&E Home Video (1995)
Portrait of a remarkable native American princess, ambassador, stateswoman, and peacemaker whose brief life left an indelible mark on a fledgling nation. Interviews with Pocahontas's descendants provide a perspective on her life and times.

The Potawatomi
Color. 30 min. VHS.
Schlessinger Video Productions (1993)
Examines the history and current situation of the Potawatomi of the Great Lakes region. Only a few hundred tribe members survive. Some still speak the language and practice the ways of their ancestors. For grades 5-10.

Potlatch People
Color. 26 min. 16mm.
Document Associates (1976)
With an economy based on the abundant fish of the ocean and
rivers, Northwest Coast Indians lived in communal longhouses
based on a rigid class system.

The Pueblo
Color. 30 min. VHS.
Schlessinger Video Productions (1993)
Examines the history of the Pueblo Indians of New Mexico, one of
the first tribes to make contact with European explorers. Includes a discussion of their ancient ancestors, the Anasazi. For
grades 5-10.

Pueblo of Laguna: Elders of the Tribe
Color. 20 min. 16mm.
National Audio Visual Center (No date given)
Describes the dynamic program for taking care of elders on a reser-
vation in Laguna, New Mexico.

The Pueblo Peoples: First Contact
Color. 60 min. VHS.
PBS Video (1990)
Describes the history of the Pueblo tribe at the time of their first
contact with Spanish conquistadors in the mid-1500's. Briefly
discusses Pueblo philosophy and legends.

Red Sunday: The Story of the Battle of the Little Bighorn
Color. 28 min. 16mm.
Pyramid Film and Video (1975)
An objective account of America's most famous U.S. Cavalry-
Indian confrontation. Still photographs, original drawings,
paintings, and live action are skillfully blended.

Report from Wounded Knee
Color. 10 min. 16mm.
Sterling Educational Films (1971)
Details the historical events at Wounded Knee using photographic
stills.

Sacajawea
Color. 24 min. VHS.
Southerby Productions (1984)
The true story of the young Indian woman who guided the Lewis
and Clark expedition.

Sacred Buffalo People
Color. 56 min. VHS.
Deb Wallwork Productions (1992)
Explores the powerful bond between Native Americans and the
buffalo, viewed by Indians as the sacred provider of life. Traditional beliefs, history, and modern reservation humor are woven together in the stories told today as buffalo return to the
plains. Features Indian park rangers, wildlife managers, and
dancers, along with photography of buffalo herds and examples of Indian art.

Sacred Ground
Color. 60 min. VHS.
Freewheelin' Films Ltd. (1991)
Tour of American Indian spiritual places such as Devil's Tower
and Bear Butte, and a discussion of myths and legends associ-
ated them.

The Search for Ancient Americans: Ancient Beginnings of Native American Culture
Color. 58 min. VHS.
Intellimation (1988)
Demonstrates how new technologies are changing the way archaeologists work as they examine evidence of the first peoples to reach America. Examined in detail are the Mayan, Anasazi, and Florida tribal cultures. Part of *The Infinite Voyage* series.

Searching for a Native American Identity
Color. 30 min. VHS.
Films for the Humanities & Sciences (1994)
Bill Moyers interviews husband and wife writing team Louise Erdrich and Michael Dorris who discuss their literary collaboration, their shared thinking based upon their like backgrounds as mixed-blood Native Americans, and the Native American characters who people their novels. Originally broadcast as a program in the PBS series, *A World of Ideas*.

Seminole
Color. 30 min. VHS.
Schlessinger Video Productions (1993)
Examines the history, changing fortunes, and current situation of the Seminole people. Includes facts about the role of the U.S. government, debunks myths about Native Americans, explores their spiritual relationship with nature, and discusses the role of women in their societies. For grades 5-10.

Seminole Indians
Color. 11 min. 16mm.
University of Minnesota (1951)
Seminole life on the hummocks of the Florida Everglades.

*The Shadow Catcher: Edward S. Curtis and the North
American Indian*
Color. 89 min. VHS.
Mystic Fire Video (1993)
Video release of a motion picture originally produced in 1974. Pro-
filves photographer, anthropologist and filmmaker Curtis, who
spent 34 years recording the American Indian tradition. Be-
tween 1896 and 1930 Curtis collected interviews and original
Indian stories, recorded some 10,000 songs and took 40,000 pic-
tures many of which are used in the production. Retraces his
journeys from the Pueblo regions of the Southwest, north to
British Columbia and Alaska.

Silent Enemy
Black and white. 88 min. 16mm. VHS, DVD.
Blackhawk Films (1930)
Study of the Ojibwas' struggle for food before the arrival of Euro-
pean Americans. Filmed on location near Lake Superior.

Sioux Indians: Live and Remember
Color. 29 min. VHS.
Barr Films (1987)
Focuses on the struggle of the Dakota Sioux to preserve their heri-
tage. Shows the Dakota people living in squalid camps in the
midst of natural beauty.

Sitting Bull: Chief of the Lakota Nation
Color. 50 min. VHS.
A&E Home Entertainment (1995)
Portrait of the legendary chief who led the Lakota Sioux to victory
over General Custer at Little Big Horn.

Sitting Bull: A Profile in Power
Color. 20 min. 16mm.
Learning Corporation of America (1976)
The heroic but sad saga of relations between the United States and
the Indians unfolds through an imaginary dialogue between an
interviewer and the charismatic Sioux chief.

Songs of Indian Territory Native American Music Traditions
of Oklahoma
Color. 38 min. VHS.
Full Circle Communications (1990)
Features music from the workshops and concert of "The Songs of
Indian Territory" held at the Kirkpatrick Center in Oklahoma
City, October 14, 1988, and includes on-location highlights.

Spirit: A Journey in Dance, Drums and Song
Color. 75 min. VHS.
USA Films (1998)
Stage performance of modern and traditional Native American
music, dance, and mythology. Native American flutes, percussion, chants, and keyboards provide evocative music. Narra-
tion by Chief Hawk Pope interweaves tribal legends.

The Spirit of Crazy Horse
Color. 60 min. VHS.
PBS Home Video (1990)
Milo Yellow Hair recounts the story of the Sioux tribe's struggle to
reclaim their ancestral homeland. Investigates the simmering
conflict of recent decades and offers a perspective on the choices
that lie ahead. Originally shown as part of the PBS television series, *Frontline*.

The Spirit of the Mask
Color. 50 min. VHS.
Atlas Video (1993)
Explores the spiritual and psychological powers of masks used by
Northwest Coast native peoples. Features rarely-seen ceremo-
nies, commentary by spiritual leaders and relates how these tra-
ditions were repressed by Christian Europeans.

Storytellers of the Pacific
Color. 120 minutes. VHS.
Vision Maker Video (1996)
Two-part series focusing on the identity crisis of various Pacific
cultures which, many years after colonization, slavery, and op-
pression, are attempting to reconstruct and live according to
their true culture. Areas highlighted include northern Mexico,
California, the Pacific Northwest, Alaska, Hawaii, Australia,
Samoa, and Guam. Narrated by Joy Harjo.

Strangers in Their Own Land
Color. 50 min. VHS.
Strangers in Their Own Land (1993)
Records Native American ceremonies, including an emotional Ki-
owa wedding ceremony and the initiation of a young brave into
an ancient warrior society.

The Sun Dagger (Edited version)
Color. 28 min. 16mm. VHS.
Bullfrog Films (1982)
The "dagger," an ancient Indian celestial calendar rediscovered in
1977, is presently the only known archaeological site in the
world that marks the extreme positions of both the sun and the
moon.

Sweating Indian Style: Conflicts Over Native American Ritual
Color. 57 min. VHS.
Women Make Movies (1994)
Presents opposing views on non-Native Americans' participation
in traditional American Indian rites.

Tales of Wonder: Traditional Native American Fireside Stories
Color. 60 min. VHS.
Rich-Heape Films (1998)
Collection of traditional stories of creation and myth accompanied
by music and illustrations. Appropriate for children.

Teaching Indians to Be White
Color. 28 min. VHS.
Films for the Humanities & Sciences (1993)
Shows how schools try to integrate American Indian children into
mainstream society and notes problems with turning children
away from their families and traditional values.

To Find Our Life: The Peyote Hunt of the Huichols of Mexico
Color. 65 min. 16mm.
University of California Extension Media Center (1968)
Filmed and recorded in the field in December, 1966, by anthropolo-
gist Peter T. Furst, this is the first documentary of the annual
peyote hunt and ceremonies of the Huichol Indians of Western
Mexico.

The Totem Pole
Color. 28 min. 16mm. VHS.
Educational Materials Corporation (1961)
The Kwakiutl and Haida are the Northwest Indians best known
for their totem poles. Shows the several types of poles and how
they are decorated.

Tribal Legacies: The Incas, the Mayas, the Sioux, the Pueblos
Color. 296 min. VHS.
Pacific Arts (1993)
Collection of four videos that depict the history and civilizations of
four different native peoples of the Americas: the Incas, Mayas,
Sioux, and Pueblo Indians.

Valley of the Standing Rocks
Color. 24 in. 16mm.
Thomas J. Barbre Productions (1957)
Vividly portrays the life of the Navajos on their reservation in Ari-
zona and Utah.

Walking in a Sacred Manner
Color. 23 min. 16mm.
Stephen Cross (1982)
Using the photographs of Edward S. Curtis, shows how traditional
Indian life was centered on the natural world.

Winds of Change: A Matter of Promises
Color/black and white. 58 min. VHS.
PBS Video (1990)
Navajos of Arizona and adjacent states and Lummis of Washington State focus on sovereignty, internal politics, the administration of justice, and relations with the U.S. government. Hosted
by N. Scott Momaday.

Winter on an Indian Reservation
Color. 11 min. 16mm.
Inform (1973)
Shows children on a forest reservation in the Great Lakes area; pro-
vides an intimate look at both the hardships and joys of Indian
life.

Wiping the Tears of Seven Generations
Color. 57 min. VHS.
Film Ideas (1992)
History of the Lakota people, culminating in the Bigfoot Memorial
Ride, December 1990, intended to end the century of grieving
since the Wounded Knee Massacre.

Woodland Indians of Early America
Color/black and white. 11 min. 16mm.
Cort (1958)
Depicts a family of hunter-culture Indians, illustrating the migra-
tory nature of such cultures and showing many techniques of
hunting, dress, cooking, and home building.

Yankton Sioux
Color. 30 min. VHS.
Schlessinger Video Productions (1993)
Extensive location filming takes the viewer to reservations where
children and elders discuss what it means to be a Native American today. Includes photographs, film footage, tribal music,
crafts and ceremonies. For grades 5-10.

FEATURE FILMS

The depictions of Indians in feature films (often by white actors)
have historically been misguided and have engendered considerable outrage. What follows is a select list of films that provide relatively accurate portrayals of Indian life, past and present. In some
of the films all Indians are portrayed by Indian actors; in others,
white actors fill at least some Indian roles.

Black Robe
Color. 100 min. VHS, DVD.
Samuel Goldwyn (1991)
Seventeenth century Jesuit priest is led by a party of Algonquins to
a distant mission. Generally accurate depiction of early Indian-
white relations as well as intertribal Algonquin, Iroquois, and
Huron relations and warfare. From Brian Moore's novel.
Lothaire Bluteau, Aden Young, Sandrine Holt.

Cheyenne Autumn
Color. 159 min. VHS.
Warner Bros. (1964)
Renowned director of Westerns John Ford filmed this story of
Cheyennes fleeing their reservation to return to their homeland.
Not without its flaws, this is an early but sympathetic look at
the situation of western Indians in the late nineteenth century.
Richard Widmark, Carroll Baker, Ricardo Montalban, Gilbert
Roland.

Crazy Horse
Color. 94 min. VHS.
Turner Home Entertainment (1994)
Made-for-cable look at the life of the Sioux and their warrior-
leader, Crazy Horse, who led his people to victory at the Battle
of Little Big Horn in 1876. Michael Greyeyes, Irene Bedard, Au-
gust Schellenberg, Wes Studi, Peter Horton.

Dance Me Outside
Color. 91 min. VHS.
Una-Pix Entertainment (1995)
The story of the passage into manhood of an 18-year-old Indian on
the Kidabanesee Reserve in Ontario. Adapted from a novel by
W. P. Kinsella. Ryan Black, Adam Beach, Jennifer Podemski,
Lisa LaCroix, Michael Greyeyes.

Dances with Wolves
Color. 181 min. VHS, DVD.
Orion Pictures (1990)
Troubled Civil War veteran goes West and finds in the lifestyle and
hunting grounds of the Lakota Sioux what he has been missing.
Generally hailed by critics for its faithful depiction of Indian life
and customs. Spoken Lakota is dubbed in English. Kevin Cost-
ner, Mary McDonnell, Graham Greene.

Geronimo
Color. 102 min. VHS.
Turner Home Entertainment (1993)
Made-for-cable look at the life of the Chiricahua Apaches and their
warrior-leader, Geronimo. Joseph Runningfox, Nick Ramus,
Michael Greyeyes, Tailinh Forest Flower.

Geronimo: An American Legend
Color. 115 min. VHS, DVD.
Columbia Pictures (1993)
The exploits of the Apache leader during the years 1885 and 1886
are effectively dramatized. Geronimo ultimately becomes a
larger-than-life hero and an expression of Apache cultural values. Wes Studi, Jason Patric, Gene Hackman.

House Made of Dawn
Color 90 min. VHS.
New Line Studios (1996)
Tells the story of a young American Indian named Abel, home
from a foreign war and caught between two worlds: the tradi-
tional one of his father and the other of industrial America. An
adaptation of the Pulitzer Prize winning novel by N. Scott
Momaday. Larry Littlebird, Judith Doty, Jay Varela, Mesa Bird.

The Indian in the Cupboard
Color. 98 min. VHS, DVD.
Columbia/Tristar (1995)
Fantasy based on Lynne Reid Banks's popular children's book. A young boy discovers that a toy Indian comes to life when it is locked in a cupboard. The boy also discovers that the toy is actually a historical Iroquois warrior who lived in the nineteenth century. A bond eventually develops between the boy and the warrior. Hal Scardino, Litefoot, Lindsay Crouse, David Keith.

Lakota Woman: Siege at Wounded Knee
Color. 113 min. VHS.
Turner Home Entertainment (1994)
Based on the biography of Mary Crow Dog, who went from an abused childhood and intra-tribal politics to become an eyewitness to the 1973 siege at Wounded Knee. Features an all Native American cast. Irene Bedard, Lawrence Bayne, Michael Horse, Joseph Runningfox, Floyd "Red Crow" Westerman.

The Last of the Mohicans
Color. 110 min. VHS, DVD.
20th Century Fox (1992)
Sweeping adaptation of the James Fenimore Cooper tale of colonial America during the French and Indian War. Hawkeye (Natty Bumppo) and his Indian brother Chingachgook must rescue colonists who have been captured by Indians. Daniel Day-Lewis, Madeleine Stowe, Russell Means, Eric Schweig.

Little Big Man
Color. 147 min. VHS, DVD.
CBS/Fox Video/Hiller Productions, Ltd. (1970)
Jack Crabb, 121-year-old veteran of the Old West and survivor of the Battle of the Little Bighorn, tells his story and stimulates sympathy for Indians along the way. Arthur Penn directed this offbeat epic starring Dustin Hoffman, Faye Dunaway, and Chief Dan George.

A Man Called Horse
Color. 114 min. VHS, DVD.
Cinema Center (1970)
In 1825 an English aristocrat is captured by a group of Sioux and eventually becomes their leader. A relatively realistic, even graphic, portrayal of Indian life and customs, including tribal initiations. Richard Harris, Judith Anderson, Manu Tupou.

Medicine River
Color. 96 min. VHS.
United American Video (1994)
Romantic comedy about a worldrenowned photojournalist who returns home to Medicine River after a twenty-year absence to attend his mother's funeral and is conned into staying to help with a community project. Based on the 1990 Thomas King novel. Graham Greene, Byron Chief-Moon, Tom Jackson, Sheila Tousey.

Powwow Highway
Color. 89 min. VHS.
Anchor Bay Entertainment (1989)
An over-sized Cheyenne man-child goes on a spiritual quest to New Mexico while giving a ride to a lifelong Indian activist friend. Gary Farmer, A. Martinez, Graham Greene, Wes Studi, John Trudell.

Running Brave
Color. 105 min. VHS
Buena Vista (1983)
Sentimental profile of half-Sioux athlete Billy Mills from his childhood on the Pine Ridge Reservation to his victory at the 1964 Tokyo Olympics. (The casting of a white actor in the lead Indian role caused considerable protest when the film was made.) Robbie Benson, Pat Hingle.

Shadow of the Wolf
Color. 108 min. VHS.
Triumph (1993)
Young Inuit hunter sets out to live in isolation in the Arctic wilderness. After killing a white trader, he is pursued by a Canadian mountie. Lou Diamond Phillips, Jennifer Tilly.

Smoke Signals
Color. 89 minutes. VHS, DVD.
Miramax Home Entertainment (1998)
Road movie that bills itself as the first feature film written and directed by Native Americans. Screenwriter Sherman Alexie and director Chris Eyre follow two young Indians, Victor and Thomas, as they journey from Idaho's Coeur d'Alene Indian Reservation to Arizona to collect the ashes and pickup truck of Victor's dead father. Adam Beach, Evan Adams, Gary Farmer, Cody Lightning, Irene Bedard, John Trudell.

Son of the Morning Star
Color. 186 min. VHS.
Republic Pictures Home Video (1991)
Thoughtful look at the life and times of General George Armstrong Custer. Emphasis is on the ill-conceived and disastrous battle against the Sioux at Little Bighorn. Rosanna Arquette, Dean Stockwell, and Rodney A. Grant.

Squanto: A Warrior's Tale
Color. 102 min. VHS.
Disney (1994)
Based on the life of a seventeenth-century American Indian who is abducted and brought to England by British traders. Squanto is befriended by a sympathetic monk who urges him to return to America on a peace-making mission. Adam Beach, Mandy Patinkin, Michael Gambon, Irene Bedard.

Thunderheart
Color. 118 min. VHS, DVD.
Tristar Pictures (1992)
An FBI agent who is part Sioux is sent to investigate a murder on a
   Sioux reservation and undergoes a personal transformation.
   The film is noteworthy for its portrayal of contemporary reser-
   vation life. Val Kilmer, Sam Shepard, Graham Greene.

Windtalkers
Color. 134 min. VHS, DVD.
Metro-Goldwyn-Mayer (2002)
Two Marine sergeants are assigned to protect a group of Navajo
   Marines who use their native language as the basis for a secret
   code during World War II. Nicholas Cage, Adam Beach, Roger
   Willie, Christian Slater.

Windwalker
Color. 108 min. VHS, DVD.
United American Video (1980)
Newly dead Cheyenne patriarch returns to life to save his family
   from his son, an evil twin who was stolen at birth and raised by
   the enemy Crow. In Cheyenne and Crow languages, and subti-
   tled in English. Trevor Howard, Nick Ramus, James Remar, Se-
   rene Hedin.

WEB SITES

Bureau of Indian Affairs
http://www.doi.gov/bureau-indian -affairs.html
The Bureau of Indian Affairs On-Line. Provides a directory of
   information on law, legislation, education, tribal services, reports, and statistics concerning American Indians.

Guide to Native American Studies Programs in the United States and Canada. Ed. Robert M. Nelson. University of Richmond.
http://www.richmond.edu/faculty/ ASAIL/guide/guide.html
Comprehensive survey of U.S. and Canadian Native American Studies programs being offered as majors, minors, and certifications at the baccalaureate level or above.

Internet Public Library
http://www.ipl.org/ref/native/
Provides information on primarily contemporary Native North American authors with bibliographies of their published works, biographical information, and links to online resources including interviews, online texts, and tribal Web sites.

Labriola National American Indian Data Center
Tempe: Arizona State University.
http://www.asu.edu/lib/archives/ labriola.htm
The Labriola National American Indian Data Center's research collection brings together current and historic information on government, culture, religion and world view, social life and customs, tribal history, and information on individuals from the United States, Canada, Sonora, and Chihuahua, Mexico.

Mashantucket Pequot Museum and Research Center
Mashantucket, Conn.
http://www.mashantucket.com/
Tribally owned-and-operated complex brings to life the story of the Mashantucket Pequot Tribal Nation, and serves as a major resource on the history of the tribe, the histories and cultures of other tribes, and the region's natural history. Information about the museum's collections, research library, exhibits, and events is available through the Web site.

Native American Book Resources on the World Wide Web
http://www.hanksville.org/NAresources/indices/NAbooks.htm
Includes links to Web sites on Native American authors, books
available online, organizations, journals, book lists with Native
American content, libraries, presses, book reviews, and book
stores online that specialize in Native American material.

Native American Sites. Ed. Lisa A. Mitten. University of
Pittsburgh.
http://www.pitt.edu/~lmitten/indians.html
Provides access to home pages of individual Native Americans
and nations, and to other sites that provide solid information
about American Indians. Links are provided to information on
individual Native nations, organizations, businesses, Indian
education, languages, powwows and festivals, Native music,
and contemporary Native American issues.

Smithsonian Institution National Museum of the American Indian
http://www.si.edu/cgi-bin/nav.cgi
Home page of the Smithsonian Institution's National Museum of
the American Indian in New York City. Provides information
about the museum's collections, exhibitions, publications, recordings, and education resources. Includes research information and links to other Native American sites.

Smithsonian Institution National Museum of Natural History
http://nmnhwww.si.edu/anthro/ outreach/Indbibl/
Bibliography for educators and parents of children K-12, compiled
by the Anthropology Outreach Office of the Smithsonian's National Museum of Natural History. Produced in response to
concerns about choosing culturally sensitive and historically
accurate books for children about American Indians and Alaska
Natives.

SOUND RECORDINGS

Creation's Journey: Native American Music
Compact Disc
Smithsonian/Folkways (1994)
Ceremonial, social, and contemporary music of Native Americans
from the United States, Canada, Mexico, and Bolivia. Music by
Comanche, Navajo, Seneca, Micmac, Cherokee, Kwakiutl, Zapo-
tec, and other native performers.

500 Nations: A Musical Journey
Compact Disc.
Epic Soundtrax (1994)
Sound track from the CBS television miniseries, *500 Nations*. Music
by Peter Buffett.

Honor the Earth Powwow: Songs of the Great Lakes Indians
Compact Disc.
Ryko (1991)
Songs of the Ojibwa, the Menominee and Winnebago. Recorded
July, 1990, at a powwow at the Lac Court Oreilles Reservation,
Wisconsin.

Music for the Native Americans
Compact Disc.
Capitol Records (1994)
Soundtrack for the Turner Broadcasting Systems mini-series, *The
Native Americans*. Songs composed and performed by Robbie
Robertson and the Red Road Ensemble and other Native Amer-
ican musicians.

Music of New Mexico: Native American Traditions
Compact Disc. 68 min.
Smithsonian Folkways (1992)
Traditional and contemporary music by Pueblo, Navajo, and
Apache musicians from New Mexico.

Proud Heritage A Celebration of Traditional American Indian Music
Compact Disc.
Indian House (1996)
An anthology of American Indian music sung in various Indian
languages including Navajo, Pueblo, Ponca, Kiowa, Creek, and
Sioux.

Songs of Earth, Water, Fire, and Sky: Music of the American Indian.
Compact Disc.
New World Records (1991)
An anthology of music recorded on various Indian reservations
and at powwows. Includes traditional songs of Pueblo, Seneca,
Arapaho, Plains, Creek, Yurok, Navajo, and Cherokee tribes.

*Talking Spirits: Music from the Hopi, Zuni, Laguna & San Juan
Pueblos.*
Compact Disc.
Music of the World (1992)
Tribal songs and dances recorded on location in New Mexico and
Arizona by James Lascelles during the 1980s. Sung in a variety
of Native American languages.

CD-ROMS

Exploring the Lost Maya
Sumeria (1996)
Contains historical material written by leading Maya scholar
Robert Sharer, interactive maps of major Maya sites, nineteenth
century lithographs and historical photos, an interactive multi-
media time line of Maya history, movies on several facets of
Maya culture, and travel information for those planning to visit
the sites.

500 Nations: Stories of the North American Indian Experience
Microsoft Home (1995)
Based on a Jack Leustig film of the same title. Hosted by Kevin
    Costner. Multimedia presentation of the history of North Amer-
    ican Indians. Includes over 2,000 images, three-dimensional
    video, computer-generated recreations, animated sequences,
    spoken segments, and music.

Maya
Hull, Quebec: The Museum (1995)
Depicts Maya architecture, art, and lifestyle primarily through
    photographs. Includes a section on the making of the IMAX
    film, *Mystery of the Maya*. Published in collaboration with the
    National Film Board of Canada and the Instituto Mexicano de
    Cinematografia. Narrated by Geoff Winter.

Pomo Indians
Compiled by Jeannine Davis-Kimball and Randal S. Brandt.
Berkeley: California Indian Library Collections, University of
    California, Berkeley (1994)
Interactive, multimedia collection divided into ten searchable cate-
    gories, each containing photographs, sound recordings, and
    textual material. The exhaustive Pomo bibliography is search-
    able by author, title, periodical, series, keyword, and holdings.

Museums, Archives, and Libraries

Select list of museums, archives, and libraries in four parts: museums in the United States; museums in Canada; libraries and archives in the United States; libraries and archives in Canada. Each part is arranged alphabetically, first by state, territory, or province, then by city.

MUSEUMS IN THE UNITED STATES

ALABAMA

Alabama Museum of Natural History
Smith Hall, University of Alabama
Tuscaloosa, 35487-0340
Resource center of Southeastern Indians; ties with Moundville Archaeological Park.

ALASKA

Alaska State Museum
395 Whittier Street
Juneau, 99801-1718
Alaskan Native Gallery; Subarctic and Northwest Coast items.

Totem Heritage Center
601 Deermount
(mailing address: 629 Dock Street)
Ketchikan, 99901
Programs and artifacts in Northwest Coast arts; index to all Alaska totem poles.

ARIZONA

Arizona State Museum
University of Arizona
Tucson, 85721
Extensive collections from the historic and prehistoric peoples of
the area.

Colorado River Indian Tribes Museum
Route 1, Box 23B
Parker, 85344
Artifacts from Mojave, Chemehuevi, Hopi, and Navajo as well as
prehistoric cultures.

Gila River Arts and Crafts Center
P.O. Box 457
Sacaton, 85247
Museum and crafts reflect all tribes of the area.

Heard Museum
22 E. Monte Vista Road
Phoenix, 85004-1480
Southwest emphasis; inventory of 8,200 Native American artists.
Library of 40,000 volumes includes Fred Harvey Company doc-
uments and photo archives.

Museum of Northern Arizona
Fort Valley Road
(mailing address: Route 4, P.O. Box 720)
Flagstaff, 86001
Southwest Anglo and Indian art, with Hopi and Navajo emphasis.
Harold S. Colton Memorial Library of 24,000 volumes.

Navajo Tribal Museum
Highway 264
(mailing address: P.O. Box 308)
Window Rock, 86515
Four Corners archaeology and ethnography, including re-creation
of 1870-1930 era trading post.

ARKANSAS

Arkansas State Museum
P.O. Box 490
State University, 72467
Emphasizes northeastern Arkansas tribes such as the Osage,
Caddo, Chickasaw, and others.

CALIFORNIA

Bowers Museum of Cultural Art
2002 North Main Street
Santa Ana, 92706
Collection of 85,000 items focuses on the fine arts of indigenous
peoples, including pre-Columbian and Native American.

Fowler Museum of Cultural History
University of California, Los Angeles
405 Hilgard Avenue
Los Angeles, 90024-1549
Extensive archaeological and ethnographic collections include Na-
tive American materials.

Maturango Museum
100 E. Las Flores
(mailing address: P.O. Box 1776)
Ridgecrest, 93556
A small regional museum focusing on one of the richest petroglyph areas in the United States at China Lake.

Natural History Museum of Los Angeles County
Times-Mirror Hall of Native American Cultures; Hall of Pre-
Columbian Cultures
900 Exposition Boulevard
Los Angeles, 90007
Excellent permanent displays, with changing exhibitions on con-
temporary issues in art and culture. The Pre-Columbian Hall
covers cultures from Mexico to Peru.

Southwest Museum
234 Museum Drive
(mailing address: P.O. Box 558)
Los Angeles, 90065
Collections range from Alaska to South America, with permanent
displays focusing on the Southwest, Great Plains, California,
and Northwest Coast. Braun Research Library contains 50,000
volumes, 100,000 photos, 900 recordings, and archival material.

COLORADO

Denver Art Museum
100 W. 14th Avenue Parkway
Denver, 80204
Art collection includes Indian clothing, Southwest pottery and
kachinas, and Northwest Coast carvings. Frederick H. Douglas
Library includes 6,000 volumes.

Denver Museum of Natural History
2001 South Colorado Boulevard
Denver, 80205
Strong on Paleo-Indian culture, including the original Folsom
spear point; a 24,000-volume library.

Southern Ute Cultural Center and Gallery
Highway 172
(mailing address: P.O. Box 737)
Ignacio, 81137
Early history; contemporary bead and leather work.

CONNECTICUT

Institute for American Indian Studies (IAIS)
38 Curtis Road
(mailing address: P.O. Box 1260)
Washington, 06793-0260
Continental coverage, but focus is on Northeast Woodlands. Reconstructed Indian village, with Indian Habitats Trail; 250,000 artifacts and a 2,000-volume library.

Peabody Museum
Yale University
170 Whitney
New Haven, 06511-8161
Extensive holdings include both archaeological and ethnographic materials of the Americas.

DELAWARE

Delaware State Museum
316 South Governors Avenue
Dover, 19901
Eastern prehistory; 1,000-volume library; State Archaeological Collection.

DISTRICT OF COLUMBIA

U.S. National Museum of Natural History
Smithsonian Institution
Washington, 20560

FLORIDA

Ah-Tha-Thi-Ki Museum
3240 North 64th Avenue
Hollywood, 33024
Artifacts and activities document and preserve Seminole traditions; village, burial site, nature trails.

Florida State Museum
University of Florida
Gainesville, 32601
Pearsall Collection of ethnographic items ranges from Seminole to Inuit.

GEORGIA

New Echota
Route 3
Calhoun, 30701
Restoration of Cherokee capital of 1825-1838. Trail of Tears material.

IDAHO

Nez Perce National Historic Park
Highway 95
(mailing address: P.O. Box 93)
Spalding, 83551
Prehistoric as well as historic regional items. Park notes sites of Indian-U.S. battles. A 600-volume library and archive of 3,000 photos.

ILLINOIS

Field Museum of Natural History
Roosevelt Road at Lake Shore Drive
Chicago, 60605
Extensive Native American collections, including Pawnee earth
lodge replica. Webber Resource Center houses books and audio-
visual materials on indigenous cultures.

INDIANA

Eiteljorg Museum of American Indian and Western Art
500 West Washington Street
Indianapolis, 46204
Extensive collection that emphasizes Northeast Woodlands, great
Plains, and Southwest culture areas.

IOWA

Putnam Museum of History and Natural Science
1717 West 12th Street
Davenport, 52804
Regional ethnographic collections and important Mississippian
materials.

KANSAS

Indian Center Museum
650 North Seneca
Wichita, 67203
Collection reflects Indian art and religion.

KENTUCKY

J. B. Speed Art Museum
2035 South Third Street
(mailing address: P.O. Box 2600)
Louisville, 40201-2600
Collection emphasizes regional materials and the Great Plains, complemented by a 14,000-volume art library that includes the Frederick Weygold Indian Collection.

LOUISIANA

Tunica-Biloxi Regional Indian Center and Museum
Highway 1
(mailing address: P.O. Box 331)
Marksville, 71351
Focuses on descendants of the mound builders. The tribal museum is built in a classic Mississippian style. Collections include colonial Indian-European materials returned to the tribe under the Indian Graves and Repatriation Act.

MAINE

Peary-MacMillan Arctic Museum and Studies Center
Hubbard Hall, Bowdoin College
Brunswick, 04011
MacMillan collection of Inuit and Subarctic material culture.

MASSACHUSETTS

Peabody Museum of Archaeology and Ethnology
11 Divinity Avenue
Harvard University
Cambridge, 02138
Worldwide collection of 2,000,000 artifacts has a North and South American focus; 180,000-volume library.

MICHIGAN

Cranbrook Institute of Science
500 Lone Pine Road
(mailing address: P.O. Box 801)
Bloomfield Hills, 48303-0801
Collection reflects all North American culture areas.

MINNESOTA

Mille Lacs Indian Museum
HCR 67
(mailing address: P.O. Box 95)
Onamia, 56359
Ojibwa and Dakota artifacts illustrate traditional lifeways.

Minnesota Historical Society's Grand Mound and Interpretive Center
Route 7
(mailing address: P.O. Box 453)
International Falls, 56649
Burial mounds with extensive exhibits of Woodland, Laurel, and Blackduck cultures.

MISSISSIPPI

Grand Village of the Natchez Indians
400 Jefferson Davis Boulevard
Natchez, 39120
Artifacts explore the culture of the descendants of the Mississippian mound builders.

MISSOURI

St. Louis Science Center
5050 Oakland Avenue
St. Louis, 63110

MONTANA

Museum of the Plains Indian and Crafts Center
U.S. 89
(mailing address: P.O. Box 400)
Browning, 59417
Northern Plains material culture; reconstruction of 1850's Blackfeet camp.

NEBRASKA

Fur Trade Museum
East Highway 20, HC 74
(mailing address: P.O. Box 18)
Chadron, 69337

Museum of Nebraska History
131 Centennial Mall North
Lincoln, 68508
Anthropology and art of the central Plains tribes.

NEVADA

Lost City Museum
721 South Highway 169
Overton, 89040
Reconstructed pueblo and kiva; archaeological museum; 400-volume library.

NEW JERSEY

Montclair Art Museum
3 South Mountain Avenue
Montclair, 07042
Rand Collection of Native American art. Art history library of
13,000 volumes.

New Jersey State Museum
205 West State Street
Trenton, 08625
Local material as well as Plains, Arctic, Southwest, and Northeast
collections.

NEW MEXICO

Maxwell Museum of Anthropology
University of New Mexico
Roma and University, N.E.
Albuquerque, 87131-1201
Extensive Southwest collections. Library of 12,500 volumes and
photo archives.

Museum of Indian Arts and Culture
708 Camino Lejo
(mailing address: P.O. Box 2087)
Santa Fe, 87504
Exhibits focus on Pueblo, Apache, and Navajo cultures. A 20,000-
volume library on the anthropology of the Southwest.

Western New Mexico University Museum
(mailing address: P.O. Box 43)
Silver City, 88061
Eisele collection of classic Mimbres pottery.

NEW YORK

American Museum of Natural History
79th Street and Central Park West
New York, 10024-5192
Exhibitions are especially strong on the cultures of the Arctic and
  Pacific Northwest.

National Museum of the American Indian
George Gustav Heye Center
Alexander Hamilton Custom House
3753 Broadway at 155th Street
New York, 10032
The first of three planned facilities of the National Museum of the
  American Indian, part of the Smithsonian Institution, opened in
  New York in 1994.

Seneca Iroquois National Museum
Broad Street Extension
(mailing address: P.O. Box 442)
Salamanca, 14779
Special wampum belt exhibit; typical nineteenth century elm-bark
  longhouse reconstruction; contemporary art.

NORTH CAROLINA

Indian Museum of the Carolinas
607 Turnpike Road
Laurinburg, 28352
Exhibits feature Southeast cultures and lifeways.

Native American Resource Center
Pembroke State University
Pembroke, 28372
Eastern Woodlands materials; North and South America.

NORTH DAKOTA

North Dakota Heritage Center
612 East Boulevard
Bismarck, 58505
Plains cultures. A 100,000-volume library on ethnology and history.

Turtle Mountain Chippewa Heritage Center
Highway 5
(mailing address: P.O. Box 257)
Belcourt, 58316
Promotes tribal history and traditions. Contemporary art gallery.

OHIO

Cincinnati Museum of Natural History
1301 Western Avenue
Cincinnati, 45203
Good selection of mound builder artifacts from the Ohio Valley.

Cleveland Museum of Natural History
1 Wade Oval Drive
University Circle
Cleveland, 44106-1767
Research fields include archaeology and physical anthropology. A 50,000-volume natural history library.

OKLAHOMA

Cherokee Heritage Center
Willis Road
(mailing address: P.O. Box 515)
Tahlequah, 74465
Reconstructed village; contemporary arts and crafts.

Museum of the Great Plains
601 Ferris Avenue
Lawton, 73502
Artifacts, library, and photo archives relating to Plains tribes.

The Philbrook Museum of Art, Inc.
2727 South Rockford Road
Tulsa, 74114
Clark Field Basket Collection; Lawson Collection of Indian clothing; Philbrook Collection of American Indian paintings; Lawson Indian library.

Seminole Nation Museum and Library
6th and Wewoka
(mailing address: P.O. Box 1532)
Wewoka, 74884

OREGON

High Desert Museum
59800 South Highway 97
Bend, 97702

Museum of Natural History
University of Oregon
1680 East 15th Avenue
Eugene, 97403-1224
Collection includes 13,000-year-old Fort Rock Cave artifacts.

PENNSYLVANIA

Carnegie Museum of Natural History
4400 Forbes Avenue
Pittsburgh, 15213-4080
Wide coverage, including Arctic and Northwest Coast collections.

RHODE ISLAND

Haffenreffer Museum of Anthropology
Brown University
Bristol, 02809
Arctic and Subarctic materials, including Archaic Period remains
  of the Red Paint People of Maine.

SOUTH CAROLINA

McKissick Museum
University of South Carolina
Columbia, 29208
Catawba pottery and baskets. Folk Art Resource Center.

SOUTH DAKOTA

Indian Museum of North America
Avenue of the Chiefs, Black Hills
Crazy Horse, 57730

Sioux Indian Museum and Crafts Center
515 West Boulevard
Rapid City, 57709

W. H. Over State Museum
414 East Clark
Vermillion, 57069-2390
Plains material culture and contemporary painting.

TENNESSEE

Frank H. McClung Museum
University of Tennessee
1327 Circle Park Drive
Knoxville, 37996-3200

Tennessee State Museum
505 Deaderick Street
Nashville, 37243-1120
Strong in prehistoric Mississippian culture.

TEXAS

Alabama-Coushatta Museum
U.S. Highway 190
Route 3
(mailing address: P.O. Box 540)
Livingston, 77351

Panhandle-Plains Historical Museum
2401 Fourth Avenue
Canyon, 79016
Hall of the Southern Plains. South and Southwest Indian focus;
10,000-volume library.

Texas Memorial Museum
University of Texas
24th and Trinity
Austin, 78705
Broad focus on the anthropology of the American Indian.

Witte Memorial Museum
3801 Broadway
San Antonio, 78209
Samples most North American culture areas.

UTAH

College of Eastern Utah Prehistoric Museum
451 East 400 North
Price, 84501
Focuses on Anasazi and Fremont cultures.

Utah Museum of Natural History
University of Utah
Salt Lake City, 84112
Regional, Great Basin, and Southwestern materials.

VIRGINIA

Jamestown Settlement
(mailing address: P.O. Box JF)
Williamsburg, 23187
Reconstruction of Indian village and Powhatan's lodge.

Mattaponi Museum
West Point, 23181
Important collection of archaeological materials.

Pamunkey Indian Museum
(mailing address: P.O. Box 2050)
King William, 23086
Contemporary and prehistoric art and artifacts.

WASHINGTON

The Burke Museum
University of Washington, DB-10
Seattle, 98195
Northwest Coast and Pacific Rim collections.

Makah Cultural and Research Center
(mailing address: P.O. Box 160)
Neah Bay, 98257
Features remains from the Ozette site, a Late Period pre-contact
  Makah village buried and preserved in a mudslide. Magnifi-
  cent Northwest Coast Tradition assemblage of 60,000 artifacts.

Seattle Art Museum
100 University Street
(mailing address: P.O. Box 22000)
Seattle, 98122-9700
Excellent collection of Northwest Coast art.

Yakima Nation Cultural Heritage Center
Toppenish, 98948

WEST VIRGINIA

Grave Creek Mound State Park
Moundsville, 26041
Largest mound produced by the Adena ceremonial complex, which flourished around 500 B.C.E. to 100 C.E.

WISCONSIN

Lac du Flambeau Chippewa Museum
(mailing address: P.O. Box 804)
Lac du Flambeau, 54538
Eighteenth century dugout canoe, artifacts, and seasonal activities displays.

Logan Museum of Anthropology
700 College Street
Beloit College
Beloit, 53511-5595
Physical and cultural anthropological materials from the Great Lakes, Plains, and Southwest culture areas.

Milwaukee Public Museum
800 West Wells Street
Milwaukee, 53233
Collections cover North America. A 125,000-volume library.

Neville Public Museum
129 South Jefferson Street
Green Bay, 54301
Archaic Period materials from the Old Copper and Red Ochre cultures.

WYOMING

Anthropology Museum
University of Wyoming
Laramie, 82071

MUSEUMS IN CANADA

ALBERTA

Glenbow Museum
130 Ninth Avenue, S.E.
Calgary, AB T2G 0P3

Provincial Museum of Alberta
12845 102nd Avenue
Edmonton, AB T5N 0M6
Regional materials; Inuit; northern Plains.

BRITISH COLUMBIA

Campbell River Museum
1235 Island Highway
Campbell Island, BC V9W 2C7
Arts of the Indian groups of northern Vancouver Island.

'Ksan Indian Village

(mailing address: P.O. Box 326)

Hazelton, BC B0J 1Y0

A center for the display, preservation, and promotion of Gitksan arts and crafts skills. Seven traditional buildings.

Museum of Anthropology

University of British Columbia

Vancouver, BC V6T 1Z1

Major Northwest Coast collections. Center for promotion of traditional arts and customs.

Museum of Northern British Columbia

(mailing address: P.O. Box 669)

Prince Rupert, BC V8J 3S1

Northwest Coast artifacts. Promotes contemporary carving and craft skills.

Royal British Columbia Museum

675 Belleville Street

Victoria, BC V8V 1X4

Traditional Kwakiutl dance houses; Thunderbird Park totem pole exhibits; art demonstrations.

MANITOBA

Eskimo Museum

La Verendrye Street

(mailing address: P.O. Box 10)

Churchill, MB R0B 0E0

Inuit materials include kayaks dating back hundreds of years. Also, Subarctic materials from Chippewa and Cree cultures.

Manitoba Museum of Man and Nature

190 Rupert Avenue

Winnipeg, MB R3B 0N2

NEW BRUNSWICK

New Brunswick Museum
277 Douglas Avenue
Saint John, NB F2K 1E5
Regional and pre-Algonquian artifacts.

NEWFOUNDLAND

Newfoundland Museum
285 Duckworth Street
St. John's, NF A1C 1G9
Exhibits cover the six major tribal groups of Labrador and New-
foundland.

NORTHWEST TERRITORIES

Dene Cultural Institute
(mailing address: P.O. Box 207)
Yellowknife, NT X1A 2N2

Northern Life Museum
110 King Street
(mailing address: P.O. Box 420)
Fort Smith, NT X0E 0P0
Arctic and Subartic tools and artifacts.

NOVA SCOTIA

Nova Scotia Museum
1747 Summer Street
Halifax, NS B3H 3A6
Artifacts of the Micmac.

ONTARIO

Museum of Indian Archaeology and Lawson Prehistoric Village
1600 Attawandaron Road
London, ON N6G 3M6
Exhibits cover five phases of culture dating back to Paleo-Indian times. On-site excavation.

North American Indian Travel College
The Living Museum
RR 3
Cornwall Island, ON K6H 5R7

Royal Ontario Museum
100 Queen's Park Crescent
Toronto, ON M5S 2C6
Ontario prehistory.

Thunder Bay Art Gallery
1080 Keewatin Street
(mailing address: P.O. Box 1193)
Thunder Bay, ON P7C 4X9
Traditional items as well as contemporary art.

PRINCE EDWARD ISLAND

Micmac Indian Village
(mailing address: P.O. Box 51)
Cornwall, PEI C0A 1H0

QUEBEC

Abenakis Museum
Route 226
Odanak, PQ J0G 1H0
Displays reflect tribal traditions and lore.

Canadian Museum of Civilization
100 Laurier Street
Hull, PQ J8X 4H2
Spectacular collection of national cultural materials.

McCord Museum
McGill University
690 Sherbrook Street W.
Montreal, PQ H3A 1E9

SASKATCHEWAN

Regina Plains Museum
1801 Scarth Street
Regina, SK S4P 2G9
Metis history and the Riel Rebellions are covered in addition to
    Plains material.

Saskatchewan Museum of Natural History
Wascana Park
Regina, SK S4P 3V7
Native Peoples Gallery focusing on Subarctic tribes.

YUKON TERRITORY

MacBride Museum
(mailing address: P.O. Box 4037)
Whitehorse, YT Y1A 3S9
Artifacts of the Yukon region.

LIBRARIES AND ARCHIVES IN THE UNITED STATES

ALABAMA

Alabama Department of Archives and History
624 Washington Avenue
Montgomery, 36130

ARIZONA

Navajo Nation Library System
Drawer K
Window Rock, 86515
Collection has 23,000 books, 1,000 manuscripts, and films and tapes. Files of the *Navajo Times*. Two libraries in Window Rock and one in Navajo, New Mexico.

Smoki People Library
P.O. Box 123
Prescott, 86302
Library of 600 volumes covers North and South American Indian ceremonials and dances.

Tohono Chul park, Inc.
7366 North Paseo del Norte
Tucson, 85704
Nature center, ethnic art exhibitions, and 800-volume library on Southwest culture and environment.

Western Archaeological and Conservation Center
1415 North Sixth Avenue
(mailing address: P.O. Box 41058, Tucson, 85717)
Tucson, 85705
Focus on Southwest prehistory and ethnography: 17,000-volume library, 100 periodicals, and 160,000-item photo archive.

ARKANSAS

Southwest Arkansas Regional Archives (SARA)

P.O. Box 134
Washington, 71862
History of Caddo Indians and Southwest Arkansas.

CALIFORNIA

American Indian Resource Center

Public Library of Los Angeles County
6518 Miles Avenue
Huntington Park, 90255
Special collections on Indians of North America; 9,000 volumes.

Malki Museum Archives

11-795 Fields Road
Banning, 92220
Oral history project tapes; field notes of J. P. Harrington and others;
  manuscript and photo archives.

Native American Studies Library

University of California at Berkeley
103 Wheeler
Berkeley, 94720
Reports of the Bureau of Indian Affairs; Indian Claims Commission materials; special California Indian collection; extensive
  holdings.

Rupert Costo Library
UCR Library Special Collections
University of California at Riverside
Riverside, 92517
The 15,000-volume collection is countrywide in scope with a California concentration. Houses the American Indian Historical Society Archives, donated by the Costos. Manuscripts, field notes, and 300 books cover the customs and medicines of the Chinantec Indians of Oaxaca.

Scientific Library
San Diego Museum of Man
Balboa Park
1350 El Prado
San Diego, 92101
Wide coverage of the Americas, including physical anthropology, archaeology, and ethnology.

COLORADO

Koshare Indian Museum, Inc.
115 West 18th Street
La Junta, 81050
The 10,000-volume Special Koshare Collection focuses on Native America and Western United States.

National Indian Law Library
Native American Rights Fund
1522 Broadway
Boulder, 80302-6296
Documents, periodicals, and 7,500 books on U.S.-Indian relations and law.

Taylor Museum Reference Library
Colorado Springs Fine Arts Center
30 West Dale Street
Colorado Springs, 80903
Art of the Southwest; Hispanic and colonial folk art. Collection
  houses 30,000 volumes; extensive biographies of folk artists.

Ute Mountain Tribal Research Archive and Library
Tribal Compound
(mailing address: P.O. Box CC)
Towaoc, 81334
Includes 2,500 books as well as 30,000 archival items, including
  tribal government documents.

CONNECTICUT

Mashantucket Pequot Research Library
Indiantown Road
Ledyard, 06339

DISTRICT OF COLUMBIA

American Folklife Center
U.S. Library of Congress
Thomas Jefferson Building - G152
Washington, 20540
Biggest collection of early Indian recordings, including the Frances
  Densmore Collection of 3,600 cylinders and the Helen Heffron
  Roberts Collection from the Northwest Coast and California.

National Anthropological Archives
Natural History Museum MRC 152
10th and Constitution Avenue
Washington, 20560
Extensive collections of recordings, photographs, field notes, and
  manuscripts of the Bureau of Ethnology.

Natural Resources Library

U.S. Department of the Interior
Mail Stop 1151
18th and C Streets, N.W.
Washington, 20240
More than 600,000 volumes and extensive periodicals and archival items, including materials on American Indians.

GEORGIA

Hargrett Rare Books and Manuscript Library

University of Georgia
Athens, 30602

ILLINOIS

Newberry Library

D'Arcy McNickle Center for the History of the American Indian
60 West Walton Street
Chicago, 60610
More than 100,000 volumes, including the E. E. Ayer Collection.

INDIANA

Fulton County Historical Society Library

Route 3
(mailing address: P.O. Box 89)
Rochester, 46975
Collection houses 4,000 volumes, including coverage of Potawatomi removal to Kansas in 1838 (the Trail of Death).

Lilly Library

Indiana University
Bloomington, 47405
Collection includes Indian accounts of Custer's defeat at the Battle of the Little Bighorn.

KANSAS

Mennonite Library and Archives
Bethel College
300 East 27th Street
North Newton, 67117-9989
Includes 26,000 books. Petter Manuscript Collection on the Cheyenne; H. R. Voth Manuscript and Photo Collection on the Hopi.

Mid-America All Indian Center Library
650 North Seneca
Wichita, 67203
Includes 3,000 books and 200 bound periodical volumes on Indian art, history, and culture. Blackbear Bosin Collection of publications and personal papers.

LOUISIANA

Grindstone Bluff Museum Library
(mailing address: P.O. Box 7965)
Shreveport, 71107
Contains 6,000 books and 2,000 periodical volumes on regional archaeology and ethnology; emphasis on Caddo Indians.

MASSACHUSETTS

Fruitlands Museums and Library
102 Prospect Hill Road
Harvard, 01451

Mashpee Archives Building
Mashpee, 02649

MICHIGAN

Custer Collection
Monroe County Library System
Monroe, 48161
Contains 4,000 books and archival materials on Custer and the West.

MINNESOTA

Minnesota Historical Society
Divison of Archives and Manuscripts
345 Kellogg Boulevard West
St. Paul, 55102-1906
Materials relating to the Ojibwa and Dakota.

MISSOURI

Missouri Historical Society Library
Jefferson Memorial Building
Forest Park
St. Louis, 63112
Northern Plains; papers of William Clark from Lewis and Clark expedition.

MONTANA

Dr. John Woodenlegs Memorial Library
Dull Knife Memorial College
P.O. Box 98
Lame Deer, 59043-0098
Cheyenne history; oral history collection. Contains 10,000 volumes.

NEBRASKA

Joslyn Art Museum
Art Reference Library
2200 Dodge Street
Omaha, 68102
Native American art covered in collection of 25,000 volumes, 3,000
bound periodicals, and 20,000 slides.

Native American Public Broadcasting Consortium Library
P.O. Box 83111
Lincoln, 68501
Special Collection of Native American video programs (171 titles).
Audio program "Spirits of the Present." NAPBC quarterly
newsletter. Materials available by mail.

Nebraska State Historical Society Library
P.O. Box 82554
Lincoln, 68501
Anderson Collection of Brule Sioux photographs. Library has
70,000 volumes.

NEW JERSEY

Firestone Library Collections of Western Americana
Princeton University
Princeton, 08544

NEW MEXICO

Mary Cabot Wheelwright Research Library
704 Camino Lejo
Santa Fe, 87502
Contains 10,000 volumes; archives on Navajo religion and sand-
painting.

Millicent Rogers Museum Library
P.O. Box A
Taos, 87571
Registry of New Mexico Hispanic artists, including a number of Indian artists.

Museum of New Mexico Photo Archives
P.O. Box 2087
Santa Fe, 87504

NEW YORK

Akwesasne Library
Route 37-RR 1
(mailing address: P.O. Box 14-C)
Hogansburg, 13655

Iroquois Indian Museum Library
P.O. Box 9
Bowes Cave, 12042-0009
Contains 1,500 volumes; 500 archival items; exhibition catalogs.

Museum of the American Indian Library
9 Westchester Square
Bronx, 10461
Contains 40,000 volumes; archives.

Seneca Nation Library
Allegany Branch
P.O. Box 231
Salamanca, 14779
Cattaraugus Branch
Irving, 14981

NORTH CAROLINA

State Archives
109 East Jones Street
Raleigh, 27601-2807

OHIO

Ohio Historical Society Archives and Library
1982 Velma Avenue
Columbus, 43211

OKLAHOMA

Chickasaw Nation Library
Arlington and Mississippi Streets
Ada, 74830

Gilcrease Library
1400 Gilcrease Museum Road
Tulsa, 74127
John Ross (Cherokee chief) and Peter Pitchlynn (Choctaw chief)
papers; 50,000 volumes.

**Oklahoma Historical Society Archives and Manuscript
Division**
2100 North Lincoln Boulevard
Oklahoma City, 73105
State Indian Agency records; Dawes Commission papers; 125,000
photographs.

OREGON

Siletz Library and Archives
119 East Logsden Road, Building II
Siletz, 97380

PENNSYLVANIA

Free Library of Philadelphia
Logan Square
Philadelphia, 19103

University Museum Library
33rd and Spruce Streets
University of Pennsylvania
Philadelphia, 19104
Brinton Collection on Indian linguistics; Delaware materials.

SOUTH DAKOTA

Center for Western Studies
Augustana College
P.O. Box 727
Sioux Falls, 57197
Great Plains history. Collection has 30,000 volumes, 1,500 linear
feet of manuscripts.

TEXAS

Fikes Hall of Special Collections
DeGolyer Library
Southern Methodist University
Dallas, 75275

National Archives
Southwest Region
501 Felix at Hemphill, Building 1
P.O. Box 6216
Fort Worth, 76115
Bureau of Indian Affairs records for Oklahoma.

UTAH

Ute Tribal Museum, Library, and Audio-Visual Center
Fort Duchesne, 84026

WASHINGTON

Jamestown Klallam Library
Blyn, 98382

Special Collections
University of Washington
Seattle, 98195

WEST VIRGINIA

**ERIC Clearinghouse on Rural Education and Small Schools
(CRESS) Library**
1031 Quarrier Street
(mailing address: P.O. Box 1348)
Charleston, 25325
Microfiche containing 300,000 documents. Indian/Hispanic issues.

WISCONSIN

Fairlawn Historical Museum
Harvard View Parkway
Superior, 54880
George Catlin lithographs; David F. Berry Collection of Indian
photographs and portraits.

Hoard Historical Museum Library
407 Merchant Avenue
Fort Atkinson, 53538
Rare Black Hawk War materials.

WYOMING

McCracken Research Library
Buffalo Bill Historical Center
P.O. Box 1000
Cody, 82414

LIBRARIES AND ARCHIVES IN CANADA

ALBERTA

Canadian Circumpolar Library
University of Alberta
Edmonton, AB T6G 2J8

University of Lethbridge Library
Special Collections
4401 University Drive
Lethbridge, AB T1K 3M4
Native American studies; English literature; education.

BRITISH COLUMBIA

Alert Bay Library and Museum
199 Fir Street
Alert Bay, BC B0N 1A0

Kamloops Museum and Archives
207 Seymour Street
Kamloops, BC V2C 2E7
Interior Salish and Shuswap material.

University of British Columbia Library
1956 Main Hall
Vancouver, BC V6T 1Z1

MANITOBA

Department of Indian Affairs and Northern Development Regional Library
275 Portage Avenue
Winnipeg, MB R3B 3A3

People's Library
Manitoba Indian Cultural Education Centre
119 Sutherland Avenue
Winnipeg, MB R2W 3C9

NEW BRUNSWICK

Education Resource Centre
University of New Brunswick
D'Avray Hall
P.O. Box 7500
Fredericton, NB E3B 5H5

NORTHWEST TERRITORIES

Thebacha Campus Library
Arctic College
Fort Smith, NT X0E 0P0

NOVA SCOTIA

Nova Scotia Human Rights Commission Library
P.O. Box 2221
Halifax, NS B3J 3C4
Rights of indigenous peoples, women, and others; 4,000 books.

ONTARIO

Department of Indian Affairs and Northern Development Departmental Library
Ottawa, ON K1A 0H4

University of Sudbury Library and Jesuit Archives
Sudbury, ON P3E 2C6

QUEBEC

Canadian Museum of Civilization Library
100 Laurier Street
Hull, PQ J8X 4H2

SASKATCHEWAN

Gabriel Dumont Institute of Native Studies and Applied Research Library
121 Broadway
Regina, SK S4N 0Z6
Indian History archives; 30,000 volumes.

Indian Federated College Library
University of Regina
Regina, SK S4S 0A2
Collection has 15,000 volumes. Branch library of 4,000 volumes on Saskatoon campus.

Saskatchewan Provincial Library
1352 Winnipeg Street
Regina, SK S4P 3V7
Has a 4,000-volume Indian collection. Strong in languages.

Organizations, Agencies, and Societies

All Indian Pueblo Council
Founded: 1958
P.O. Box 3256
Albuquerque, NM 87190

**American Indian Council of
Architects and Engineers**
Founded: 1976
P.O. Box 230685
Tigard, OR 97223

**American Indian Culture
Research Center**
Founded: 1967
Box 98
Blue Cloud Abbey
Marvin, SD 57251

**American Indian Graduate
Center**
Founded: 1969
4520 Montgomery Boulevard
NE
Ste. 1-B
Albuquerque, NM 87109

**American Indian Health Care
Association**
Founded: 1975
245 E. 6th Street
Ste. 499
St. Paul, MN 55101

**American Indian Heritage
Foundation**
Founded: 1973
6051 Arlington Boulevard
Falls Church, VA 22044

**American Indian Higher
Education Consortium**
Founded: 1972
513 Capitol Court NE
Ste. 100
Washington, DC 20002

**American Indian Horse
Registry**
Founded: 1961
Route 3, Box 64
Lockhart, TX 78644

**American Indian Liberation
Crusade**
Founded: 1952
4009 S. Halldale Avenue
Los Angeles, CA 90062

**American Indian Library
Association**
Founded: 1979
50 E. Huron Street
Chicago, IL 60611

American Indian Lore Association
Founded: 1957
960 Walhonding Avenue
Logan, OH 43138

American Indian Movement (AIM)
Founded: 1968
710 Clayton Street
Apartment 1
San Francisco, CA 94117

American Indian Registry for the Performing Arts
Founded: 1983
1717 N. Highland Avenue
Ste. 614
Los Angeles, CA 90028

American Indian Research and Development
Founded: 1982
2424 Springer Drive
Ste. 200
Norman, OK 73069

American Indian Science and Engineering Society
Founded: 1977
1630 30th Street
Ste. 301
Boulder, CO 80301

Americans for Indian Opportunity
Founded: 1970
3508 Garfield Street NW
Washington, DC 20007

Arrow, Incorporated (Americans for Restitution and Righting of Old Wrongs)
Founded: 1949
1000 Connecticut Avenue NW
Ste. 1206
Washington, DC 20036

Associated Community of Friends on Indian Affairs
Founded: 1869
Box 1661
Richmond, IN 47375

Association of American Indian Physicians
Founded: 1971
Building D
10015 S. Pennsylvania
Oklahoma City, OK 73159

Association of Community Tribal Schools
Founded: 1982
c/o Dr. Roger Bordeaux
616 4th Avenue W
Sisseton, SD 57262-1349

Association on American Indian Affairs
Founded: 1923
432 Park Ave. S.
New York, NY 10016

Bureau of Catholic Indian Missions
Founded: 1874
2021 H Street NW
Washington, DC 20006

Cherokee National Historical Society
Founded: 1963
P.O. Box 515
Tahlequah, OK 74465

Coalition for Indian Education
Founded: 1987
3620 Wyoming Boulevard NE
Ste. 206
Albuquerque, NM 87111

Concerned American Indian Parents
Founded: 1987
CUHCC Clinic
2016 16th Avenue S
Minneapolis, MN 55404

Continental Confederation of Adopted Indians
Founded: 1950
960 Walhonding Avenue
Logan, OH 43138

Council for Indian Education
Founded: 1970
517 Rimrock Road
Billings, MT 59102

Council for Native American Indians
Founded: 1974
280 Broadway
Ste. 316
New York, NY 10007

Council of Energy Resource Tribes (CERT)
Founded: 1975
1999 Broadway
Ste. 2600
Denver, CO 80202

Crazy Horse Memorial Foundation
Founded: 1948
The Black Hills
Avenue of the Chiefs
Crazy Horse, SD 57730

Creek Indian Memorial Association
Founded: 1923
Creek County House Museum
Town Square
Okmulgee, OK 74447

Dakota Women of All Red Nations (DWARN)
Founded: 1978
c/o Lorelei DeCora
P.O. Box 423
Rosebud, SD 57570

First Nations Development Institute
Founded: 1980
69 Kelley Road
Falmouth, VA 22405

Gathering of Nations
Founded: 1984
P.O. Box 75102
Sta. 14
Albuquerque, NM 87120-1269

Indian Arts and Crafts Association
Founded: 1974
122 La Veta Drive NE
Ste. B
Albuquerque, NM 87108

Indian Heritage Council
Founded: 1988
Henry Street
Box 2302
Morristown, TN 37816

Indian Law Resource Center
Founded: 1978
508 Stuart Street
Helena, MT 59601

Indian Rights Association
Founded: 1882
1801 Market Street
Philadelphia, PA 19103-1675

Indian Youth of America
Founded: 1978
609 Badgerow Building
Sioux City, IA 51101

Institute for American Indian Studies
Founded: 1971
38 Curtis Road
P.O. Box 1260
Washington, CT 06793-0260

Institute for the Development of Indian Law
Founded: 1971
c/o K. Kirke Kickingbird
Oklahoma City University
School of Law
2501 Blackwelder
Oklahoma City, OK 73106

Institute for the Study of American Cultures
Founded: 1983
The Rankin
1004 Broadway
Columbus, GA 31901

Institute for the Study of Traditional American Indian Arts
Founded: 1982
P.O. Box 66124
Portland, OR 97290

Institute of American Indian Arts
Founded: 1962
P.O. Box 20007
Santa Fe, NM 87504

International Indian Treaty Council
Founded: 1974
710 Clayton Street
Number 1
San Francisco, CA 94117

Inter-Tribal Indian Ceremonial Association
Founded: 1921
Box 1
Church Rock, NM 87311

Lone Indian Fellowship and Lone Scout Alumni
Founded: 1926
1104 St. Clair Avenue
Sheboygan, WI 53081

National American Indian Court Clerks Association
Founded: 1980
1000 Connecticut Avenue NW
Ste. 1206
Washington, DC 20036

National American Indian Court Judges Association
Founded: 1968
1000 Connecticut Avenue NW
Ste. 401
Washington, DC 20036

National Center for American Indian Alternative Education
Founded: 1960
941 E. 17th Ave.
Denver, CO 80218

National Center for American Indian Enterprise Development
Founded: 1969
953 E. Juanita Avenue
Mesa, AZ 85204

National Congress of American Indians
Founded: 1944
900 Pennsylvania Avenue SE
Washington, DC 20003

National Council of BIA
   Educators
Founded: 1967
6001 Marble NE
Ste. 10
Albuquerque, NM 87110

National Indian Council on
   Aging
Founded: 1976
6400 Uptown Boulevard NE
City Centre
Ste. 510-W
Albuquerque, NM 87110

National Indian Counselors
   Association
Founded: 1980
Learning Research Center
Institute of American Indian
   Arts
P.O. Box 20007
Santa Fe, NM 87504

National Indian Education
   Association
Founded: 1970
1819 H Street NW
Ste. 800
Washington, DC 20006

National Indian Health Board
Founded: 1969
1385 S. Colorado Boulevard
Ste. A-708
Denver, CO 80222

National Indian Social
   Workers Association
Founded: 1970
410 NW 18th Street
Number 101
Portland, OR 97209

National Indian Training and
   Research Center
Founded: 1969
2121 S. Mill Avenue
Ste. 216
Tempe, AZ 85282

National Indian Youth
   Council
Founded: 1961
318 Elm Street SE
Albuquerque, NM 87102

National Native American
   Cooperative
Founded: 1969
P.O. Box 1030
San Carlos, AZ 85550-1000

National Urban Indian
   Council
Founded: 1977
10068 University Station
Denver, CO 80210

Native American (Indian) Chamber of Commerce
Founded: 1990
c/o Native American Cooperative
P.O. Box 1000
San Carlos, AZ 85550-1000

Native American Community Board
Founded: 1984
P.O. Box 572
Lake Andes, SD 57356-0572

Native American Educational Services College
Founded: 1974
2838 West Peterson
Chicago, IL 60659

Native American Indian Housing Council
Founded: 1974
900 2nd Street NE
Ste. 220
Washington, DC 20002

Native American Policy Network
Founded: 1979
Barry University
11300 2nd Avenue NE
Miami, FL 33161

Native American Rights Fund (NARF)
Founded: 1970
1506 Broadway
Boulder, CO 80302

North American Indian Association
Founded: 1940
22720 Plymouth Road
Detroit, MI 48239

North American Indian Chamber of Commerce
Founded: 1983
P.O. Box 5000
San Carlos, AZ 85550-1000

North American Indian Museums Association
Founded: 1979
c/o George Abrams
260 Prospect Street
Number 669
Hackensack, NJ 07601-2608

North American Indian Women's Association
Founded: 1970
9602 Maestor's Lane
Gaithersburg, MD 20879

North American Native
  American Indian
  Information and Trade
  Center
Founded: 1991
P.O. Box 1000
San Carlos, AZ 85550-1000

Order of the Indian Wars
Founded: 1979
P.O. Box 7401
Little Rock, AR 72217

Pan-American Indian
  Association
Founded: 1984
P.O. Box 244
Nocatee, FL 33864

Seventh Generation Fund for
  Indian Development
Founded: 1977
P.O. Box 10
Forestville, CA 95436

Smoki People
Founded: 1921
P.O. Box 123
Prescott, AZ 86302

Survival of American Indians
  Association
Founded: 1964
7803-A Samurai Drive SE
Olympia, WA 98503

Tekakwitha Conference
  National Center
Founded: 1939
P.O. Box 6768
Great Falls, MT 59406-6768

Tiyospaya American Indian
  Student Organization
Founded: 1986
P.O. Box 1954
St. Petersburg, FL 33731

United Indians of All Tribes
  Foundation
Founded: 1970
Daybreak Star Arts Center
Discovery Park
P.O. Box 99100
Seattle, WA 98199

United Native Americans
Founded: 1968
2434 Faria Avenue
Pinole, CA 94564

United South and Eastern
  Tribes
Founded: 1969
1101 Kermit Drive
Ste. 302
Nashville, TN 37217

Culture Areas of North America

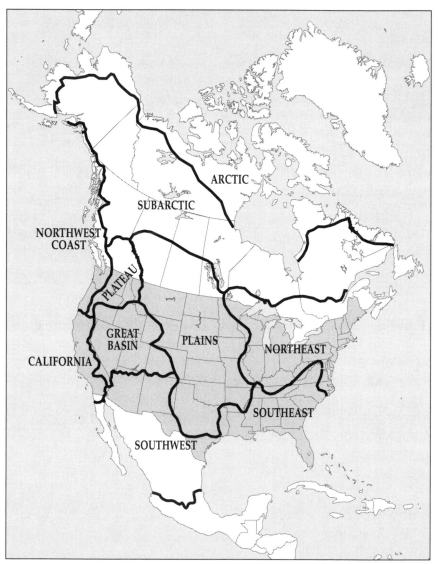

Tribes by Culture Area

Major tribal groups are listed below their geographical culture areas; language groups represented appear after the culture-area heading.

Arctic

Language groups: Eskimo-Aleut (Aleut, Inuit-Iñupiaq, Yupik)

Aleut
Inuit
Yupik

California

Language groups: Athapaskan, Chimariko, Chumashan, Esselen, Karok, Maiduan, Palaihnihan, Pom oan, Salinan, Shastan, Uto-Aztecan, Wintun, Wiyot, Yanan, Yokutsan, Yukian, Yuman, Yurok

Achumawi
Atsugewi
Cahuilla
Chemehuevi
Chumash
Costano
Cupeño
Diegueño
Esselen
Fernandeño
Gabrielino
Hupa
Juaneño
Kamia
Karok
Kato
Luiseño
Maidu
Mattole

Miwok
Patwin
Pomo
Quechan
Salinan
Serrano
Shasta
Tolowa
Tubatulabal
Wailaki
Wappo
Wintun
Wiyot
Yahi
Yana
Yokuts
Yuki
Yurok

Great Basin

Language groups: Hokan, Numic (Shoshonean)

Bannock
Gosiute
Kawaiisu
Mono (Monache)
Numaga (Northern Paiute)

Panamint
Paviotso (Northern Paiute)
Shoshone
Ute
Washoe

Northeast

Language groups: Algonquian, Iroquoian, Siouan

Abenaki
Algonquin
Cayuga
Erie
Fox
Huron
Illinois
Kaskaskia
Kickapoo
Lenni Lenape
Mahican
Maliseet
Massachusett
Menominee
Miami
Micmac
Mohawk
Nanticoke
Narragansett
Neutral
Nottaway

Oneida
Onondaga
Ottawa
Pamlico
Passamaquoddy
Pennacook
Penobscot
Pequot
Petun
Piankashaw
Potawatomi
Sauk
Secotan
Seneca
Shawnee
Susquehannock
Tuscarora
Wampanoag
Wappinger
Winnebago

Northwest Coast
Language groups: Athapaskan, Chinook, Penutian, Salish

Alsea
Bella Bella
Bella Coola
Chehalis
Chinook
Coast Salish
Coos
Eyak
Gitksan
Haida
Klamath

Klikitat
Kwakiutl
Nootka (Nuu-Chah-Nulth)
Quileute
Quinault
Siuslaw
Takelma
Tillamook
Tlingit
Tsimshian
Umpqua

Plains
Language groups: Algonquian, Athapaskan, Caddoan, Kiowa-Tanoan, Siouan, Uto-Aztecan

Apache of Oklahoma
Arapaho
Arikara
Assiniboine
Atsina
Blackfoot (Blood, Piegan,
    Siksika)
Caddo
Cheyenne
Comanche
Crow
Hidatsa
Iowa
Kansa (Kaw)

Kiowa
Mandan
Missouri
Omaha
Osage
Oto
Pawnee
Ponca
Quapaw
Sarsi
Sioux (Santee, Teton, Yankton)
Tonkawa
Waco
Wichita

Plateau
Language groups: Penutian, Sahaptin, Salishan

Coeur d'Alene	Okanagan
Colville	Palouse
Flathead	Sanpoil
Kalispel	Shuswap
Klamath	Spokane
Klikitat	Tenino
Kutenai	Thompson
Lake	Tyigh
Lillooet	Umatilla
Methow	Walla Walla
Mical	Wanapam
Modoc	Wauyukma
Molala	Wenatchi
Nez Perce	Yakima

Southeast
Language groups: Algonquian, Atakapa, Caddoan, Chitimacha, Iroquoian, Muskogean, Natchez, Siouan, Timucuan, Tunican, Yuchi

Ais	Catawba
Alabama	Cheraw
Anadarko (Hasinai Confed-	Cherokee
eracy)	Chiaha
Apalachee	Chickasaw
Apalachicola	Chitimacha
Atakapa	Choctaw
Bayogoula	Coushatta
Biloxi	Creek
Calusa	Guale
Cape Fear	Guasco (Hasinai Confederacy)

Hitchiti
Houma
Jeaga
Manahoac (Mahock)
Mobile
Nabedache (Hasinai
    Confederacy)
Natchez
Ocaneechi
Ofo
Pamlico
Pawokti
Powhatan Confederacy

Seminole
Texas (Hasinai Confederacy)
Timucua
Tiou
Tohome
Tunica
Tuscarora
Tuskegee
Tutelo
Waccamaw
Yamasee
Yazoo
Yuchi

Southwest

Language groups: Athapaskan, Keres, Kiowa-Tanoan, Uto-Aztecan, Yuman, Zuni

Acoma
Apache (including Chiricahua,
    Jicarilla, and Mescalero)
Cochiti
Havasupai
Hopi
Isleta
Jemez
Karankawa
Laguna
Nambe
Navajo
Picuris
Pima
Pojoaque

San Felipe
San Ildefonso
San Juan
Sandia
Santa Ana
Santa Clara
Santo Domingo
Taos
Tesuque
Tohono O'odham
Walapai
Yaqui
Yavapai
Zia
Zuñi

Subarctic

Language Groups: Algonquian, Athapaskan, Eskimo-Aleut

Ahtna
Beaver
Carrier
Chilcotin
Chipewyan
Cree
Dogrib
Haida
Han
Hare
Ingalik
Inland Tlingit

Koyukon
Kutchin
Montagnais
Mountain
Naskapi
Saulteaux
Slave
Tagish
Tanaina
Tanana
Tsetsaut
Yellowknife

Bibliography

The following select bibliography of works on American Indians is organized into four categories: General Studies and Reference, History, Culture Areas (with eight subsections), and Contemporary Life. —C.A.B.

GENERAL STUDIES AND REFERENCE

American Indian Tribes. 2 vols. Pasadena, Calif.: Salem Press, 2000.

Barrett, Carole A., ed. *American Indian History.* 2 vols. Pasadena, Calif.: Salem Press, 2002.

Bataille, Gretchen M., ed. *Native American Women: A Biographical Dictionary.* New York: Garland, 1993.

Bataille, Gretchen M., and Kathleen M. Sands. *American Indian Women Telling Their Lives.* Lincoln: University of Nebraska Press, 1984.

Berlo, Catherine. *Spirit Beings and Sun Dancers: Black Hawk's Vision of the Lakota World.* New York: George Braziller, 2000.

Berlo, Catherine, and Ruth Phillips. *Native North American Art.* New York: Oxford History of Art, 1998.

Bierhorst, John. *The Mythology of North America.* New York: William Morrow, 1985.

Boas, Franz. *Handbook for American Indian Languages.* 3 parts. Bureau of American Ethnology, Bulletin 40. Washington, D.C.: U.S. Government Printing Office, 1911.

Bowden, Henry Warner. *American Indians and Christian Missions.* Chicago: University of Chicago Press, 1981.

Brumble, H. David. *An Annotated Bibliography of American Indian and Eskimo Autobiographies.* Lincoln: University of Nebraska Press, 1981.

Campbell, Lyle, and Marianne Mithune, eds. *The Languages of Native America: Historical and Comparative Assessment.* Austin: University of Texas Press, 1979.

Coe, Michael, et al. *Atlas of Ancient America.* New York: Facts on File, 1986.

Cohen, Felix. *Felix Cohen's Handbook of Federal Indian Law*. 2d ed. Charlottesville, Va.: Michie/Bobbs-Merrill, 1982.

Culin, Stewart. *Games of the North American Indians*. Bureau of American Ethnology, Annual Report 24 (1902-1903). Washington, D.C.: U.S. Government Printing Office, 1907.

Curtis, Natalie. *The Indians' Book*. New York: Harper and Brothers, 1923.

Dawdy, Doris O., comp. *Annotated Bibliography of American Indian Painting*. Contributions from the Museum of the American Indian, Heye Foundation, vol. 21, pt. 2. New York: Museum of the American Indian, Heye Foundation, 1968.

Dobyns, Henry F. *Native American Historical Demography: A Critical Bibliography*. Newberry Library Center for the History of the American Indian Bibliographical Series. Bloomington: Indiana University Press, 1976.

Dockstader, Frederick J. *Indian Art in America: The Arts and Crafts of the North American Indians*. Greenwich, Conn.: New York Graphics Society, 1961.

Driver, Harold. *Indians of North America*. Chicago: University of Chicago Press, 1975.

Eggan, Fred, ed. *Social Anthropology of North American Tribes*. Chicago: University of Chicago Press, 1966.

Erdoes, Richard, and Alfonso Ortiz, eds. *American Indian Myths and Legends*. New York: Pantheon Books, 1984.

Feest, Christian F. *Native Arts of North America*. New York: Oxford University Press, 1980.

Gill, Sam D. *Native American Religions: An Introduction*. Belmont, Calif.: Wadsworth, 1982.

Gill, Sam D., and Irene F. Sullivan, comps. *Dictionary of Native American Mythology*. Santa Barbara, Calif.: ABC-CLIO, 1992.

Green, Rayna. *Native American Women: A Contextual Bibliography*. Bloomington: Indiana University Press, 1983.

Haas, Marilyn L. *Indians of North America: Sources for Library Research*. Hamden, Conn.: Library Professional Publications, 1983.

Hamilton, Charles, ed. *Cry of the Thunderbird*. Norman: University of Oklahoma Press, 1972.

Hamlin-Wilson, Gail, ed. *Biographical Dictionary of the Indians of the Americas*. 2 vols. Newport Beach, Calif.: American Indian Publishers, 1991.

Harris, R. Cole, ed. *Historical Atlas of Canada: From the Beginning to 1800*. Toronto: University of Toronto Press, 1987.

Heard, J. Norman. *Handbook of the American Frontier: Four Centuries of Indian-White Relations*. 3 vols. Metuchen, N.J.: Scarecrow Press, 1987-1992.

Hill, Edward E., comp. *Guide to the Records of the National Archives of the United States Relating to American Indians*. Washington, D.C.: National Archives and Records Service, 1981.

Hirschfelder, Arlene B., et al. *Guide to Research on North American Indians*. Chicago: American Library Association, 1983.

Hirschfelder, Arlene B., and Paulette Molin, comps. *The Encyclopedia of Native American Religions: An Introduction*. New York: Facts on File, 1992.

Hodge, Frederick W., ed. *Handbook of American Indians North of Mexico*. 2 vols. Washington, D.C.: U.S. Government Printing Office, 1907-1910.

Horr, David A., comp. and ed. *American Indian Ethnohistory*. 118 vols. New York: Garland, 1974.

Hoxie, Frederick E., ed. *Indians in American History: An Introduction*. Arlington Heights, Ill.: Harlan Davidson, 1988.

Hoxie, Frederick E., and Harvey Markowitz, comps. *Native Americans: An Annotated Bibliography*. Pasadena, Calif.: Salem Press, 1990.

Hultkrantz, Ake. *The Religions of the American Indians*. Translated by Monica Setterwall. Berkeley: University of California Press, 1967.

Hurt, R. Douglas. *Indian Agriculture in America: Prehistory to the Present*. Lawrence: University Press of Kansas, 1987.

Jenness, Diamond. *The Indians of Canada*. Ottawa: F. A. Acland, 1932.

Johnson, Steven L. *Guide to American Indian Documents in the Congressional Series Set, 1817-1899*. New York: Clearwater, 1977.

Josephy, Alvin M., Jr., ed., and William Brandon. *The American Heritage Book of Indians*. New York: American Heritage, 1961.

Kapplar, Charles. *Indian Affairs: Laws and Treaties.* 2 vols. Washington, D.C.: U.S. Government Printing Office, 1904-1941.

Klein, Barry T., ed. *Reference Encyclopedia of the American Indian.* 2 vols. 4th ed. New York: Todd, 1986.

Krech, Shepard, III. *Native Canadian Anthropology and History: A Selective Bibliography.* Winnipeg: Rupert's Land Research Centre, University of Winnipeg, 1986.

Krupat, Arnold. *For Those Who Come After: A Study of Native American Autobiography.* Berkeley: University of California Press, 1985.

Laubin, Reginald, and Gladys Laubin. *Indian Dances of North America.* Norman: University of Oklahoma Press, 1977.

Leacock, Eleanor Burke, and Nancy O. Lurie, eds. *North American Indians in Historical Perspective.* Prospect Heights, Ill.: Waveland Press, 1988.

Liberty, Margot, ed. *American Indian Intellectuals.* St. Paul, Minn.: West, 1978.

Littlefield, Daniel F., Jr., and James W. Parin. *A Biobibliography of Native American Writers, 1772-1924.* Metuchen, N.J.: Scarecrow Press, 1981.

_____. *A Biobibliography of Native American Writers, 1772-1924: Supplement.* Metuchen, N.J.: Scarecrow Press, 1981.

Markowitz, Harvey. *American Indian Biographies.* Pasadena, Calif.: Salem Press, 1998.

_____. *Ready Reference: American Indians.* 3 vols. Pasadena, Calif.: Salem Press, 1995.

Marriott, Alice Lee, and Carol Rachlin. *American Indian Mythology.* New York: Thomas Y. Crowell, 1964.

Murdock, George Peter, and Timothy J. O'Leary. *Ethnographic Bibliography of North America.* 4th ed. 5 vols. New Haven, Conn.: Human Relations Area Files Press, 1975.

Nabokov, Peter. *Native American Testimony.* New York: Harper & Row, 1979.

Nabokov, Peter, and Robert Easton. *Native American Architecture.* New York: Oxford University Press, 1989.

Orchard, William C. *Beads and Beadwork of the American Indian.* New York: Museum of the American Indian, Heye Foundation, 1929.

_____. *The Technique of Porcupine-Quill Decoration Among the North American Indians*. New York: Museum of the American Indian, Heye Foundation, 1971.

Prucha, Francis Paul. *A Bibliographical Guide to the History of Indian-White Relations in the United States*. Chicago: University of Chicago Press, 1977.

_____, ed. *Documents of United States Indian Policy*. 2d ed., expanded. Lincoln: University of Nebraska Press, 1990.

_____. *Indian-White Relations in the United States: A Bibliography of Works Published 1975-1980*. Lincoln: University of Nebraska Press, 1982.

Ronda, James, and James Axtell. *Indian Missions: A Critical Bibliography*. Newberry Library Center for the History of the American Indian Bibliographical Series. Bloomington: Indiana University Press, 1978.

Ruoff, A. Lavonne, and Karl Kroeber. *American Indian Literatures in the United States: A Basic Bibliography for Teachers*. New York: Association for the Study of American Indian Literature, 1983.

Schusky, Ernest L., ed. *Political Organization of Native North Americans*. Washington, D.C.: University of America Press, 1980.

Smith, Jane F., and Robert M. Kvasnicka, eds. *Indian-White Relations: A Persistent Paradox*. Washington, D.C.: Howard University Press, 1976.

Snipp, C. Mathew. *American Indians: The First of This Land*. New York: Russell Sage Foundation, 1989.

Snow, Dean R. *The American Indians: Their Archaeology and Prehistory*. New York: Thames and Hudson, 1976.

_____. *Native American Prehistory: A Critical Bibliography*. Newberry Library Center for the History of the American Indian Bibliographical Series. Bloomington: Indiana University Press, 1979.

Spencer, Robert F., Jesse D. Jennings, et al. *The Native Americans*. New York: Harper & Row, 1977.

Stewart, Omer C. *Peyote Religion: A History*. Norman: University of Oklahoma Press, 1987.

Stuart, Paul. *Nations Within a Nation: Historic Statistics of American Indians*. Westport, Conn.: Greenwood Press, 1987.

Sturtevant, William C., gen. ed. *Handbook of North American Indians*. Washington, D.C.: U.S. Government Printing Office, 1978.

Sullivan, Lawrence E., ed. *Native American Religions: North America*. New York: Macmillan, 1987.

Swann, Brian. *Smoothing the Ground: Essays on Native American Oral Literature*. Berkeley: University of California Press, 1983.

Taylor, Colin. *Native American Weapons*. Norman: University of Oklahoma, 2001.

Tedlock, Dennis, and Barbara Tedlock, eds. *Teachings from the American Earth: Indian Religion and Philosophy*. New York: Liveright Press, 1975.

Thornton, Russell, and Mary K. Gramsmick. *Sociology of American Indians: A Critical Bibliography*. Newberry Library Center for the History of the American Indian Bibliographical Series. Bloomington: Indiana University Press, 1980.

Tyler, S. Lyman. *A History of Indian Policy*. Washington, D.C.: U.S. Department of the Interior, Bureau of Indian Affairs, 1973.

Ullom, Judith C., ed. *Folklore of the North American Indians: An Annotated Bibliography*. Washington, D.C.: Library of Congress, 1969.

Underhill, Ruth M. *Red Man's Religion*. Chicago: University of Chicago Press, 1965.

Utley, Robert M., and Wilcomb B. Washburn. *The American Heritage History of the Indian Wars*. New York: American Heritage, 1977.

Vogel, Virgil. *American Indian Medicine*. Norman: University of Oklahoma Press, 1970.

Waldman, Carl. *Atlas of the North American Indians*. New York: Facts on File, 1985.

Washburn, Wilcomb E. *History of Indian-White Relations*. Vol. 4 in *Handbook of North American Indians*. Washington, D.C.: U.S. Government Printing Office, 1988.

_____, comp. and ed. *The American Indian and the United States*. 4 vols. New York: Random House, 1973.

HISTORY

Adams, David Wallace. *Education for Extinction: American Indians and the Boarding School Experience, 1875-1928*. Lawrence: University of Kansas Press, 1995.

Adams, Howard. *Prison of Grass: Canada from the Native Point of View*. Toronto: New Press, 1975.

Axtell, James. *The European and the Indian: Essays in the Ethnohistory of Colonial North America*. New York: Oxford University Press, 1981.

Berkhofer, Robert F., Jr. *Salvation and the Savage: An Analysis of Protestant Missions and American Indian Response 1787-1862*. Lexington: University of Kentucky Press, 1965.

Bowden, Henry W. *American Indians and Christian Missions: Studies in Cultural Conflict*. Chicago: University of Chicago Press, 1981.

Brown, Dee A. *Bury My Heart at Wounded Knee: An Indian History of the American West*. New York: Henry Holt, 1970.

Brown, Jennifer S. H. *Strangers in Blood: Fur Trade Company Families in Indian Country*. Vancouver: University of British Columbia Press, 1980.

Burt, Larry W. *Tribalism in Crisis: Federal Indian Policy, 1953-1961*. Albuquerque: University of New Mexico Press, 1982.

Calloway, Colin G. *Crown and Calumet: British-Indian Relations, 1783-1815*. Norman: University of Oklahoma Press, 1987.

Child, Brenda. *Boarding School Seasons: American Indian Families, 1900-1940*. Lincoln: University of Nebraska Press, 2000.

Cook, Sherburne F. *The Conflict Between the California Indian and White Civilization*. Berkeley: University of California Press, 1974.

Cronon, William. *Changes in the Land: Indians, Colonists, and the Ecology of New England*. New York: Hill & Wang, 1983.

Crosby, Alfred W., Jr. *The Columbian Exchange: Biological and Cultural Consequences of 1492*. Westport, Conn.: Greenwood Press, 1972.

Crow Dog, Leonard, and Richard Erdoes. *Crow Dog: Four Generations of Sioux Medicine Men*. New York: HarperCollins, 1995.

Curtis, Edward S. *In a Sacred Manner We Live*. Barre, Mass.: Barre Publishers, 1972.

Debo, Angie. *And Still the Waters Run*. New York: Gordian Press, 1966.

_____. *The Rise and Fall of the Choctaw Republic*. 2d ed. Norman: University of Oklahoma Press, 1967.

Dickason, Olive P. *The Myth of the Savage and the Beginnings of French Colonialism in the Americas*. Edmonton: University of Alberta Press, 1984.

Dippie, Brian W. *Custer's Last Stand: The Anatomy of a Myth*. Lincoln: University of Nebraska Press, 1994.

_____. *The Vanishing American: White Attitudes and United States Indian Policy*. Lawrence: University of Kansas Press, 1991.

Ellis, Clyde. *To Change Them Forever: Indian Education at the Rainy Mountain Boarding School, 1893-1920*. Norman: University of Oklahoma Press, 1996.

Erdoes, Richard. *Ohitika Woman: Mary Brave Bird*. New York: Harper Perennial, 1994.

Fixico, Donald L. *Termination and Relocation: Federal Indian Policy, 1945-1966*. Albuquerque: University of New Mexico Press, 1986.

Foreman, Grant. *Indian Removal: The Emigration of the Five Civilized Tribes of Indians*. Norman: University of Oklahoma Press, 1932.

Fox, Richard Allan, Jr. *Archeology, History, and Custer's Last Battle: The Little Big Horn Reexamined*. Norman: University of Oklahoma Press, 1993.

Fritz, Henry. *The Movement for Indian Assimilation, 1860-1890*. Philadelphia: University of Pennsylvania Press, 1963.

Getty, Ian A. L., and Antoine S. Lussier. *As Long as the Sun Shines and Water Flows: A Reader in Canadian Native Studies*. Vancouver: University of British Columbia Press, 1983.

Green, Michael D. *The Politics of Indian Removal: Creek Government and Society in Crisis*. Lincoln: University of Nebraska Press, 1982.

Hagan, William T. *American Indians*. Rev. ed. Chicago: University of Chicago Press, 1979.

Hanke, Lewis. *Aristotle and the American Indians*. Chicago: Henry Regnery, 1959.

Hauptman, Laurence. *The Iroquois and the New Deal.* Syracuse, N.Y.: Syracuse University Press, 1981.

Hauptman, Laurence M., and James D. Wherry. *The Pequots in Southern New England: The Fall and Rise of an American Indian Nation.* Norman: University of Oklahoma Press, 1993.

Horsman, Reginald. *Expansion and American Indian Policy, 1783-1812.* East Lansing: Michigan State University Press, 1967.

Hoxie, Frederick E. *A Final Promise: The Campaign to Assimilate the Indians, 1880-1920.* Lincoln: University of Nebraska Press, 1984.

Huddleston, Lee Eldridge. *Origins of the American Indians: European Concepts, 1492-1729.* Austin: University of Texas Press, 1967.

Jackson, Helen Hunt. *A Century of Dishonor: A Sketch of the United States Government's Dealings with Some of the Indian Tribes.* New York: Harper and Brothers, 1881.

Jacobs, Wilbur R. *Dispossessing the American Indian: Indians and Whites on the Colonial Frontier.* New York: Charles Scribner's Sons, 1972.

Jaenen, Cornelius J. *Friend and Foe: Aspects of French-Amerindian Cultural Contact in the Sixteenth and Seventeenth Centuries.* New York: Columbia University Press, 1976.

Jennings, Francis. *The Invasion of America.* New York: W. W. Norton, 1975.

John, Elizabeth A. H. *Storms Brewed in Other Men's Worlds: The Confrontation of Indians, Spanish, and French in the Southwest, 1540-1795.* Lincoln: University of Nebraska Press, 1975.

Jones, Dorothy V. *License for Empire: Colonialism by Treaty in Early America.* Chicago: University of Chicago Press, 1982.

Keller, Robert H. *American Protestantism and United States Indian Policy, 1869-82.* Lincoln: University of Nebraska Press, 1983.

Kennedy, John H. *Jesuit and Savage in New France.* New Haven, Conn.: Yale University Press, 1950.

La Flesche, Francis. *The Middle Five.* Lincoln: University of Nebraska Press, 1978.

Lame Deer, Archie Fire, and Richard Erdoes. *Lame Deer, Seeker of Visions.* New York: Pocket Books, 1978.

Lindsey, Donal F. *Indians at Hampton Institute, 1877-1923*. Urbana: University of Illinois Press, 1995.

Little Bear, Leroy, and Menno Boldt, eds. *Pathways to Self-Determination*. Toronto: University of Toronto Press, 1984.

Little Coyote, Bertha, and Dorothy Giglio. *Leaving Everything Behind: The Songs and Memories of a Cheyenne Woman*. Norman: University of Oklahoma Press, 1998.

Lomawaima, K. Tsianina. *They Called It Prairie Light: The Story of Chilocco Indian School*. Lincoln: University of Nebraska Press, 1994.

McBeth, Sally. *Ethnic Identity and the Boarding School Experience of West-Central Oklahoma American Indians*. Washington, D.C.: University Press of America, 1983.

McDonnell, Janet A. *The Dispossession of the American Indian, 1887-1934*. Bloomington: University of Indiana Press, 1991.

McLoughlin, William G. *After the Trail of Tears: The Cherokees' Struggle for Sovereignty, 1839-1880*. Chapel Hill: The University of North Carolina Press, 1993.

Mihesuah, Devon A. *Cultivating the Rosebuds: The Education of Women at the Cherokee Female Seminary, 1851-1909*. Urbana: University of Illinois Press, 1993.

Milanich, Jerald T., and Susan Milbruth, eds. *First Encounters: Spanish Explorations in the Caribbean and the United States, 1492-1570*. Gainesville: University of Florida Press, 1989.

Miller, J. R. *Skyscrapers Hide the Heavens: A History of Indian-White Relations in Canada*. Toronto: University of Toronto Press, 1989.

Mooney, James. *The Ghost Dance Religion and the Sioux Outbreak of 1890*. Bureau of American Ethnology, Annual Report 14 (1892-1893). Washington, D.C.: U.S. Government Printing Office, 1896.

Morrison, Kenneth M. *The Embattled Northeast: The Elusive Ideal of Alliance in Abnaki-Euramerican Relations*. Berkeley: University of California Press, 1984.

Nash, Gary B. *Red, White, and Black: The Peoples of Early America*. Englewood Cliffs, N.J.: Prentice-Hall, 1974.

Priest, Loring Benson. *Uncle Sam's Stepchildren: The Reformation of*

United States Indian Policy, 1865-1887. New Brunswick, N.J.: Rutgers University Press, 1942.

Prucha, Francis Paul. *The Great Father: The United States Government and the American Indians*. Lincoln: University of Nebraska Press, 1986.

Ray, Arthur J. *Indians in the Fur Trade: Their Role as Trappers, Hunters, and Middlemen in the Lands Southwest of Hudson Bay, 1660-1870*. Toronto: University of Toronto Press, 1974.

Reyhner, Jon, and Jeanne Eder. *A History of Indian Education*. Billings: Eastern Montana College, 1989.

Riney, Scott. *The Rapid City Indian School, 1898-1933*. Norman: University of Oklahoma Press, 1999.

St. Pierre, Mark. *Madonna Swan: A Lakota Woman's Story*. Norman: University of Oklahoma Press, 1991.

Salisbury, Neal. *Manitou and Providence: Indians, Europeans, and the Making of New England*. New York: Oxford University Press, 1982.

Satz, Ronald N. *American Indian Policy in the Jacksonian Era*. Lincoln: University of Nebraska Press, 1975.

Sheehan, Bernard W. *Savagism and Civility: Indians and Englishmen in Colonial Virginia*. New York: Cambridge University Press, 1980.

————. *Seeds of Extinction: Jeffersonian Philanthropy and the American Indian*. Chapel Hill: University of North Carolina Press, 1973.

Szasz, Margaret C. *Indian Education in the American Colonies, 1607-1783*. Albuquerque: University of New Mexico Press, 1988.

Trennert, Robert A., Jr. *Alternative to Extinction: Federal Indian Policy and the Beginnings of the Reservation System, 1846-51*. Philadelphia: University of Pennsylvania Press, 1975.

Trigger, Bruce G. *Natives and Newcomers: Canada's "Heroic Age" Reconsidered*. Montreal: McGill-Queen's University Press, 1985.

Utley, Robert M. *The Indian Frontier of the American West, 1846-1890*. Albuquerque: University of New Mexico Press, 1984.

————. *The Lance and the Shield: The Life and Times of Sitting Bull*. New York: Ballantine Books, 1994.

Vennum, Thomas, Jr. *American Indian Lacrosse: Little Brother of War.* Washington, D.C.: Smithsonian Institution Press, 1994.

Viola, Herman J. *Diplomats in Buckskin: A History of the Indian Delegations in Washington City.* Washington, D.C.: Smithsonian Institution Press, 1981.

_____. *Little Bighorn Remembered: The Untold Story of Custer's Last Stand.* New York: Random House, 1999. A compilation of Indian accounts gathered from all tribes who had a presence at the Battle of the Little Big Horn.

Washburn, Wilcomb E. *The Assault on Indian Tribalism: The General Allotment Law (Dawes Act) of 1887.* Philadelphia: J. B. Lippincott, 1975.

Weaver, Sally M. *Making Canadian Indian Policy: The Hidden Agenda, 1968-70.* Toronto: University of Toronto Press.

White, Richard. *The Roots of Dependency: Subsistence, Environment, and Social Change Among the Choctaws, Pawnees, and Navajos.* Lincoln: University of Nebraska Press, 1983.

CULTURE AREAS

Arctic and Subarctic

Boas, Franz. *The Central Eskimo.* Bureau of American Ethnology, Annual Report 6 (1884-1885). Washington, D.C.: U.S. Government Printing Office. 1888.

Chance, Norman A. *The Eskimo of North Alaska.* New York: Holt, Rinehart and Winston, 1966.

Condon, Richard G. *Inuit Youth: Growth and Change in the Canadian Arctic.* New Brunswick, N.J.: Rutgers University Press, 1987.

Cruikshank, Julie in collaboration with Angela Sidney, Kitty Smith, and Annie Ned. *Life Lived Like a Story: Life Stories of Three Yukon Native Elders.* Lincoln: University of Nebraska Press, 1990.

Damas, David. *Arctic.* Vol. 5 in *Handbook of North American Indians.* Washington, D.C.: Smithsonian Institution, 1984.

Dumond, Don E. *The Eskimos and Aleuts.* Rev. ed. London: Thames and Hudson, 1987.

Helm, June. *The Indians of the Subarctic: A Critical Bibliography.* Newberry Library Center for the History of the American Indian Bibliographical Series. Bloomington: Indiana University Press, 1976.

_____, ed. *Subarctic.* Vol. 6 in *Handbook of North American Indians.* Washington, D.C.: Smithsonian Institution, 1981.

Krech, Shepard, III, ed. *The Subarctic Fur Trade: Native Social and Economic Adaptations.* Vancouver: University of British Columbia Press, 1984.

Nelson, Richard K. *Hunters of the Northern Forest.* Chicago: University of Chicago Press, 1973.

_____. *Hunters of the Northern Ice.* Chicago: University of Chicago Press, 1969.

Oswalt, Wendell H. *Eskimos and Explorers.* Novato, Calif.: Chandler and Sharp, 1979.

Ray, Dorothy Jean. *Aleut and Eskimo Art: Tradition and Innovation in South Alaska.* Seattle: University of Washington Press, 1981.

VanStone, James W. *Athapaskan Adaptations: Hunters and Fishermen of the Subarctic Forests.* Chicago: Aldine, 1974.

California

Bean, Lowell J. *Mukat's People: The Cahuilla Indians of Southern California.* Berkeley: University of California Press, 1973.

Chartkoff, Joseph L., and Kerry K. Chartkoff. *The Archaeology of California.* Stanford, Calif.: Stanford University Press, 1984.

Grant, Campbell. *The Rock Painting of the Chumash: A Study of a California Indian Culture.* Berkeley: University of California Press, 1965.

Heizer, Robert F., ed. *California.* Vol. 8 in *Handbook of North American Indians.* Washington, D.C.: Smithsonian Institution, 1978.

_____. *The Indians of California: A Critical Bibliography.* Newberry Library Center for the History of the American Indian Bibliographical Series. Bloomington: Indiana University Press, 1976.

Heizer, Robert F., and Albert B. Elsasser, comps. *A Bibliography of California Indians: Archaeology, Ethnography, and Indian History.* New York: Garland, 1977.

Heizer, Robert F., and Theodora Kroeber, eds. *Ishi, the Last Yahi: A Documentary History*. Berkeley: University of California Press, 1979.

Heizer, Robert F., and Mary A. Whipple, comps. and eds. *The California Indians: A Source Book*. 2d rev., enlarged ed. Berkeley: University of California Press, 1971.

Kroeber, Theodora, and Robert F. Heizer. *Almost Ancestors: The First Californians*, edited by F. David Hales. San Francisco: Sierra Club Books, 1968.

Ray, Verne F. *Primitive Pragmatists: The Modoc Indians of Northern California*. Seattle: University of Washington Press, 1963.

Shipek, Florence C. *Pushed into the Rocks: Southern California Indian Land Tenure, 1769-1986*. Lincoln: University of Nebraska Press, 1987.

Great Basin

Bunte, Pamela A., and Robert J. Franklin. *From the Sands to the Mountain: Change and Persistence in a Southern Paiute Community*. Lincoln: University of Nebraska Press, 1987.

D'Azevedo, Warren L. *Great Basin*. Vol. 11 in *Handbook of North American Indians*. Washington, D.C.: Smithsonian Institution, 1986.

_____, ed. and comp. *The Washo Indians of California and Nevada*. University of Utah Anthropological Papers 67. Salt Lake City: University of Utah Press, 1963.

Densmore, Frances. *Northern Ute Music*. Bureau of American Ethnology, Bulletin 75. Washington, D.C.: U.S. Government Printing Office, 1922.

Fowler, Don D., ed. *Great Basin Cultural Ecology: A Symposium*. Desert Research Institute Publications in the Social Sciences 8. Reno, Nev.: Publications Office of the Desert Research Institute, 1972.

Hopkins, Sarah Winnemucca. *Life Among the Piutes: Their Wrongs and Claims*. New York: G. P. Putnam's Sons, 1883.

Knack, Martha. *Life Is with People*. Socorro, N.Mex.: Ballena Press, 1980.

Knack, Martha, and Omer C. Stewart. *As Long as the River Shall Run: An Ethnohistory of Pyramid Lake Indian Reservation*. Berkeley: University of California Press, 1984.

Laird, Carobeth. *Mirror and Pattern: George Laird's World of Chemehuevi Mythology*. Banning, Calif.: Malki Museum Press, 1984.

Madsen, Brigham D. *The Bannock of Idaho*. Caldwell, Idaho: Caxton Printers, 1958.

Steward, Julian H. *Basin-Plateau Aboriginal Sociopolitical Groups*. Bureau of American Ethnology, Bulletin 120. Washington, D.C.: U.S. Government Printing Office, 1938.

Stewart, Omer C. *Indians of the Great Basin: A Critical Bibliography*. Newberry Library Center for the History of the American Indian Bibliographical Series. Bloomington: Indiana University Press, 1982.

Northeast

Anson, Bert. *The Miami Indians*. Norman: University of Oklahoma Press, 1970.

Barnouw, Victor. *Wisconsin Chippewa Myths and Tales and Their Relation to Chippewa Life*. Madison: University of Wisconsin Press, 1977.

Black Hawk (Ma-ka-tai-me-she-kia-kiak). *An Autobiography*, edited by Donald Jackson. Urbana: University of Illinois Press, 1955.

Brose, David S., et al. *Ancient Art of the American Woodlands Indians*. New York: Harry N. Abrams, in association with the Detroit Institute of Arts, 1985.

Clifton, James A. *The Prairie People: Continuity and Change in Potawatomi Indian Culture, 1665-1965*. Lawrence: Regents Press of Kansas, 1977.

Densmore, Frances. *Chippewa Customs*. Bureau of American Ethnology, Bulletin 86. Washington, D.C.: U.S. Government Printing Office, 1929.

_____. *Chippewa Music*. 2 vols. Bureau of American Ethnology, Bulletins 45 and 53. Washington, D.C.: U.S. Government Printing Office, 1910-1913.

_____. *Uses of Plants by the Chippewa Indians*. Bureau of American Ethnology, Annual Report 44 (1926-1927). Washington, D.C.: U.S. Government Printing Office, 1928.

Edmunds, R. David. *The Potawatomis: Keepers of the Fire*. Norman: University of Oklahoma Press, 1978.

Gibson, Arrell M. *The Kickapoos: Lords of the Middle Border*. Norman: University of Oklahoma Press, 1963.

Hagan, William T. *The Sac and the Fox Indians*. Norman: University of Oklahoma Press, 1958.

Hale, Horatio E., ed. *The Iroquois Book of Rites*. Brinton's Library of Aboriginal American Literature 11. Philadelphia: D. G. Brinton, 1883.

Hickerson, Harold. *The Chippewa and Their Neighbors: A Study in Ethnohistory*. Prospect Heights, Ill.: Waveland Press, 1988.

Kinietz, W. Vernon. *The Indians of the Western Great Lakes, 1615-1760*. Ann Arbor: University of Michigan Press, 1940.

Landes, Ruth. *Ojibwa Religion and the Mdewiwin*. Madison: University of Wisconsin Press, 1968.

_____. *Ojibwa Sociology*. Columbia University Contributions to Anthropology 29. New York: Columbia University Press, 1937.

Lyford, Carrie A. *Iroquois Crafts*. Lawrence, Kans.: Haskell Institute Press, 1945.

_____. *Ojibway Crafts*. Lawrence, Kans.: Haskell Institute Press, 1943.

Mason, Ronald J. *Great Lakes Archaeology*. New York: Academic Press, 1981.

Morgan, Lewis Henry. *League of the Ho-de-no-sau-nee or Iroquois*. Rochester, N.Y.: Sage and Brothers, 1851.

Morgan, William N. *Prehistoric Architecture in the Eastern United States*. Cambridge, Mass.: MIT Press, 1980.

Mountain Wolf Woman. *Mountain Wolf Woman, Sister of Crashing Thunder: The Autobiography of a Winnebago Indian*, edited by Nancy O. Lurie. Ann Arbor: University of Michigan Press, 1961.

Quimby, George I. *Indian Life in the Upper Great Lakes: 11,000 B.C. to A.D. 1800*. Chicago: University of Chicago Press, 1960.

Radin, Paul. *The Winnebago Tribe*. Bureau of American Ethnology, Annual Report 37 (1915-1916). Washington, D.C.: U.S. Government Printing Office, 1923.

_____, ed. *The Autobiography of a Winnebago Indian*. University of California Publications in American Archaeology and Ethnology, vol. 16, no. 7. Berkeley: University of California Press, 1920.

Ritzenthaler, Robert E., and Pat Ritzenthaler. *The Woodland Indians of the Western Great Lakes*. Garden City, N.Y.: Natural History Press, 1970.

Salisbury, Neal. *The Indians of New England: A Critical Bibliography*. Newberry Library Center for the History of the American Indian Bibliographical Series. Bloomington: Indiana University Press, 1982.

Snow, Dean R. *The Archaeology of New England*. New York: Academic Press, 1980.

Tanner, Helen Hornbeck, et al. *Atlas of Great Lakes Indian History*. Norman: University of Oklahoma Press, 1986.

Tooker, Elisabeth. *The Indians of the Northeast: A Critical Bibliography*. Newberry Library Center for the History of the American Indian Bibliographical Series. Bloomington: Indiana University Press, 1978.

_____, ed. *Native North American Spirituality of the Eastern Woodlands: Sacred Myths, Dreams, Visions, Speeches, Healing Formulas, Rituals, and Ceremonies*. Mahwah, N.J.: Paulist Press, 1979.

Trigger, Bruce G. *The Huron: Farmers of the North*. New York: Holt, Rinehart and Winston, 1969.

_____, ed. *Northeast*. Vol. 15 in *Handbook of North American Indians*. Washington, D.C.: Smithsonian Institution, 1978.

Vennum, Thomas, Jr. *Wild Rice and the Ojibway People*. St. Paul: Minnesota Historical Society, 1988.

Wallace, Anthony F. C. *The Death and Rebirth of the Seneca*. New York: Alfred A. Knopf, 1969.

Webb, William S., and Charles E. Snow. *The Adena People*. Knoxville: University of Tennessee Press, 1974.

Northwest Coast and Plateau

Amoss, Pamela. *Coast Salish Spirit Dancing: The Survival of an Ancestral Religion.* Seattle: University of Washington Press, 1978.

Boas, Franz. *Kwakiutl Ethnography,* edited by Helen Codere. Chicago: University of Chicago Press, 1966.

Codere, Helen. *Fighting with Property: A Study of Kwakiutl Potlatching and Warfare 1792-1930.* New York: J. J. Augustin, 1950.

Drucker, Philip. *Cultures of the North Pacific Coast.* San Francisco: Chandler, 1965.

Fahey, John. *The Flathead Indians.* Norman: University of Oklahoma Press, 1974.

Grumet, Robert S. *Native Americans of the Northwest Coast: A Critical Bibliography.* Newberry Library Center for the History of the American Indian Bibliographical Series. Bloomington: Indiana University Press, 1979.

Haines, Francis. *The Nez Percé: Tribesmen of the Columbian Plateau.* Norman: University of Oklahoma Press, 1955.

Inverarity, Robert B. *Art of the Northwest Coast Indians.* Berkeley: University of California Press, 1950.

Kirk, Ruth, and Richard D. Daughtery. *Exploring Washington Archaeology.* Seattle: University of Washington Press, 1978.

Miller, Jay, and Carol Eastman, ed. *The Tsimshian and Their Neighbors on the North Pacific Coast.* Seattle: University of Washington Press, 1984.

Mourning Dove (Humishuma). *Coyote Stories,* edited by Jay Miller. Lincoln: University of Nebraska Press, 1990.

————. *Mourning Dove: A Salishan Autobiography,* edited by Jay Miller. Lincoln: University of Nebraska Press, 1990.

People of 'Ksan. *Gathering What the Great Nature Provided: Food Traditions of the Gitksan.* Vancouver: Douglas and McIntyre and Seattle: University of Washington Press, 1980.

Ruby, Robert H., and John A. Brown. *A Guide to the Indian Tribes of the Pacific Northwest.* Norman: University of Oklahoma Press, 1986.

Samuel, Cheryl. *The Chilkat Dancing Blanket.* Seattle: Pacific Search Press, 1982.

Spradley, James, ed. *Guests Never Leave Hungry: The Autobiography of James Sewid, a Kwakiutl Indian*. New Haven, Conn.: Yale University Press, 1969.

Stewart, Hilary. *Artifacts of the Northwest Coast Indians*. Saanichton, British Columbia: Hancock House Publishers, 1973.

_____. *Cedar: Tree of Life to the Northwest Coast Indians*. Seattle: University of Washington Press, 1984.

_____. *Indian Fishing: Early Methods on the Northwest Coast*. Seattle: University of Washington Press, 1977.

Plains

Albers, Patricia, and Beatrice Medicine. *The Hidden Half: Studies in Plains Indian Women*. Lanham, Md.: University Press of America, 1983.

Baird, W. David. *The Quapaw Indians: A History of the Downstream People*. Norman: University of Oklahoma Press, 1981.

Berthrong, Donald J. *The Southern Cheyennes*. Norman: University of Oklahoma Press, 1963.

Black Elk, as told to John G. Neihardt. *Black Elk Speaks*. New York: William Morrow, 1932.

Blaine, Martha R. *The Pawnees: A Critical Bibliography*. Newberry Library Center for the History of the American Indian Bibliographical Series. Bloomington: Indiana University Press, 1980.

Blish, Helen H. *A Pictographic History of the Oglala Sioux, Drawings by Amos Bad Heart Bull*. Lincoln: University of Nebraska Press, 1967.

Bowers, Alfred W. *Mandan Social and Ceremonial Organization*. Chicago: University of Chicago Press, 1950.

Brown, Joseph E. *The Sacred Pipe: Black Elk's Account of the Seven Rites of the Oglala Sioux*. Norman: University of Oklahoma Press, 1953.

DeMallie, Raymond, ed. *The Sixth Grandfather: Black Elk's Teachings Given to John G. Neihardt*. Lincoln: University of Nebraska Press, 1984.

DeMallie, Raymond, and Douglas R. Parks, eds. *Sioux Indian Religion*. Norman: University of Oklahoma Press, 1987.

Densmore, Frances. *Cheyenne and Arapaho Music.* Southwest Museum Papers 10. Los Angeles: Southwest Museum, 1936.

_____. *Mandan and Hidatsa Music.* Bureau of American Ethnology, Bulletin 80. Washington, D.C.: U.S. Government Printing Office, 1923.

_____. *Pawnee Music.* Bureau of American Ethnology, Bulletin 93. Washington, D.C.: U.S. Government Printing Office, 1929.

_____. *Teton Sioux Music.* Bureau of American Ethnology, Bulletin 61. Washington, D.C.: Government Printing Office, 1918.

Dorsey, George A. *The Cheyenne.* Field Columbian Museum Anthropological Series, vol. 9, nos. 1 and 2. Chicago: The Museum, 1905.

Ewers, John C. *The Blackfeet: Raiders on the Northwestern Plains.* Norman: University of Oklahoma Press, 1958.

_____. *Blackfoot Crafts.* Lawrence, Kans.: Haskell Institute Printing Department, 1945.

_____. *The Horse in Blackfoot Culture.* Bureau of American Ethnology, Bulletin 159. Washington, D.C.: U.S. Government Printing Office, 1955.

Fletcher, Alice C. *The Hako: A Pawnee Ceremony.* Bureau of American Ethnology, Annual Report 22. (1900-1901). Washington, D.C.: U.S. Government Printing Office, 1904.

Fletcher, Alice C., and Francis La Flesche. *The Omaha Tribe.* 2 vols. Bureau of American Ethnology, Annual Report 27 (1905-1906). Washington, D.C.: U.S. Government Printing Office, 1911.

Fowler, Loretta. *Arapahoe Politics, 1851-1978.* Lincoln: University of Nebraska Press, 1982.

Frison, George. *Prehistoric Hunters of the High Plains.* New York: Academic Press, 1978.

Gilmore, Melvin R. *Uses of Plants by the Indians of the Missouri River Region.* Bureau of American Ethnology, Annual Report 33 (1911-1912). Washington, D.C.: U.S. Government Printing Office, 1919.

Grinnell, George B. *The Cheyenne Indians: Their History and Ways of Life.* 2 vols. New Haven, Conn.: Yale University Press, 1923.

Hassrick, Royal B. *The Sioux: Life and Customs of a Warrior Society.* Norman: University of Oklahoma Press, 1964.

Hoebel, E. Adamson. *The Plains Indians: A Critical Bibliography.* Newberry Library Center for the History of the American Indian Bibliographical Series. Bloomington: Indiana University Press, 1979.

Holder, Preston. *The Hoe and the Horse on the Plains.* Lincoln: University of Nebraska Press, 1970.

Hyde, George E.. *Spotted Tail's Folk: A History of the Brule Sioux.* Norman: University of Oklahoma Press, 1961.

Iverson, Peter, ed. *The Plains Indians of the Twentieth Century.* Norman: University of Oklahoma Press, 1985.

Llewellen, Karl N., and E. Adamson Hoebel. *The Cheyenne Way: Conflict and Case Law in Primitive Jurisprudence.* Norman: University of Oklahoma Press, 1941.

Lowie, Robert H. *The Crow Indians.* New York: Farrar and Rinehart, 1935.

————. *Indians of the Plains.* New York: McGraw-Hill, 1954.

————. *Myths and Traditions of the Crow Indians.* Anthropological Papers of the American Museum of Natural History, vol. 25, pt. 1. New York: Order of Trustees, 1918.

————. *Social Life of the Crow Indians.* Anthropological Papers of the American Museum of Natural History, vol. 9, pt. 2. New York: Order of Trustees, 1912.

Lyford, Carrie A. *Quill and Beadwork of the Western Sioux.* Lawrence, Kans.: Printing Department, Haskell Institute, 1940.

Mandelbaum, David G. *The Plains Cree.* Anthropological Papers of the American Museum of Natural History, vol. 37, pt. 2. New York: Order of Trustees, 1940.

Murie, James R. *Ceremonies of the Pawnee.* 2 parts, edited by Douglas R. Parks. 2 vols. Washington, D.C.: Smithsonian Institution Press, 1981.

Newkumet, Vynola Beaver, and Howard L. Meridith. *Hasinai: A Traditional History of the Caddo Confederacy.* College Station: Texas A&M University Press, 1988.

Petersen, Karen D. *Plains Indian Art from Fort Marion.* Norman: University of Oklahoma Press, 1971.

Plenty Coups. *American: The Life Story of a Great Indian, Plenty-*

coups, Chief of the Crows, edited by Frank B. Linderman. New York: World Book, 1930.

Powell, Peter J. *The Cheyennes, Ma'heo'o's People: A Critical Bibliography*. Newberry Library Center for the History of the American Indian Bibliographical Series. Bloomington: Indiana University Press, 1980.

_____. *People of the Sacred Mountain: A History of the Northern Cheyenne Chiefs and Warrior Societies, 1830-1879.* 2 vols. San Francisco: Harper & Row, 1981.

Powers, William K. *Yuwipi: Vision and Experience in Oglala Ritual*. Lincoln: University of Nebraska Press, 1982.

Standing Bear, Luther. *My People the Sioux*. Boston: Houghton Mifflin, 1928.

Stands in Timber, John, and Margot Liberty. *Cheyenne Memories*. New Haven, Conn.: Yale University Press, 1967.

Unrau, William E. *The Emigrant Indians of Kansas: A Critical Bibliography*. Newberry Library Center for the History of the American Indian Bibliographical Series. Bloomington: Indiana University Press, 1979.

Voget, Fred W. *The Shoshoni-Crow Sun Dance*. Norman: University of Oklahoma Press, 1984.

Walker, James R. *Lakota Belief and Ritual*, edited by Raymond J. DeMallie and Elaine A. Jahner. Lincoln: University of Nebraska Press, 1980.

_____. *Lakota Myth*, edited by Elaine A. Jahner. Lincoln: University of Nebraska Press, 1983.

_____. *Lakota Society*, edited by Raymond J. DeMallie. Lincoln: University of Nebraska Press, 1982.

Wedel, Waldo R., ed. *A Plains Archaeology Source Book: Selected Papers of the Nebraska Historical Society*. New York: Garland, 1985.

Weist, Katherine M., and Susan R. Sharrock. *An Annotated Bibliography of Northern Plains Ethnohistory*. Missoula: Department of Anthropology, University of Montana, 1985.

Wildschut, W., and John C. Ewers. *Crow Indian Beadwork*. New York: Museum of the American Indian, Heye Foundation, 1959.

Will, George F., and George E. Hyde. *Corn Among the Indians of the Upper Missouri*. St. Louis, Mo.: William Harvey Minor Co., 1917.

Wissler, Clark, ed. *Societies of the Plains Indians*. American Museum of Natural History, Anthropological Papers, vol. 11., pts. 1-13. New York: The Trustees, 1912-1916.

Wood, W. Raymond, and Margot Liberty, eds. *Anthropology on the Great Plains*. Lincoln: University of Nebraska Press, 1980.

Zimmerman, Larry J. *Peoples of Prehistoric South Dakota*. Lincoln: University of Nebraska Press, 1985.

Southeast

Baird, W. David. *The Chickasaw People*. Phoenix: Indian Tribal Series, 1974.

_____. *The Choctaw People*. Phoenix: Indian Tribal Series, 1973.

_____. *Peter Pitchlynn: Chief of the Choctaws*. Norman: University of Oklahoma Press, 1972.

Blu, Karen I. *The Lumbee Problem: The Making of an American Indian People*. Cambridge, England: Cambridge University Press, 1980.

Densmore, Frances. *Choctaw Music*. Bureau of American Ethnology, Bulletin 136. Washington, D.C.: U.S. Government Printing Office, 1943.

_____. *Seminole Music*. Bureau of American Ethnology, Bulletin 161. Washington, D.C.: U.S. Government Printing Office, 1956.

Edmunds, R. David. *The Shawnee Prophet*. Lincoln: University of Nebraska Press, 1983.

Fogelson, Raymond D. *The Cherokees: A Critical Bibliography*. Newberry Library Center for the History of the American Indian Bibliographical Series. Bloomington: Indiana University Press, 1978.

Gilliland, Marion Spjut. *The Material Culture of Key Marco, Florida*. Gainesville: University Presses of Florida, 1975.

Green, Michael D. *The Creeks: A Critical Bibliography*. Newberry Library Center for the History of the American Indian Bibliographical Series. Bloomington: Indiana University Press, 1979.

Hudson, Charles M., ed. *Ethnology of the Southeastern Indians*. New York: Garland, 1985.

_____. *The Southeastern Indians*. Knoxville: University of Tennessee Press, 1976.

Kidwell, Clara Sue, and Charles Roberts. *The Choctaws: A Critical Bibliography*. Newberry Library Center for the History of the American Indian Bibliographical Series. Bloomington: Indiana University Press, 1980.

King, Duane H., ed. *The Cherokee Indian Nation: A Troubled History*. Knoxville: University of Tennessee Press, 1979.

McReynolds, Edwin C. *The Seminoles*. Norman: University of Oklahoma Press, 1957.

Merrell, James H. *The Indians' New World: Catawbas and Their Neighbors from European Contact Through the Era of Removal*. Chapel Hill: University of North Carolina Press, for the Institute of Early American History and Culture, Williamsburg, Virginia, 1989.

Milanich, Jerald T., and Charles H. Fairbanks. *Florida Archaeology*. New York: Academic Press, 1980.

Mooney, James. *Myths of the Cherokee*. Bureau of American Ethnology, Annual Report 19 (1897-1898). Washington, D.C.: U.S. Government Printing Office, 1900.

_____. *The Sacred Formulas of the Cherokees*. Bureau of American Ethnology, Annual Report 7 (1885-1886). Washington, D.C.: U.S. Government Printing Office, 1891.

Rountree, Helen C. *The Powhatan Indians of Virginia: Their Traditional Culture*. Norman: University of Oklahoma Press, 1989.

Swanton, John R. *The Indians of the Southeastern United States*. Bureau of American Ethnology, Bulletin 137. Washington, D.C.: U.S. Government Printing Office, 1946.

_____. *Myths and Tales of the Southeastern Indians*. Bureau of American Ethnology, Bulletin 88. Washington, D.C.: U.S. Government Printing Office, 1929.

Walthall, John A. *Prehistoric Indians of the Southeast: Archaeology of Alabama and the Middle South*. Tuscaloosa: University of Alabama Press, 1980.

Southwest

Basso, Keith H., ed. *Western Apache Raiding and Warfare, from the Notes of Grenville Goodwin*. Tucson: University of Arizona Press, 1971.

Benedict, Ruth. *Zuni Mythology*. 2 vols. New York: Columbia University Press, 1935.

Bunzel, Ruth L. *The Pueblo Potter: A Study of Creative Imagination in Primitive Art*. New York: Columbia University Press, 1929.

Cordell, Linda S. *Prehistory of the Southwest*. Orlando, Fla.: Academic Press, 1984.

Densmore, Frances. *Papago Music*. Bureau of American Ethnology, Bulletin 90. Washington, D.C.: U.S. Government Printing Office, 1929.

Dobyns, Henry F., and Robert C. Euler. *Indians of the Southwest*. Newberry Library Center for the History of the American Indian Bibliographical Series. Bloomington: Indiana University Press, 1980.

Dozier, Edward P. *Hano: A Tewa Indian Community in Arizona*. New York: Holt, Rinehart and Winston, 1966.

Eggan, Fred. *Social Organization of the Western Pueblos*. Chicago: University of Chicago Press, 1950.

Ferguson, T. J., and Richard E. Hart. *A Zuni Atlas*. Norman: University of Oklahoma Press, 1985.

Foster, Morris. *Being Comanche: A Social History of an American Indian Community*. Tucson: University of Arizona Press, 1991.

Frisbie, Charlotte J. *Navajo Medicine Bundles or Jish: Acquisition, Transmission, and Disposition in the Past and Present*. Albuquerque: University of New Mexico Press, 1987.

Goodman, James M. *The Navajo Atlas: Environments, Resources, People, and History of the Dine Bikeyah*. Norman: University of Oklahoma Press, 1982.

Haile, O. F. M., Fr. Berard, comp. and trans. *Navajo Coyote Tales: The Curly To Aheeddliinii Version*, edited by Karl Luckert. Lincoln: University of Nebraska Press, 1984.

Iverson, Peter. *Carlos Montezuma and the Changing World of American Indians*. Albuquerque: University of New Mexico Press, 1982.

————. *The Navajo Nation*. Westport, Conn.: Greenwood Press, 1981.

————. *The Navajos: A Critical Bibliography*. Newberry Library Center for the History of the American Indian Bibliographical Series. Bloomington: Indiana University Press, 1976.

Kent, Kate Peck. *Navajo Weaving: Three Centuries of Change*. Santa Fe, N.Mex.: School of American Research Press, 1985.

————. *Prehistoric Textiles of the Southwest*. Santa Fe: School of American Research and Albuquerque: University of New Mexico Press, 1983.

Kluckhohn, Clyde. *Navaho Witchcraft*. Boston: Beacon Press, 1962.

Laird, W. David. *Hopi Bibliography, Comprehensive and Annotated*. Tucson: University of Arizona Press, 1977.

Lamphere, Louise. *To Run After Them: Cultural and Social Bases of Cooperation in a Navajo Community*. Tucson: University of Arizona Press, 1977.

Leighton, Dorothea, and John Adair. *People of the Middle Place: A Study of the Zuni Indians*. New Haven, Conn.: Human Relations Area Files Press, 1966.

Lister, Robert H., and Florence C. Lister. *Chaco Canyon: Archaeology and Archaeologists*. Albuquerque: University of New Mexico Press, 1981.

Melody, Michael Edward. *The Apache: A Critical Bibliography*. Newberry Library Center for the History of the American Indian Bibliographical Series. Bloomington: Indiana University Press, 1977.

————. *The Tewa World: Space, Time, Being, and Becoming in a Pueblo Society*. Chicago: University of Chicago Press, 1969.

Ortiz, Alfonso, ed. *New Perspectives on the Pueblos*. Albuquerque: University of New Mexico Press, 1972.

————, ed. *Southwest*. Vol. 9 in *Handbook of North American Indians*. Washington: Smithsonian Institution, 1979.

————, ed. *Southwest*. Vol. 10 in *Handbook of North American Indians*. Washington, D.C.: Smithsonian Institution, 1983.

Parsons, Elsie C. *Pueblo Indian Religion*. 2 vols. Chicago: University of Chicago Press, 1939.

Reichard, Gladys A. *Navaho Indian Religion: A Study of Symbolism.* 2 vols. New York: Pantheon Books, 1950.

Stevenson, Matilda C. *The Zuni Indians: Their Mythology, Esoteric Fraternities, and Ceremonies.* Bureau of American Ethnology, Annual Report 23 (1901-1902). Washington, D.C.: U.S. Government Printing Office, 1904.

Tanner, Clara Lee. *Prehistoric Southwestern Craft Arts.* Tucson: University of Arizona Press, 1976.

_____. *Southwest Indian Painting: A Changing Art.* 2d ed. Tucson: University of Arizona Press, 1973.

Underhill, Ruth M. *Papago Woman.* New York: Holt, Rinehart and Winston, 1979.

Whitewolf, Jim. *The Life of a Kiowa Apache Indian*, edited by Charles S. Brant. New York: Dover, 1969.

Wills, W. H. *Early Prehistoric Agriculture in the American Southwest.* Santa Fe, N.Mex.: School of American Research Press, 1988.

CONTEMPORARY LIFE

Ambler, Marjane. *Breaking the Iron Bonds: Indian Control of Energy Development.* Lawrence: University Press of Kansas, 1990.

Berkhofer, Robert, Jr. *The White Man's Indian.* New York: Alfred A. Knopf, 1978.

Deloria, Vine, Jr. *Behind the Trail of Broken Treaties: An Indian Declaration of Independence.* New York: Delta, 1974.

_____. *God Is Red.* New York: Grosset & Dunlop, 1973.

Fixico, Donald L. *The Urban Indian Experience in America.* Albuquerque: University of New Mexico Press, 2000.

Fuchs, Estelle, and Robert Havighurst. *To Live on This Earth.* Garden City, N.Y.: Doubleday, 1972.

Hagan, William T. *Indian Police and Judges: Experiments in Acculturation and Control.* Lincoln: University of Nebraska Press, 1980.

Hertzberg, Hazel W. *The Search for an American Indian Identity: Modern Pan-Indian Movements.* Syracuse, N.Y.: Syracuse University Press, 1971.

Highwater, Jamake. *The Sweet Grass Lives On: Fifty Contemporary North American Indian Artists.* New York: Lippincott and Thomas Y. Crowell, 1980.

Hobson, Geary, ed. *The Remembered Earth: An Anthology of Contemporary Native American Literature.* Albuquerque: University of New Mexico Press, 1979.

Hyer, Sally. *One House, One Voice, One Heart: Native American Education at Santa Fe Indian School.* Santa Fe: Museum of New Mexico Press, 1990.

Johnston, Basil. *Indian School Days.* Norman: University of Oklahoma Press, 1989.

McNickle, D'Arcy. *The Surrounded.* New York: Dodd, Mead, 1936.

Mihesuah, Devon A. *American Indians: Stereotypes and Realities.* Atlanta: Clarity Press, 1996.

_____. *Repatriation Reader: Who Owns American Indian Remains?* Lincoln: University of Nebraska Press, 2000.

Milloy, John S. *A National Crime: The Canadian Government and the Residential School System, 1879-1986.* Winnipeg: The University of Manitoba Press, 1999.

Momaday, N. Scott. *House Made of Dawn.* New York: Harper & Row, 1968.

O'Brien, Sharon. *American Indian Tribal Governments.* Norman: University of Oklahoma Press, 1989.

Red Horse, John, et al. *The American Indian Family: Strengths and Stresses.* Isleta, N.Mex.: American Indian Social Research and Development Associates, 1981.

Rosen, Kenneth. *The Man to Send Rain Clouds: Contemporary Stories by American Indians.* New York: Viking Press, 1974.

Silko, Leslie M. *Ceremony.* New York: Viking Press, 1977.

Smith, Paul Chaat, and Robert Allen Warrior. *Like a Hurricane: The Indian Movement from Alcatraz to Wounded Knee.* New York: New Press, 1996.

Waddell, Jack O., and O. Michael Watson, eds. *The American Indian in Urban Society.* Boston: Little, Brown, 1971.

Welch, James. *Winter in the Blood.* New York: Harper & Row, 1974.

Web Resources

American Indian Heritage Foundation (AIHF)
http://www.indians.org/
This national foundation, dedicated to assisting underprivileged
Native Americans, maintains a resource page with links to federally recognized tribes, Native American literature and art essays and links, and a broad array of other links organized
topically.

American Indian History and Related Issues
http://www.csulb.edu/projects/ais/
A wide-ranging list of links to sites dealing with mostly modern
American Indian history. Contains links to tribal home pages,
federal departments, image banks, cultural resources, and
much more.

American Indian History as Told by American Indians
http://www.manataka.org/page10.html
Links to over one hundred U.S. and Canadian Native American
sites with information on American Indian history from a native perspective.

American Indian Library Association (AILA)
http://www.nativeculture.com/lisamitten/aila.html
The affiliate of the American Library Association devoted to Native American libraries, librarians, and collections, offering access to the AILA newsletter and listservs.

American Indian Resources
http://jupiter.lang.osaka-u.ac.jp/~krkvls/naindex.html
A collection of links for academic research in Native American
studies. Includes links to oral and written tribal histories, primary source documents, maps, and bibliographies.

American Indian Tribal Directory
http://www.indians.org/tribes/tribes.html
Site of the American Indian Heritage Foundation, with a useful directory to all federally recognized tribes and resource library.

Black-Indian History Resources
http://anpa.ualr.edu/f_black_indian.htm
A fascinating site on the intermixing of African Americans and the Five Civilized Tribes.

CodeTalk
http://www.codetalk.fed.us/
Hosted by the U.S. Department of Housing and Urban Development, Office of Native American Programs, a federal Web site designed as a central electronic resource for all government offices and programs affecting Native Americans. Links to most federal government offices dealing with Indian affairs.

Diversity and Ethnic Studies: Recommended American Indian Web Sites
http://www.public.iastate.edu/~savega/amer_ind.htm
A list of academically reliable Web sites, including links to a number of online journals and newspapers.

Doe & Moffitt Libraries, Native American Collections
http://www.lib.berkeley.edu/doemoff/gov_ntvam.html
The University of California at Berkeley maintains this site, which offers comprehensive links for researching Native American history and culture, including bibliographies and directories; guides and handbooks; law and civil rights; treaties and federal programs; congressional publications; statistical indexes and guides; basic statistics; census data; declassified federal documents and federal surveillance files; special collections; California documents; and Internet resources.

Edward S. Curtis's *The North American Indian*
http://memory.loc.gov/ammem/award98/ienhtml/
  curthome.htmlE
Allows search on the text and images of this controversial yet
  highly influential publication, issued 1907-1930. Curtis's monu-
  mental twenty-volume work contains more than two thousand
  photogravure images and narrative, representing traditional
  customs and lifeways of eighty Indian tribes. Organized by
  tribes and culture areas. The site features more than fifteen hundred illustrations and more than seven hundred plates, brows-
  able or searchable by subject, tribe, or geographic locale.

First Nation Information Project
http://www.johnco.com/firstnat/index.html
A very thorough resource for information on all aspects of life
  among the Canadian First Nations.

First Nations Histories
http://www.tolatsga.org/Compacts.html
Provides short histories of all Canadian First Nations, along with
  bibliographies and maps.

Harvard University Pluralism Project
http://www.pluralism.org
A search page offers access to a list and links to Native American
  spiritual centers nationwide.

Index of Native American Resources on the Internet
http://www.hanksville.org/NAresources/
A comprehensive index to Internet resources, frequently updated.

Indian Affairs: Laws and Treaties
http://digital.library.okstate.edu/kappler/index.htm
A digitized edition of Charles J. Keppler's 1904 work on the relations between the U.S. government and Native American
  tribes.

Indian Peoples of the Northern Great Plains
http://libmuse.msu.montana.edu:4000/NAD/nad.home
A searchable photographic database.

Indian Trusts Assets Management
http://www.doi.gov/indiantrust/index.html
The U.S. Department of the Interior's Web site covering issues regarding Indian Trusts, with updates on the ongoing legal disputes.

Institute of American Indian Arts (IAIA)
http://www.iaiancad.org/
Established in 1962 by the United States Bureau of Indian Affairs (BIA), the is now an independent two-year college, contemporary Indian art musuem, and member of the American Indian Higher Education Consortium located in Santa Fe, New Mexico. Its site offers information about programs and exhibitions, a tour of the collection, and access to the virtual library by tribe, subject, or geographical locale.

Internet Law Library: Indian Nations and Tribes
http://www.nsulaw.nova.edu/library/ushouse/31.htm
Links to numerous sites with information on legal relations between the U.S. government and Native American tribes. Includes a number of links dealing with treaties.

National Indian Gaming Association (NIGA)
http://www.indiangaming.org
The main advocacy group for Indian gambling enterprises, offering access to government officials, a virtual library and other resources aimed at advancing Indian gaming.

National Museum of the American Indian

http://www.nmai.si.edu/

The Web site for this, one of the Smithsonian museums, lists a calendar of events, exhibitions, and links to the New York, Maryland, and Washington, D.C., facilities. Nearly one million artifacts are in the collection, and an interactive database, planned for inauguration in 2005, will give researchers and the public access to information about many of these pieces.

Native American Authors

http://www.ipl.org/div/natam/

Maintained by the University of Michigan's School of Information, this is an interactive search by authors, book titles, and tribes, including biographical information and bibliographical information and links to news stories and other sources for hundreds of Native American authors.

Native American Documents Project

http://www.csusm.edu/nadp/

Provides primary source documentation of the allotment system, published reports of the Bureau of Indian Affairs in the 1870's, and information on the Rogue River War and the Silitz reservation.

Native American History and Studies

http://www.tntech.edu/www/acad/hist/nativam.html

A collection of historical links hosted by the history department at Tennessee Technological University.

Native American Music Awards (Nammys)

http://www.nativeamericanmusic.com/

Supports and promotes contemporary Native American artists thourgh the Nammys (which began in 1998) as well as the Native American Music Hall of Fame.

Native American Research Page

http://maple.lemoyne.edu/~bucko/indian.html

A collection of links to resources on all aspects of Native American culture and life.

Native American Rights Fund (NARF)

http://www.narf.org/

Legal activist group dedicated to advancing and defending Native American civil rights and liberties. Maintains pages listing current cases, calls to action, and the National Indian Law Library.

NativeCulture.com

http://www.nativeculture.com

An organized set of links to indigenous culture sites by tribe, arts, and teaching tools. Arts are further categorized under arts, dance, media, music, literature, and "hand arts."

NativeWeb

http://www.nativeweb.org/

Maintained by academicians and Web technicians, NativeWeb describes itself as "an international, nonprofit, educational organization dedicated to using telecommunications including computer technology and the Internet to disseminate information from and about indigenous nations, peoples, and organizations around the world; to foster communication between native and non-native peoples; to conduct research involving indigenous peoples' usage of technology and the Internet; and to provide resources, mentoring, and services to facilitate indigenous peoples' use of this technology." Hosts sub-sites such as NativeTech, links to resources, news stories, and other resources related to Native American culture. Accepts donations.

The Newberry Library

http://www.newberry.org

Located in Chicago, the Newberry maintains one of the world's finest collections of books on American Indian culture and history, the Edward E. Ayer Collection. The site offers a searchable catalog.

Office of Tribal Justice

http://www.usdoj.gov/otj/

The Web site of the division of the U.S. Department of Justice that deal with Native American issues. Includes a statement of the Department of Justice's sovereignty policy.

On This Date in North American Indian History

http://americanindian.net/

A site dedicated to timelines of Native American historical events.

Smithsonian Institution: Native American History and Culture

http://www.si.edu/resource/faq/nmai/start.htm

Links to Native American resources at the Smithsonian, including a number of online museum exhibits. The "Native American Portraits from the National Portrait Gallery" exhibit features many historically important Native Americans.

Treaty Negotiations Office of the Attorney General of British Columbia

http://www.gov.bc.ca/tno/

Contains information about treaties between Canada and First Nations, with updates on current legislation and negotiations.

Tribal Law and Policy Institute

http://www.tribal-institute.org/lists/tlpi.htm

The site of a Native American nonprofit institute dedicated to increasing resources for tribal judicial systems and operations.

American Indian Culture

Category Index

Ceremonies, Dances, and Festivals

Contemporary Life and Issues

Culture Area Index

Subject Index

religion, 415; medicine bundle, 454; shields, 656; tobacco, 729

Voluntary Relocation Program, 604, 769

Wailaki, 40

Wakan, 589, 624, 626

Walam Olum, 777

Walapai, 43, 79

Walla Walla, 94

Wampanoag, 45, 622

Wampum, 617, 652, 778-780, 783

Wappinger, 45

War bonnets, 287, 349, 781-782, 787

War dances, 787

War helmets, 88

War shirts, 236

War societies, 823

War Twins, 768

Warfare, 148, 151, 191, 463, 783-790; demography, 217; guns, 337; Plains culture, 781; scalping, 638; slavery, 662; weapons, 791-794. *See also* Weapons; Category Index under "Weapons and Warfare"

WARN. *See* Women of All Red Nations

Warrior societies, 671-673

Warrior, Clyde, 528

Wasco, 94

Washita, Battle of the, 899

Washoe, 43, 56, 79; basketry, 80

Wattle and daub construction, 26, 59, 388, 790-791

Weapons, 109, 148, 396, 791-794; guns, 337-339; technology, 721;

tomahawks, 730-731; warfare, 788. *See also* Category Index

Weaving, 794-798; Plateau bags, 94

Weirs, 291, 633, 799-801

Wenebojo, 630

Western Pueblo tribes (Hopi, 178

Whales, 801-803

Wheat, 9

Wheels, 751

Whistles, 495

White Buffalo Society, 156, 803-804

White Deerskin Dance, 804-805

Whitman, Richard Ray, 70

Wichita, 90, 781

Wickiups, 42-43, 196, 713, 805-806

Wigwams, 46, 67, 806-807

Wild rice, 8, 808-809

Windigo, 810

Winnebago, 45, 83, 459, 808

Winnemucca, Sarah, 819

Wintercounts, 91, 542, 811-812

Wintun, 40, 75

Wishram, 94

Witchcraft, 371, 668, 812-813

Wivot, 547, 561

Wiyot, 40

Wodziwob, 600

Wolf Society, 672

Women, 308-319, 814-821; shamans, 450

Women of All Red Nations (WARN), 529, 820

Women, non-kin-based societies and, 676, 685, 804

Women's societies, 803, 822-823

Woodlands, 31, 117